FAST FAMILIES, VIRTUAL CHILDREN

FAST FAMILIES, VIRTUAL CHILDREN

A Critical Sociology of Families and Schooling

Ben Agger and Beth Anne Shelton

Paradigm Publishers

Boulder • London

Copyright © 2007 Paradigm Publishers

Published in the United States by Paradigm Publishers, 3360 Mitchell Lane, Suite E, Boulder, CO 80301 USA.

Paradigm Publishers is the trade name of Birkenkamp & Company, LLC, Dean Birkenkamp, President and Publisher.

Library of Congress Cataloging-in-Publication Data

Agger, Ben.
        Fast families, virtual children : a critical sociology of families and schooling / Ben Agger and Beth Anne Shelton.
                p. cm.
Includes bibliographical references and index.
ISBN-13   978-1-59451-339-8 (cloth: alk. paper)
ISBN-10   1-59451-339-2 (cloth: alk. paper)
ISBN-13   978-1-59451-340-4 (pbk. : alk. paper)
ISBN-10   1-59451-340-6 (pbk. : alk. paper)
1. Family. 2. Work and family. 3. Children of working parents. 4. Children—Social conditions—21st century. 5. Education. 6. Educational sociology. 7. Civilization, Modern—21st century. I. Shelton, Beth Anne. II. Title.
Q519.A44 2007
06.8709182'1—dc22

                                                            2006039048

Designed and Typeset by Straight Creek Bookmakers.

11 10 09 08 07 1 2 3 4 5

Contents

Preface

Most people want a family—a partner and perhaps also children. They want an intimate life that sustains them. But families are often thwarted by external social forces that weigh heavily on all of us. We want to understand these pressures, especially as they impact children, and to help make possible the families and relationships of our dreams. Our book is about the degradation of family life and childhood in a fast, frenetic society. People may search for familylike intimacy not inside the four walls of their homes but at work, where they temporarily escape the pressures of home life. They eat on the run, throwing away their money on unhealthful "fast" foods. Our book also addresses the degradation of childhood as adults expect kids to join a pre-labor force in which they must work hard at school, complete hours of homework, and then spend their "free" time in extracurricular activities organized and evaluated by adults (think of Little League baseball or dance classes). One of our primary challenges in this book is to bring the children back into sociology and social theory, from which they have been missing.

Work, family, and school are interlocking domains. Indeed, we contend that the boundaries separating these social institutions are increasingly fragile, making it difficult for parents to shield their children and themselves from the outside world. This collapsing of boundaries is characteristic of what some writers call a postmodern society. We examine these boundaries carefully as we draw attention to the ways in which work has become familylike (think of collegiality and office dating). We also examine how families have become work as parents and kids rush around trying to get everything done, with precious little downtime. There is an interesting parallel between adults doing more work at home ("telework")—their home/work—and kids confronting prodigious amounts of school homework.

This book is not only a diagnosis, though. We identify positive features of families and schools in order to deploy "family" and "school" as useful metaphors of social relationships built on intimacy, mutuality, and democracy. We all want the experiences of being cherished by loved ones and educated by teachers and mentors who care. We believe children need to be protected from the busy, burdensome outside world for as long as possible.

We have seen the effects of this intrusive, rushed outside world on our own family. Recently, our twelve-year-old son was watching prime-time television with us when an ad for Viagra came on. He asked what it was. We did not want to have to explain the medicine's use to him because we wanted him to live in childish innocence for a few more short years. We are tempted to throw out our television, but that seems like burying our heads in the sand. Instead, networks need to make better choices about what they screen at 7:30 p.m., long before most kids' bedtimes.

We have also experienced the overburdening of children firsthand. On Halloween, our son wanted to go trick-or-treating. It may have been the last time he would don a costume and go door-to-door. However, several of his teachers assigned hours of homework that night, forcing him to choose between having fun and filling in some rote worksheets. The teachers knew it was an exciting holiday for kids, but they did not care. We helped him make the right choice—he enjoyed Halloween. Similarly, when our daughter was in junior high school, she was assigned mountains of homework over the short Thanksgiving break. And last year, her first year of high school, she was kept busy doing homework over the Christmas break. Of course, her teachers were not working during those all-American vacations, but they felt that their students should not be idle during holiday vacations, which are supposed to be much-needed respites from school and a time for family and friends.

In what follows, we examine the blurred boundary between work and family, especially for women. The 1960s women's movement liberated women to get college diplomas and pursue careers. Working women also augmented family incomes, thus improving the economic circumstances of their husbands and children. However, women are stressed and overloaded, largely because changes in women's labor force participation have not been accompanied by changes in gender roles and the work/family interface. Thus, women perform a "second shift" of meal preparation and child care once they return home from work. They are members of a new hurried and harried class.

Women's husbands suffer also because their own work lives are stressful, family time is frantic, and their wives are stretched so thin. Finally—and this is one of the main arguments of our book—children get the short end of the stick because they are neglected by parents who work long hours. Children are neglected when they return home from school to an empty house. Children are also increasingly burdened with adultlike expectations of their school and sports performances as they are positioned to "build a résumé" that will get them into the best colleges and then have the best job opportunities—putting them on the same treadmill as their parents.

We address the impact of rapid information and communication technologies on people's work and family lives. We note that people seek sustaining and intimate relations in the workplace; the family home becomes merely a hotel in which family members have hurried and occasional contact. We interpret the yearning for family as a sign that people are not getting their needs met in contemporary families. We also address the impact of fast family and work lives on children. We observe that childhood is being attenuated as children are confronted with adultlike expectations of their productivity (of homework) and performativity (the tendency to evaluate everything kids do, from sports to lunchroom comportment).

We focus particularly on schooling as a site of the erosion of childhood. Kids are warehoused in factory- and prisonlike settings in which the "guards"—teachers—are underpaid and overburdened. Kids become little workers (a pre–labor force) whose blissful idleness, spent in unstructured play, is threatening to envious adults. These adults defend the acceleration of childhood as an expedient in a competitive world. Just as family has become a symbol of democratic and reciprocal human relationships, school can serve the same function if we view schooling as an important component of the public sphere—a place where citizens gather in education and celebration. This would require major shifts in the ways we think about the value and purpose of education, which would not remain rote learning, with fill-in-the-blank answers, but become a lifelong process of self-discovery and the edification of others. Transforming schooling would require us to view kids as basically good and educable rather than following the authoritarian model currently found in most American schools in which kids are viewed as basically bad, leading to prisonlike restrictions on behavior, dress, and movement.

We conclude with a children's bill of rights and a corresponding agenda of adult responsibilities. Children have the right to be children, and parents have the responsibility not to abdicate parenting to schools, peers, video games, television, and the Internet. Above all, we must protect childhood as a distinctive developmental stage and not allow it to become nothing more than a period of preparation for obtaining college admission followed by a career.

Acknowledgments

We are indebted to several people who assisted with this project at crucial junctures. Dean Birkenkamp supported this project enthusiastically and with his usual critical insight and expert guidance. He has wonderfully collegial relationships with authors, which is why we clamor to publish with Paradigm.

Julie Kirsch, in charge of producing and copyediting the book, was far more than a style editor, although she does a great job of that. She helped us articulate our arguments more clearly, understanding, sometimes better than we did, what we were trying to say and helping us say it more effectively.

Finally, Megan Hartzell, a sociology instructor at University of Nevada, Las Vegas, graciously allowed Paradigm to test market a draft of our book in her marriage and family class. She composed acute and helpful comments and suggestions for revision, and her students gave us valuable input about how to improve our arguments and analyses for undergraduates. We are indebted to all of our "editors" at UNLV!

Finally, we acknowledge our children, Sarah and Oliver, who put up with parents who analyze and overanalyze every single aspect of their lives! Our kids and their friends give us access to a "kids' world" that can be inaccessible to adults who enter it without a roadmap. Unfortunately, as we argue here, the adult world encroaches too much on children. We want a sociology and social science that view children as citizens, and we want a world in which kids can be kids.

1

Mapping Families in Fast Capitalism

This is a book about our family. As such, it is necessarily biographical and autobiographical. Our lives, and our kids' lives, provide insights and data. This book is not value free; we are partisan. We want to slow down childhood and remake families, schools, and, thus, all of society. This is also a book about your family and many families. One of our main contentions is that "the family" of nuclear lore has been dispersed into many different configurations. We spend much of this book analyzing the causes and consequences of these transformations. We view "family," or actually families, as a utopian ideal, a source of radical energy at a time when we all want and need "family," including in our working lives. We also view the concept of "school" as potentially progressive. Together, family/families and schooling can become progressive ideals that energize a movement of women, progressive men, gays, lesbians, and even children in the ongoing struggle against fundamentalist "traditional" values. In this opening chapter, we map families in the early twenty-first century in their increasing diversity. We also explore assumptions about human nature that inform differing parenting and schooling styles.

This is also a book about gender,* the ways in which men and women play out their sexual identities and orientations. Men and women have tended to play rather bifurcated roles, with men viewed as the stronger (and perhaps more emotionally obtuse) sex and women viewed as the weaker (but more intuitive and nurturant) sex. The Victorians created a sexual division of labor, with women staying home and tending the household and children and men entering paid labor. This division creates differences in power between men and women. The ways in which

---

*The ways in which women and men are taught to express their sexual identities, usually, in this society, sharply divided into masculine versus feminine identities; gender is learned, whereas one's sex is more or less biologically fixed.

1

we have structured our family lives revolve around our definitions and practices of gender, as we explore.

This book is intended to be a contribution to sociologies of family and marriage, childhood and children, schools and schooling, gender roles and gender inequality. Our book is different from many standard texts in these fields in that we have a definite theoretical perspective, which we derive from critical theory,* feminist theory,† and postmodernism.‡ We use theory to illuminate the assumptions underlying families, childhood, and schooling. But a sociological background is not required—this book is also addressed to general readers who live in families, work, and send kids to school. These readers want to bring up kids who are unburdened by the world, to promote more enlightening schooling, and to enjoy more meaningful work. We provide footnotes to define terms and describe theorists perhaps unfamiliar to readers, encouraging them to do further reading in the sources that inspire us.

MANY FAMILIES

On May 17, 2004, gay and lesbian marriages were legalized in Massachusetts. Gay marriage has received much notice in the press because the issue is contentious, dividing conservatives and progressives as few issues have since abortion and, before that, the rights of women and Americans of color (Donlan 2005; Neilan 2003). Conservatives quickly proposed an amendment to the U.S. Constitution to ban gay marriages, fearing that such marriages will destroy the fabric of American culture and morality. Progressives hailed the Massachusetts court decision as a landmark ruling that recognizes the various ways people live. This debate over gay marriage and civil unions mirrors the broader discussion of what is or should be considered a family.

As sociologists we take the position that family is the way in which people live together. It is the way you split up or pool the household's income(s); how you raise children; whether you have children in the

---

*Theories of the Frankfurt School that stress the role of big government and media in perpetuating capitalism into the twenty-first century.

†A social theory emphasizing the importance of gender roles and gender inequality for understanding women's lives.

‡A European theory that challenges Marxism as overly economic and stresses the importance of culture, media, and discourse for understanding human behavior; associated with Derrida, Foucault, Baudrillard, and Lyotard, who sometimes reject Habermas's project of modernity as an overly optimistic theory of progress.

first place, and whether you conceived or adopted them; whether there are one or more adults living under one roof; whether there are actually several roofs under which family members live; who initiates having sex; how much television is watched; who makes decisions about what to have for dinner, whether to buy a new house, and how to teach the kids about religion and politics; who goes shopping and does the driving; and who helps kids with homework.

Families are the places and ways in which these, and many more, issues are decided. These are private decisions in the sense that most people do not allow people outside of the household to make them, but they are public decisions in that they are often heavily influenced by the larger social, economic, cultural, and political institutions surrounding us. For example, the more the husband earns, the less likely the wife is to work for pay outside the home (Jacobson 1998; Lehrer 1999). The less time women spend working for pay, the more time they spend on housework and the more we reinforce the idea that women stay home and men go out to work (Blair-Loy 2003). Indeed, the image of wealthy women tending the household suggests that the only reason less wealthy women work is that they must, for economic reasons.

The United States is nearly alone among Western industrial countries in lacking both a national health-care plan and a child-care plan (Kamerman and Kahn 1991). Canada, our near neighbor, has had publicly funded medical insurance for many years (Ostry 2006). And Canadians are now debating how to implement a child-care policy (Greenaway 2006). Canada also recently legalized same-sex marriage (Andrew Mills 2005). European countries are also far ahead of the United States in their family-leave and child-care policies (Kamerman and Kahn 1995). We are interested sociologically in why the United States is so different from these other countries, especially when the United States is so similar to most of these countries and regions economically and politically. A good deal of the answer to this question involves—again—the notion of what a family is and how people should best conceptualize the relationships among person, government, and church.

When President George W. Bush gave his victory speech the morning after the 2004 election, making way for his second term of office, he said that he stood for "faith and family." These are code words, as many voters recognize. This code embraces a narrow definition of the family as "nuclear," a sociological term connoting a heterosexual couple, legally married, with children and the father usually working for wages outside the home and the mother often staying home to raise kids and tend the household. It is said that Bush's victory hinged on his perceived support of traditional values, which supposedly differentiated him from his Democratic opponent, John Kerry. At the heart of these differences are people's views about women's roles in the family, abortion rights, and same-sex marriage and civil unions.

A book about family, then, must contend with the various overlapping and sometimes contradictory meanings of the term. Moreover, we address the idea of family as much as the empirical forms families take. Idealized notions of family often signify what people lack in their lives, or what families are not, as much as they describe the family arrangements people construct for themselves. The family, then, is both absent and present, something for which people yearn and something that people invent, even if their inventions defy conventional wisdom about what a family should look like.

By some accounts, fewer than one in four households is made up of a married couple living with their minor children, only a subgroup of which is composed of families where only the father is employed (Fields 2004). This sitcom-style family was idealized mainly by men who benefit from women who are subordinate and by the Victorians, who, during Queen Victoria's era in the late nineteenth century, wanted to persuade women and their children to retreat from factory work and instead take up residence in the family home. This was because industrial technologies could perform jobs formerly staffed by humans; men were allowed to keep their wages, while women were encouraged to find other work, albeit uncompensated work that would suit their supposed nature as helpmates and nurturers. Women would lose wages but in return receive deliverance from the din and dangers of the factory. They would also gain the "family wage," supposedly paid out by the husband in return for getting his shirts ironed and receiving sexual favors and for, yes, being loved, cherished, and obeyed. Feminists contend that the family wage is a myth in that employers pay men wages blind to the number of their dependents. The Victorians set up the "nuclear family,"* as sociologists term it, in order to establish a sexual division of labor that would supposedly prove beneficial to men, women, and children. The motivation for this was not to oppress women but to set up a sharing of roles, with women and men each doing what they supposedly did best. Women would perform important but uncompensated duties such as childrearing,

---

* A family composed of a father, mother, and children still living at home; traditionally, the father was employed outside the home and the mother stayed home to raise the children and maintain the home.

cooking, and cleaning. Upper-class Victorian women would hire a nanny to care for their kids and would spend their time planning their families' social lives.

Why do only a minority of Americans inhabit this sort of family? And what are the consequences of this fact? These are complicated and interrelated issues. Suffice it to say that the very fact that the male-headed nuclear family is increasingly a thing of the past makes a lot of people "deviants," by which sociologists mean that they deviate from norms governing their behavior. Here the norms are to get married and have kids biologically, with the wife staying home to care for the family and household and the husband leaving in the morning with briefcase, laptop, or, in increasingly rare cases these days, hard hat and lunch pail. There are many people "doing" family differently or not doing it at all.

There are four ways in which people could be said to "do" family. They do not take the forms of family from a textbook but invent them in meeting the challenges in their daily lives. We contend that many people improvise their families, producing forms and styles that can be quite unconventional. People are flexible and dextrous in negotiating family life, requiring us to look beyond textbooks and marriage manuals to sample the diversity of their improvisations.

Marriage

You love your partner. You have been dating and perhaps even cohabiting for a while. You pool your money. Do you apply for a marriage license and vow to stay together until death? To get married in most American states you have to be heterosexual. In some states, only civil unions are acknowledged between gay and lesbian partners, with only one state, Massachusetts, currently allowing same-sex marriage. (Connecticut, Vermont, and California allow "legal unions" of gay people that are stronger than civil unions and similar to marriage except in name.) This is very different from Canada and Europe, where gay and lesbian marriage is increasingly common (Gardner 2003). So, if you are not straight in the United States, you are automatically a deviant because you cannot get married except in Massachusetts. Even if you are straight, you may not want to get married. Let's say that you have been married twice before and feel burned by the institution of marriage. No more wedding vows for you! But you still love your partner and want to have a relationship with her/him, perhaps even to move in together. Disavowing the married state automatically makes you a deviant from the norms of the nuclear family and possibly a sinner if you choose to cohabit without being married, "living in sin," the old-fashioned term for cohabiting—pretending that you are married, living under one roof, having sex, sharing finances.

Patriarchy

It is deep-seated in Christianity that men should make the major decisions in the family, a political arrangement called *patriarchy*.* From male authority in the family stems male authority in the larger political arena. Philip Blumstein and Pepper Schwartz (1983) find that in married couples and in cohabiting straight couples and gay male couples, the highest earner (typically, the male) makes the decisions. Only in couples without any men—lesbian—is power shared nearly equally. Male rule is said to be biblical, and it has been a norm of the nuclear family. Only with 1960s feminism did women begin to question male rule in the family along with a host of other dubious family practices such as women having to stay home.

Children

We have children and do all the things that child-centered families do—go to the latest Pixar movie, take the kids to play miniature golf, vacation where there are other families with kids. Single people, before they become coupled, often do not have kids. We cannot say they never do because by now, with the prevalence of divorce and childbearing outside of marriage, nearly half of American children live in families headed by only one parent (presumably, these are families, too). In any event, it is not cast in stone that single and even coupled adults need, want, or must have children. In addition, it was assumed for a century that couples would acquire children by reproducing themselves biologically. Biological offspring were written into the legal code of the nuclear family. That has begun to change now, as children join families through adoption and via the recombinant postmodern families (as Judith Stacey [1990] calls them) that follow in the wake of divorces and recouplings. Adoption is on the rise both because it is increasingly acceptable for women not to have kids biologically and because many of them cannot, perhaps because they have delayed childbirth until

---

* Rule by men, either in the larger political and economic systems or in families.

well into their thirties and forties, having attended college and then established careers (Child Welfare Information Gateway 2004; Della Cava, Phillips, and Engel 2004).

Sexual Division of Labor

Although the Victorians did not use the term "sexual division of labor,"* that is what they had in mind as they tried to persuade women to leave nineteenth-century factories and retreat into maternal domesticity. They tried to make this attractive to women by telling them that they would share in a wage paid the husband in order to care for his family, a wage that would reflect the number of a husband's dependents. By sexual division of labor, feminist sociologists are referring to the assignment of paid work to men and unpaid housework to women, all the way from changing diapers to cooking meals. In a sense, it could be said that the lot of women and children was improved by their removal from the factory, even though another perspective on this would stress that women lost relational power as they lost their wages.

As technology advanced, women and children were encouraged to leave the labor force so that men could have jobs. In post–World War II capitalism, beginning in the early 1960s, women were encouraged, especially by other women, to leave the home and go out to work. This is beneficial to capitalism† because it generates more household income and thus more spending, hallmarks of an "affluent society" (Galbraith 1984). However, the entry of women into the workforce has had a massive impact on the traditional family with a stay-at-home wife. It has also affected children, schooling, leisure time, and even men.

Each of these four features of families—marriage, patriarchy, children, and sexual division of labor—can be viewed as a choice, something that changes or can change. People who make up a family can be married, or they might not be. Men might make the important decisions in families, or women might, or the power may be shared. Or perhaps there is not only one decision maker, in which case the older kids probably get votes, too. Some families have kids, and others do not. Or custody of children may be split between two parents in separate households,

---

*A feminist term for the way in which men perform paid labor outside the household and women perform unpaid housework and child care; stems from the Victorian era.

†An economic system such as that of the United States in which the means of production, such as businesses and technology, are owned privately, not by the government.

in which case there are really two families—the family with the kids on certain days and the family without the kids on those same days. There are other important features, too, such as the sexual orientation of the spouses, whether older relatives live with the family, commuting relationships, and the status of the family when the children are alone at home, such as after school.

This last type of family is quite postmodern. By postmodern we mean flexible, diverse, and different from the standards of post–World War II society during the 1950s. The Victorians never imagined that kids a hundred years later might become the adults, while the real adults are nowhere to be seen. Almost 16 percent of grade school children spend at least some of their time in self-care (U.S. Census Bureau 2003). Little attention is paid to kids home alone ("latchkey" children) and thus becoming, in effect, parents. This has been hilariously (and sociologically) treated by Hollywood in the series of movies that began with *Home Alone.* The precocious but annoying youngest sibling is left behind when his family rushes to catch a Christmas flight to Paris. By the time the parents discover that the child is missing and return home, the little one has had a series of hilarious adventures, including staving off some burglars. He is the man of the house, and he is loving it! This gives latchkey a new meaning. America flocked to the movie because they could relate to the pressures that led the family to "misplace" one of their own brood, who then fends for himself creatively.

The nuclear family enshrined by certain conservative versions of the New Testament is declining as people, of necessity and by choice, craft other types of relationships that better suit them. Women work, men stay home, power is shared; kids take care of themselves; gays and lesbians establish lifelong committed relationships and even bear or adopt children. Certain people might not like these "other" relationships enough to call them families, but they command our attention as social scientists. And we choose to call them families because we realize that there is no single correct way to "do" intimacy, home life, and nurturing. There are only families, plural.

DEFENSES AND CRITIQUES OF THE FAMILY: FROM FRANKFURT TO FEMINISM, AND BEYOND

This is not to say that people, in complete freedom, have chosen alternative forms of family, and thus their own private utopias (imagined perfect societies) of humanized social relationships, as they might select gourmet foods off the shelves of their local specialty stores. Family, like work and most other social arrangements, is born of people's efforts to deal with "contingencies," the various circumstances into which we find ourselves thrust by accidents of birth and by the ebb and flow of our adult relationships. We agree with Judith Stacey (1990), Dorothy Smith (1987), and others who view gender and family from a social-constructionist and ethnomethodological perspective that people are quite creative in their modes of adaptation to, and transformation of, these contingent circumstances; they are not the rote role players depicted by Parsons* (1951) in his writings on the social system and family systems. The social-constructionist and ethnomethodological perspectives stress people's creativity in achieving their own meanings and identities from their everyday lives, and they stress the ways in which social reality is negotiated among its participants using language. However, people's lives—our own—are not perfect, especially where there are real gaps between the lives we lead and the better world we seek.

One might call these gaps "history," or simply the distance between what is and what we believe ought to be. This is not an infinite distance, because people struggle mightily to better themselves and give their children hope and a head start, but they have usually fallen short for most of human history, often drastically short. The life expectancy in fifteenth-century Europe was about twenty-eight; in the early twenty-first century, a fifth of Americans or more are still locked into poverty; in the 1960s and 1970s millions of people were killed in Vietnam in order to "free" the Vietnamese from communism; since the 1980s AIDS has been ravaging sub-Saharan Africa; and in 2005 Hurricane Katrina caused much of New Orleans to float away—and this is to name only a few instances of notable human tragedy. But still people strive, especially in their personal lives, to improve themselves and their children.

Our own theoretical perspective derives from feminism,† the Frankfurt School,‡ and postmodernism. Feminists have persuaded us that the

---

*The founder of structural functionalism who, from his position at Harvard, influenced the training of American sociologists from the 1930s to the 1960s; his writings on the family also embraced the sexual division of labor and were countered by many feminists.

†A 1960s perspective that analyzes and criticizes patriarchy, or rule by men; major feminist goals include equal pay for equal work and full political participation by women.

‡A group of German Jewish Marxist intellectuals including Herbert Marcuse, Max Horkheimer, Theodor Adorno, and Jürgen Habermas, writing from the 1920s to the present, who attempt to figure out why capitalism lasted longer than Marx predicted back in the mid-nineteenth century; they stress the importance of ideology and media in influencing people's behavior.

personal is political and that what occurs at home reflects and affects what happens in the political and economic spheres. The Frankfurt School critical theorists advise us that culture and the technologies that convey it cannot be ignored as factors in power arrangements. Postmodernists identify ways in which people (especially children) are caught in disciplinary grids that constrain them in subtle, everyday ways. These perspectives allow us to read the emphasis in schools on neatness, penmanship, punctuality, obedience to authority, and even dress codes as political stances. Our argument throughout this book is that we can no longer clearly separate personal/family from political/public/work activities and experiences, especially in a "fast" capitalism in which people text message each other, order goods online, and use chat rooms and e-mail in order to create electronic communities. Using rapid information and communication technologies, we have moved beyond early-twentieth-century capitalism in which factories had inflexible divisions of labor, produced only a few product lines, and required a large workforce of blue-collar workers. In our global, Internetworked capitalism, workers tend to be well educated and middle-class and even to identify more with management than with the working class and labor unions.

We take the feminist and Frankfurt School arguments a step further because we believe that what Jürgen Habermas[*] (1984, 1987b) calls the colonization of everyday life[†] (its invasion by outside influences) has been greatly facilitated and accelerated by rapid information and communication technologies such as the Internet and the cell phone. One of our themes is that children have been missing from sociology and social theory and we try to restore them (but see O'Neill 1994, who is one of the few to theorize children and childhood). Kids overlap the spheres of home and work, via school, which prepares them for adult life and indeed already imposes adultlike expectations on them, from homework to discipline. This helps create what we call a rote culture characterized by fill-in-the-blank answers and discouraging thinking outside the box. And we contend that children constitute a distinctive but neglected class that we call the pre–labor force.

---

[*]A second-generation member of the Frankfurt School who tries to make Marxism relevant in the twenty-first century by reinterpreting its aim not as communism but as a democratic society based on dialogue, mutuality, and reciprocity; also stresses the relevance of communication and media in capitalism.

[†]Habermas's term for the tendency of social structures to penetrate deep into the routines of personal and family life.

Feminists, Frankfurt School theorists, and postmodernists agree that the personal is political, but they have somewhat disagreed about the role of the family in capitalism. Already we must differentiate among different species of feminism and feminist theory (see Jaggar 1983) because there is disagreement among the sisterhood about families, even if there is also general agreement about the nature of patriarchy and what to do about it. Feminists believe in equality between the sexes, but they sometimes disagree about the causes and consequences of inequalities, especially with respect to what sociologists call gender roles.

As we teach in our introductory sociology and women's studies classes, the difference between sex and gender is equivalent to the difference between biology and society or history. Sex is, for the most part, "given" in our reproductive natures as either women or men. You can have a sex-change operation and alter aspects of your biological nature, thus changing your sex or at least blending your former sex with your new, desired one. But sex is fairly impervious to such attempts to transform it. Also, sexual identity (as either woman or man) tends to be a primary factor differentiating people. The vast majority of the world's population are readily identified, and identify themselves, as men or women.

Gender, on the other hand, is quite flexible, even if gender, too, seems to be bimodal—split between two opposite extremes. Gender identity (how you view yourself as man or woman) tends to have two varieties, masculinity and femininity, including all of the traits and behaviors that we view as appropriate in well-socialized adults. Gender in this sense is how you enact (and how you are taught to enact) your sexuality—what makes you a "real" man or a "real" woman. Just saying it in this way immediately invites the observation that there is much disagreement, even within genders, about what constitutes appropriateness. Some "real" men view it as okay to cry while watching tragic movies, where others view involvement in sports and sports fandom as a basic requirement of rugged masculinity.

Women also face gender expectations, which are often confusing and contradictory. Should feminists get manicures and pedicures and otherwise beautify themselves? Get married? Establish careers? Have kids? There is mounting evidence that what one might call lifestyle feminism—actually living by feminist principles in one's everyday life, in all spheres—has become a period piece of the 1960s. After the 1960s, younger "postfeminists" have rejected many of the original feminist aims, such as a restructuring of both the family and gender, and they somehow seek to combine feminism and femininity, wanting to "have it all" (Baumgardner and Richards 2000). The components of feminism our college students retain are equal pay for equal work and reproductive rights, but they do not seem particularly troubled by the dichotomous structuring of gender into clear-cut masculine and feminine characteristics and behaviors. These young women still believe, as their 1950s forebears did, that the woman should wait for the man to call, that she should allow the man to open the door, and that the man should pay the bills on a date. But they also believe that it is okay for women to get college degrees and work (Abowitz 2002).

In spite of the flexibility of gender, the work world in the United States has not become particularly flexible, as it has in European countries, as far as parental leave and child care are concerned. Women are still expected to do the second shift (housework and child care) after paid work, and their employers do not feel that it is their responsibility to help out with flex time, day care, and parental leave (Moen and Roehling 2005). "Having it all" is nearly impossible in the capitalist and male-run work world primarily because gendered roles are still with us. There may be an irresolvable contradiction between wanting a family and seeking a career in a society with fairly rigid gender roles. If a woman wants and pursues both family and work, she may find herself shouldering most of the child care and falling behind in her career if she takes years off to have children and leaves work early when her kids are sick.

The issue of the legacy of 1960s feminism is complex and interesting. Many young women reject feminism while their mothers are proud to be feminists. We conclude that feminism's most powerful critique was of gender, the very structuring of identity, attitudes, and actions into sex-appropriate categories. Gender is a trap for both women and men in that it limits people's possibilities and prevents them from combining traits, emotions, and attitudes of the opposite gender. Nancy Chodorow (1978), in her powerful *The Reproduction of Mothering*, traces sexism (negative attitudes toward and treatment of women by men) to a certain family structure that allows the man/father to be absent and the woman/mother to do most of the parenting. Using a psychoanalytic perspective but with feminist influences, Chodorow argues that it is bad for both girls and boys to be brought up only by the mother. Boys rebel against maternal authority and thus against all women. Girls become ambivalent about stay-at-home moms, especially at a time when feminism encourages women to obtain college degrees and to work. In this context, mothering is reproduced across generations, making it incredibly difficult for young people to shake free of imprisoning gender roles.

Feminist ethnomethodologists* recognize that gender is something we "do," borrowing from Harold Garfinkel's (1967) original insights into the ways in which social structure is constructed by everyday participants, especially using language. Social structures do not just "happen" to people, falling from the sky, but are actually created and re-created through everyday interactions over which people have some control. Ethnomethodology† and social constructionism‡ view the person as an "agent," a person capable of making important choices about everyday life. Seeing/saying gender this way emphasizes people's involvement in their own everyday scripts, which are not simply imposed on them by the guardians of patriarchy. To be sure, people, especially young ones, do not feel very free, or free at all, to innovate in the ways they do gender. They experience their genders as a prison, requiring girls to beautify themselves for boys and to pretend that they are the weaker sex and requiring boys to be macho and not show emotions. But the social-constructionist perspective on gender sheds much light on family, which is one of the main venues in which gender is played out. People "do" family in the sense that they interpret the roles assigned to them and deal with the practical contingencies of everyday life creatively. There are no scripts that we can consult, only the ones we imagine in our heads. And kids are especially at sea as they learn to do gender without a script ("What do I say when the boy on whom I have a crush calls me up for a date? Is it OK for me to call him?"). One of the reasons some people cling to religion is that religion seems to provide such scripts, although the interpretation of sacred texts may be unclear and involves the person in decisions about what the texts actually mean.

---

*A version of Garfinkel's perspective on ethnomethodology that examines the ways in which women and men, in their everyday lives, tend to negotiate and construct a shared (and sometimes conflicting) concept of their gender roles; stresses people's responsibilities for their own relationships and family lives.

† Garfinkel's sociology of everyday life in which he studies ways in which people creatively make sense of their sometimes confusing lives, relying heavily on conversations and communication to achieve common understandings with others.

‡ A perspective, similar to ethnomethodology, originally developed by Alfred Schutz and later by Berger and Luckmann, that stresses how people develop shared meanings through their everyday interactions that help frame what they know and their identities; people aren't simply receptacles into which knowledge is poured but active agents who, to some extent, control their own fate.

What we think of as the traditional script for family was written during the nineteenth century w.hen it was no longer necessary to have such a large labor force. And so women were convinced to reframe their gender roles. They would concentrate on raising children, now viewed as fragile and precious, around whom such holidays as Christmas would pivot. Were children not always precious? For most of history, children were simply viewed as small adults who were expected to work alongside big adults in the fields and then the factories (Shorter 1975). Adam Smith's (1998) classic treatise on capitalist economic theory, *The Wealth of Nations,* describes child labor (and we are talking about seven-year-olds here) as if it were natural. Child labor is still found in many underdeveloped countries.

In the United States, a major change to this script occurred first during World War II, when Rosie the Riveter left the American home and worked in factories doing military production while her husband (whose job she was temporarily filling) was away at war. Although the Rosies of America returned to home and hearth after the war and had babies in record numbers during the baby boom between about 1946 and 1964, the early 1960s saw women again considering entry into the workforce, and college, as Betty Friedan (1974) and other early feminists called for women's rights and women's liberation. Arguably, the experience of American women on the home front during World War II prepared the way for the massive entry of U.S. women into paid work during and after the 1960s.

This notion that women could (and should) get an education beyond high school and then embark on careers alongside men changed gender scripts,* but not completely. American women, except for hardcore radical feminists during and after the 1960s (when everyone was questioning everything, it seemed), retained the traditional script of gender in the sense that they continued to differentiate sharply between what is masculine and feminine *except* for getting an education and working. But many feminists changed the script, or at least tried to, regarding how to raise kids. Many thought and still think that it would be better for everyone, especially kids and moms, if men took their turns changing diapers and preparing infant formula, as Chodorow has persuasively argued.

These are major changes to the gender script, but certain things have not changed. Women often still define themselves, as least in

---

*Ways in which young children, teenagers, and adults are taught to play out their appropriate gender roles; powerfully influenced by peers, media, and advertising.

part, in terms of their appearance. The fashion, cosmetic, and fitness industries—all involving a kind of self-help—are huge and continue to grow, attesting to women's need to (and we lack a more nuanced term here) appear to be beautiful objects. Although certain more traditional feminists contend that women who dress up and pluck their eyebrows are in fact doing these things for themselves, many are doing it to catch the eye of men, who help them construct their gender identities by staring and admiring. Women also dress for other women as they reproduce their femininity among an appreciative and supportive audience. In this sense, women's gender identity plays out in social relationships with both sexes—men who objectify women and like-minded women who deeply understand that women define themselves by their attractiveness to men (even as they resent this). Women, although more independent than forty years ago, still sometimes succumb to defining themselves in terms of their value for men.

For their part, men, too, live by traditional gender scripts, especially equating physical prowess and other external markers of success such as money and possessions with their value as people. They also define themselves in terms of their conquests of women, and they inhabit a male culture in which women are privately deprecated and objectified. The heart of the matter here is that men and women are still objects to each other, aliens in effect. The Victorians would not have had it any other way because they wanted to demarcate women's and men's worlds, notably the spheres of domesticity and work. Many of these differences have survived women's liberation.

Indeed, in these increasingly conservative times, even the gains of the 1960s women's movement—such as *Roe v. Wade* and equal pay for equal work—are imperiled. In 1994 Bush won a second presidential term in large measure because he appealed to evangelicals in the Bible Belt in his support of the traditional heterosexual family. In their famous study *The Authoritarian Personality,* Theodor Adorno and his coauthors (Adorno, Frenkel-Brunswik, Levinson, Sanford 1950) indicate that the ruling elites divide and conquer the powerless masses by convincing one powerless group to displace their anger by scapegoating an even weaker group—Jews during the Holocaust and now gays and lesbians.

In this political and cultural climate, so-called postfeminism (women having jobs but also wearing nail polish) is quite appealing to younger women, seeming to move beyond the more strident radicalism and rhetoric of 1960s feminists. Postfeminism retains quite traditional gender scripts, differing with traditionalists mainly on whether women should be allowed to obtain a higher education and work outside the home. But the traditional emphasis on "family" has been preserved in the current call for "family values," which include for Bush and the evangelicals what they call "faith." This undoes the separation of church and state and also demonizes gay and lesbian couplings.

THE NEW RIGHT'S FAITH-BASED FAMILY
VERSUS THE NEW LEFT'S "FAMILIES"

The decline and dispersal of parental authority and role models have been inflated by the New Right* into a critique not only of the decline of the family but of a decline of all Christian values and America's dominant role in the world. The New Right arose during the 1980s as an alliance between conservative Republicans who favor the free market and evangelical "born-again" Christians. The blame is put on left-wing professors, feminists, gays and lesbians, and multiculturalists, among others. This neoconservative critique of the 1960s and its baby-boom generation (see Bloom 1987 and D'Souza 1991) began during the Reagan years, when the country began to shift toward the right in the wake of the antiwar, civil rights, and women's liberation movements, all of which were stigmatized by the Right. This backlash (see Faludi 1992) only intensified after Clinton's terms in office, even though it is fair to say that the role of the Democratic Leadership Council in pushing the party to the right has blurred the differences between Democrat and Republican (see Agger 2005). Bush's reelection has been the capstone of the conservative Christian New Right's attempt to capture federal, state, and local power across America.

Central in this ideology is the conjuncture of "faith" and "family." Under the Christian New Right's interpretation of faith and family there is little if any support for gay and lesbian marriage. Women will return to a subservient role both in and beyond the household, and children will be homeschooled or attend religious school, a "faith-based" agenda that would see the flourishing of religious educational institutions. All of this will return America to its pre-1960s course, militating against new social movements designed to win rights, wealth, and power for oppressed minorities, including women.

---

*A social and political movement beginning in the 1980s that brings together Republican ideas about a free-market economy and an evangelical interpretation of Christianity; was largely responsible for George W. Bush's election and reelection.

What is interesting about the New Right's critique of the family is that, in some superficial respects, it converges with a Frankfurt School perspective and our own perspective on the decline of the family and particularly the decline and dispersal of parental authority. However, we do not turn back the clock to an earlier era with men working and thus dominant in the marriage and women staying home to raise kids, cook meals, and do the laundry. We want to reconfigure "family" to inform all humane social relationships in both the public and private spheres. Whether everyone approves or not, "family" is being reconfigured as people devise all sorts of ways to conduct their intimate lives and raise their children.

A crucial difference, then, between the New Right's critique of the family and our own is that they view kids as basically bad and in need of stronger paternal authority and we view kids as potentially good and in need of parents who are present and play active roles in their kids' upbringing. We reject patriarchy and the accompanying denial of children's rights, rarely discussed by the New Right. In our concluding chapter, we explore these rights more fully.

We share with the New Right simply the observation that something is awry in the family, although, as we have been arguing, the cause of this is not found in the family isolated from other social institutions but in the collapsing boundaries between and among social institutions. We identify especially the intrusion into everyday life of work and other informatic tethers sucking up our time and thwarting our autonomy. We do not blame divorce, feminists, or gays and lesbians for the dissolution of families, the prevalence of latchkey children, and the shift of authority and responsibility from parents to teachers and schools. In postmodern capitalism, people are controlled and connected from morning to night by rapid information technologies that rob them of sleep, contentment, and time alone and with their families. The family is overloaded with expectations of happiness, deliverance, and meaning. These expectations were first formulated when the family promised women and children relief from factory labor and promised men succor when they returned home.

The nuclear family, idealized in images of childhood, Christmas, and Valentine's Day, was actually a warning signal. Capitalism was not working to provide for people's needs, especially their emotional and psychological ones. The family was construed as a haven in a heartless world (see Ehrenreich 1983; Lasch 1977) because the workplace did not meet people's emotional needs; indeed, it was often a hell on earth. The nurturing maternal figure, along with the figures of young children frolicking playfully and without care, was actually a utopian image of an end to alienation* and isolation. (By "alienation" we are drawing from the Marxian tradition to designate the human experience of being out of control of one's life, especially in the realm of work. According to Marx, you can be alienated without necessarily knowing it, especially if you have what he termed false consciousness.) Fast-forward to the early twenty-first century: the wives of wealthy men in the United States are the least likely of all wives to work outside the home. They do not have to work for a living. Although we can reconstruct work to be creative and fulfilling, especially in "familized" democratic work settings, this is very far from happening. To "familize" social relationships means giving relationships outside the family proper, including work relationships, familylike attributes such as intimacy and mutuality. Rich women who do not work for pay engage in volunteer work and spend time socializing and working on their tennis games and their abs. This might be a utopian model for all who hate their jobs, have too much stress, and spend little time with family and loved ones. What the New Right likes about the "traditional" family are the subservient roles of women and children, who prop up the haggard male with sustenance and affection.

We support the utopian imagery and implications of family viewed as pacified, civilized, democratic social relationships. Later, we also propose a radical image of school as community. This is the New Left† and feminist family—a group of intimates, including children, who care about each other and make lives together. By "New Left" we refer to the student movement during the 1960s that put a premium on participatory democracy in everyday life. This is not the Parsonian family with people dutifully playing roles—men earning paychecks and women doing dishes and cooking. We embrace family as a utopian ideal—community, by another name. This view of family-as-community is subversive because it rejects patriarchy (male rule), sharply divided gender roles, the denial of rights to children, assumed heterosexuality, and the compartmentalization of family as a separate sphere apart from the economy, polity, and school.

This is yet another way in which the term *family* must be decoded politically. The New Right grounds family in religion, from which it derives sanction for its patriarchal view of family. The New Left grounds

---

*A condition of being powerless and lacking control of one's life; people may not recognize that they are alienated; derived from Marx's ideas.

†A social and political movement stemming from the 1960s that values participatory democracy; originally arose as part of the civil rights and antiwar movements during the 1960s.

family in a utopian imagery of intimate community. Imagine a family sitting around the table debating what movie to watch after dinner, with give-and-take all the way around. Imagine a town debating whether to shift from fossil to renewable fuel. Imagine a nation debating whether to allow gay and lesbian marriage. As well, a broad conception of the family allows for family multiplicity—single parent, dual earner, extended, intergenerational, unmarried, gay and lesbian, as well as straight. Many family types must be acknowledged by sociology and society, just as there are many types of culture and language in the world. This diversity must be "allowed" because it already exists and deserves legitimation. Fewer than one tenth of all households are composed of an employed husband, a stay-at-home wife, and at least one dependent child (Fields 2004).

Stacey's (1990) work on the postmodern family demystifies all sorts of class, race, gender, and generational assumptions about progressive parenting, family-type differentiation, and political flexibility within families. Conservatives universalize the white Christian family of 1950s sitcom lore at the peril of a realistic topographic mapping of diverse family, parenting, and cohabiting styles. Blumstein and Schwartz's study (1983) is much closer to the mark than the New Right's "family" in that it examines at least four arrangements of intimacy—straight married, straight cohabiting, lesbian, and gay.

The New Right uses the discourse of faith and family to advance its political agenda. Family values are not empty rhetoric but a careful positioning of the Right on issues of the politics of the body, women, and children. But family can be a radical agenda, as we have been arguing, if we celebrate families' diversity, use family as a synonym for community, and point out that families in the past have not been havens in a heartless world but zones of conflict and contested terrains, even if embryos of family have elevated the self and protected people to some extent against the ravages of the outside world.

Feminism's point is that the inside world is ravaged, too. Family was never a haven for women and children, who depended economically on the beneficence of the male breadwinner. Violence against women can be understood as male rage and resentment mistakenly directed at a female scapegoat. Socialist feminists* (see Jaggar 1983; Walby 1990) urge alliances between progressive men and women as they identify their common enemy—patriarchal capitalism. Only in this way can "inside"

---

*A feminist theory that links patriarchy and capitalism, noticing that gender inequality and economic inequality go hand in hand, for example in the fact that women earn less than men do for the same job.

be connected to "outside" and both be transformed together. Feminism's intriguing point is that this change might begin at home, between spouses and among parents and children, and then spread to traditional politics. Before the 1960s, it was assumed that politics occupied only the public sphere and was not always personal. The Frankfurt School, especially Herbert Marcuse* (1969a), takes the politics of everyday life seriously because they argue that the damaged self who begins to throw over alienation in his or her own life becomes "prefiguring," auguring large structural changes that feed back into the private sphere. Both feminism and the critical theorists recognize that there is no such thing as private life, especially under a capitalism in which the purpose of all human relationships and activities is to produce economic value (or, as we argue, preeconomic value in the case of children who do homework and are evaluated performatively in all of their activities).

Feminism and the Frankfurt School coalesce with queer theory,[†] which might be regarded as one of the strongest critiques of fast society today (see Seidman 1996). Queer theorists examine the connection between sexuality and society and focus on how gays and lesbians have become a new minority group. They also express pride in their "queerness." Gays and lesbians are perhaps the biggest "moral" threat to the New Right. Where the 1950s were defined by McCarthyist witch hunts, the 1960s by Bull Connor's and Richard Daley's assaults on civil rights, and the 1980s by the Reagan Right's attacks on affirmative action, the early twenty-first century is marked by the New Right's assault on gays and lesbians, particularly as homosexuals seek to marry. Short of an unlikely constitutional amendment banning gay marriage, individual states are rushing to ban gay marriage within their provinces. This is legally unnecessary in that few states or cities allow gay and lesbian marriage. It is symbolic of anger against "difference"—here, homosexuals who seek the comforts of visible domestic unions. Even the mainstream of the Democratic Party has not come down clearly on the side of gay and lesbian marriage, preferring the "don't ask, don't tell" equivocation of Bill Clinton.

Gay and lesbian marriage scandalizes the Right because it deconstructs "family" as an essentially arbitrary set of intimate conventions. Most of these permutations are already found in the world, as we have

---

*A Frankfurt School theorist who combined the theories of Marx and Freud in order to understand how people are persuaded, against their best interests, to keep their noses to the grindstone in work beyond what is technologically necessary.

†A social and sexual theory that examines the social construction of homosexuality by a society in which heterosexuality is judged to be the norm; examines discrimination against gays and lesbians; proudly expresses "queerness" as a legitimate source of identity.

discussed—cohabitation, extended families, single-parent households, commuting marriages and relationships, adoptive kinship, homosexual unions and marriage. Yet undoing the heterosexual core of marriage and the family not only undercuts the biblical auspices of patriarchy and heterosexuality but goes much further, suggesting the family as a site of intimacy, love, and brotherhood/sisterhood that models other more public sites of these relationships and hence functions as a valuable utopian* image in these anti-utopian times (see Jacoby 1999).

The politics of faith and family are extremely intense because they deal with issues of body politics such as sexual orientation and reproductive rights that stem from feminist, gay, and lesbian politics of subjectivity (see Jacoby 1975). These issues hit home because they begin and end at home, in bedrooms, nurseries, and kitchens. Feminists and gay and lesbian activists have continued the social movements of the 1960s by other means, using the politics of the personal as a wedge against a government that would reverse affirmative action and scapegoat feminists and queers as enemies of the faith-based family. The politics of the personal is threatening to the New Right because it foretells certain intimate solidarities, such as brotherhood and sisterhood, potentially more powerful even than traditional instrumental political alliances and interest-group coalitions.

The New Right and gays and lesbians stand at opposite ends of the political spectrum. Ironically, they have in common a commitment to marriage and family that stands at odds with 1960s radical feminism[†] (Atkinson 1974; Dworkin 2002), which viewed all state regulation of sexuality and intimacy as inappropriate. The move to legalize gay and lesbian marriage—and the counterrevolution against it—operates within the framework of state-regulated sexuality, although gays and lesbians and the New Right have diametrically different takes on the issue. Although gays and lesbians may be arguing for legal homosexual marriage largely for legitimacy and to challenge the state's heterosexist monopoly on the right to marry, there is a curious way in which gay/lesbian politics of the family and those of the New Right converge. They both value marriage, an enduring public commitment to one's partner. However, for gays and lesbians marriage is a utopian bursting

---

*A perfect society without social problems, projected by philosophers and social theorists interested in achieving progress.

†A feminist theory that opposes patriarchy as a source of the oppression of women; critiques the nuclear family and even marriage; also critiques pornographic and objectifying representations of women.

asunder of heterosexual regulation and compartmentalization of sexuality, whereas for the New Right marriage is a bulwark against gays and lesbians themselves and all others who would corrupt the American way of life.

Most interesting here is the way in which gay and lesbian marriage follows Marcuse's (1955) earlier model of "erotized" human relations, developed through his interweaving of Sigmund Freud and Karl Marx. By "erotization"* Marcuse was advocating a society in which people are sensuous and feel free to touch, shake hands, and hug without necessarily having full sexual contact. He felt that this sensuousness could be the basis of community and democracy. It could also connect us to nature and to animals. According to Marcuse's perspective, gays and lesbians should not be asking for a token acknowledgment of the legitimacy of their sexuality but for a whole new order of sexualized human relations based on intimacy and community. There are liberal and radical versions of queer theory, just as there are liberal and radical versions of feminist theory. The utopian potential in gay and lesbian marriage and families is obvious and needs to be teased out so that gays and lesbians (proudly calling themselves queers) do not become yet another isolated interest group. The most radical perspective on feminist and gay/lesbian politics is one that views gender and sexual orientation as "moments" of a larger structuring hierarchy of valued over seemingly valueless activities that lies at the heart of our civilization (Agger 1993). These do not subordinate gender or sexual orientation to class but "transcode" them (Jameson 1991) into terms of each other, purposely depriving them of uniqueness and irreducibility and building bridges to other people's domination and possible liberation. Indeed, liberation would now be conceptualized as the assignment and/or acknowledgment of value to activities such as housework, child care, and homework heretofore denied them by a male heterosexist† patriarchy, as the theoretical terminology characterizes it.

Heterosexuality, although the apparent fate of nearly 90 percent of the world's population, is a prison, as is gender, if heterosexuality requires a bipolar construction of sexual orientation and subordinates one to the other. For the same reason, feminists (Agger 2002) require the overthrow of gender—masculinity "versus," and over, femininity—as the

---

*Transforming human relationships and even work into sensuous, caring activities not necessarily requiring sexual contact but involving the release of people's inherent desires to be sensuous and playful.

†Heterosexism is the intolerance of and discrimination against gays and lesbians by straight (heterosexual) people, akin to racism and sexism.

goal of women's, men's, and children's liberation. Sexual orientation, like gender, class, and race, will all dissolve when—and as—people liberate themselves from hierarchies of value and define themselves (and allow themselves to be defined) not in terms of hierarchical bipolarities that subordinate the inferior term and deny that these seemingly dichotomous categories of humanity are actually a continuum. This is highly threatening to the Right, which wants to deny its femininity, proletarian status, and nonwhite origins in the name of a dubious purity of origins and clean categories. People are sorted neatly into little boxes, some of the boxes are bigger and more resplendent than others, and finally the inferior boxes are sent to the shredder or the garbage dump. But survivors crawl out of their squashed containers, make their way to the larger, superior boxes, and worm their way inside. They then spread the word that purity, bipolarity, and hierarchy are false representations of people's complex, ambiguous, and often ambivalent natures. And this is how the revolution begins.

DEDIFFERENTIATION OF SOCIAL INSTITUTIONS

Postmodernists sometimes use the term *dedifferentiation* to refer to the blurring of boundaries between and among people and social institutions. If we have entered a postmodern stage of history (that makes for an interesting debate), its main characteristic is the blurring of boundaries among social institutions heretofore assumed to be separate.

Émile Durkheim,* one of the founders of sociology and social theory, argued in *The Division of Labor in Society* (1947) that the essence of modernity is differentiation, subdividing activities, especially work, into smaller and smaller units. We already used a Durkheimian term earlier in this chapter when we addressed the *sexual division of labor*. The division of labor† was perhaps the most important example of differentiation to Durkheim. Talcott Parsons, in his *The Structure of Social Action* (1937) and then in *The Social System* (1951), teased out

---

*One of the first European sociologists to notice that the decline of organized religion tended to make people *anomic* (directionless and devoid of meaning); Durkeim theorized that people could find meaning in their work, especially where work was done in teams of collaborating colleagues.

†Durkheim's term for the tendency of human labor in capitalism to become increasingly specialized, moving us away from work during the Middle Ages that required people to have a wide variety of skills, especially in agriculture and home maintenance.

Durkheim's and Max Weber's* (1958) legacies for sociology. He identified several separate social institutions that perform specialized functions: the economy, the political system, religion, education, media, and family. Parsons's influence on family sociology has been immense, and he has served as a foil for post-1960s feminist scholars who attack Parsons for his views of gender.

Parsons argued that men are best equipped to enter the hurly-burly world of work, accepting its risk and enjoying its rewards (Parsons and Bales 1955; also see Davis's [1937] defense of prostitution on functionalist grounds). Men are rational, instrumental, calculating, strong. Women are best suited to staying home and raising kids, providing a sheltered harbor for their male mates. Women are intuitive, emotional, spontaneous, weak. These views helped motivate early 1960s feminists such as Betty Friedan (1984) to propose greater flexibility so that both men and women could get college educations and have careers and so that both sexes could raise kids.

Friedan's feminist critique also, at least by implication, attacked one of Parsons's strongest contentions, which served as the linchpin of his theoretical perspective, often called structural functionalism.† That contention is that the family is, in effect, separate from other social institutions such as work, education, and politics. These institutions are best viewed as boundaried, demarcated from each other by separate sets of roles that people are supposed to accept, such as the roles of father and mother. Although family is tied to work via roles that turn men loose in the marketplace and keep women tethered to the home, in which they prepare men for work and children for school (which in turn prepares them for the labor force), family was for Parsons a specialized and separate domain. Indeed, Parsons, following Durkheim and Weber, argued that the crux of modernity, which follows antiquity and then feudalism, is the differentiation and specialization of social institutions such as work, family, and school and the resulting narrowing of people's roles.

---

*Early German sociologist who developed theories of the middle class, bureaucracy, and the relationship between the Protestant Reformation and the rise of capitalism; was pessimistic that people in a bureaucratic society would find meaningful lives, but he opposed Marxism as unrealistic.

†Parsons's theory, popular from the late 1930s until the 1960s, that views people as occupants of social roles situated within dominant institutions such as work, family, and education; Parsons viewed people as more or less passive, unlike the social-constructionist and ethnomethodological perspectives.

We notice that institutional boundaries associated with modernity have begun to blur, especially with women entering the workforce in record numbers after feminism set them free (to work) during and after the 1960s (Padavic and Reskin 2002). Women's entry into the labor force has had an enormous impact on schools as well as on schooling, especially where women are still widely expected to shoulder the roles of employee, mother, and PTA volunteer (Doucet 2000; Gerstel 2000). To juggle these roles, women blur the physical and temporal boundaries characteristic of an earlier stage of modernity in which the public/private distinction was clearer and even, to some extent, indelible. Women are now found "in public" and "in private." Or, perhaps better said, the so-called private sphere traditionally occupied by women, out of sight and out of mind of social theory and social science, is not so private after all.

Having kids, raising them, helping with their homework, cooking, cleaning, and even sexuality, are in fact public and political activities in that they help produce and reproduce a labor force. Both husbands and children are "produced," calling attention to women's economic contributions to capitalism. Many feminists have argued that these economic contributions have gone largely unnoticed where women do not receive a wage for their "private" economic activity but only share in their husbands' earnings, the supposed family wage. This line of argument by feminists suggests that modernity has never fully kept social and economic institutions distinct, especially where women and slaves in earlier societies shouldered an economic burden that has largely gone unacknowledged and unrewarded.

The feminist critique of the public/private distinction converges with the postmodern thesis of institutional blurring. Important postmodern theorists such as Jacques Derrida* (1994) and Michel Foucault† (1977) were also feminists and were very concerned about understanding the roles of sexuality and gender in the disciplinary society. In addition Foucault was one of the first queer theorists. Both of these theoretical perspectives seek to "valorize," or give value to, activities that have been hidden from public, political, and intellectual view. The notion

---

*A founder of postmodernism, from Algeria, who critiqued the whole Western tradition of philosophy because it sets up neat distinctions and thus ignores the fuzziness and complexity of both language and social life.

†A French postmodernist who studied the transition from harsh punishment, such as public beheadings, to more subtle forms of social control that are internalized by people who fear stepping out of line.

that activities in one realm provide value to another realm is inherently a critique of a society based on dualities and hierarchies, such as man/woman. Derrida points out that such dualities usually conceal hierarchy, such that one term of the duality (here, men) is secretly superior to the other term (here, women), which is defined in terms of its absence of the superior's qualities. This is a deconstructive reading of Freud's famous notion of women as creatures who experience penis envy, framing them as less-than-complete versions of men.

Institutional dedifferentiation*—the blurring of social boundaries of all types—is problematic for feminist and postmodern critics where it creates what Foucault called a panoptical society.[†] In *Discipline and Punish* (1977) he discusses a perfect prison in which the harsh and punitive role of the prison guard is softened through a system of self-surveillance as prisoners imagine that they are being watched and hence toe the line. This idea is also found in George Orwell's *Nineteen Eighty-Four* (2003), in which people believe that their thoughts are being monitored by Big Brother—the absolute state. The panoptical or disciplinary society exacts obedience not mainly by harsh sanctions and prohibitions but through the self, which is conditioned to constrain her or his own behavior without necessarily being told to do so.

Scholars of the Frankfurt School (such as Max Horkheimer,[‡] Theodor Adorno,[§] Herbert Marcuse, and Jürgen Habermas) made much the same argument in their discussions of "domination,"[**] an enveloping state of conformity brought about in late capitalism. Domination is so

---

*A tendency in a postmodern stage of society for the boundaries among separate institutions such as work, family, education, and media to blur.

[†] Foucault's term for a society based on people's assumption that they are constantly under surveillance; as a result, they conform without being told or forced to do so.

[‡] Frankfurt School member who, with Adorno, authored *Dialectic of Enlightenment,* a revision of Marxism after World War II that was pessimistic about radical change because of the newfound power of the culture industries centered on Madison Avenue and in Hollywood.

[§] A member of the Frankfurt School who teamed with Horkheimer to write *Dialectic of Enlightenment,* a pessimistic statement about the culture industry; Adorno also argued that the defeat of the Nazis during World War II did not eliminate authoritarianism, which he defined as the tendency of powerless people to look up to authority figures and blindly follow them, a perspective highly relevant to the global spread of religious fundamentalism today.

**The Frankfurt School's term for an overall human condition of powerlessness and the experience of having one's every activity controlled by others; an updating of Marx's concept of alienation.

pervasive and insidious that people often cannot see or sense it. They also term this "total administration," which, translated into more accessible terms, means the overwhelming of everyday life with commands to consume and conform. These commands are often transmitted through the media, especially via advertising. The Frankfurt critical theorists argue that command and control are exacted not by harsh discipline but by subtly inducing people to constrain themselves, believing, falsely, that this is the good life and they are living it (see Adorno 1978; Habermas 1970; Horkheimer 1974; Horkheimer and Adorno 1972; Marcuse 1964).

In *One-Dimensional Man* (1964) Marcuse argued that "the universe of discourse" has closed as people lose the vocabulary to imagine and discuss a qualitatively different, better society. We lose sight of utopia (see Jacoby 2005), a better society, as we immerse ourselves in a busy everyday life. Of course, life has accelerated greatly since Marcuse and his 1964 book because of television, media, the Internet, cell phones, fax machines, interstate highways, jet travel, laptops, and other fast technologies. "Instantaneity" is the experience of time as people watch global news live on CNN, send text messages and e-mail messages to people in other states, and surf the Web. This acceleration of everyday life makes it even more difficult for people to resist institutional dedifferentiation as they talk on the phone about their kids' after-school care while driving to work listening to the radio.

The casualties of this acceleration and institutional blurring are *boundaries* between nations, between people, between public and private life, between work and home, between busyness and leisure. What Max Weber (1958) called the iron cage of an earlier bureaucratic capitalism is being supplemented by an electronic cage (see Kroker and Kroker 1997) highly characteristic of the panoptical society of global surveillance, information, and communication.

What does institutional dedifferentiation mean for the family? That is precisely the question that we seek to answer in this book. Although we do not have particularly good news to report, there are signs of hope, especially if we understand the problem correctly. The problem has traditionally been defined as one of protecting the family against society, hence the image of family as a safe haven. Although we are in sympathy with defenses of family as a bulwark against eroding boundaries, especially boundaries drawn around the self and hence around sanity, it is too late in the day to retreat to a concept of family as distinct from the rest of society. We must confront the embedding of family in society, economy, culture, and school and deal with it on its own terms. The solution, as we sketch later in this book, is that we can treat family as a utopian concept and seek to "familize" other social institutions such as work, culture, and school. In other words, family becomes a normative idea—something for which we strive—functioning as a metaphor for all humane relationships, both public and private.

FAMILY AND THE NEEDY SELF

In this context of blurring boundaries, especially the boundary between work and home, the family is burdened with all sorts of expectations. These are expectations that, by and large, it cannot meet. One of the problems of modernity is that it has portrayed the good life in terms of an enhanced private life, what C. B. Macpherson (1962), the noted Canadian political theorist, called "possessive individualism."* Public life was viewed as primarily sullied, especially the workaday world in which people check their autonomy and creativity at the door. Theorists as diverse as Hannah Arendt (1959), Karl Marx (1964), Alexis de Tocqueville (1966), and the members of the Frankfurt School oppose this needy individualism, arguing instead that people become truly human only in public, through work, good works, politics, the small-town meeting. These are images stemming from the Athenian concept of the polis, the intimate city-state in which people are political animals and revel in good-natured discussion. Public life was conceived as being valuable in itself and not a sphere of inevitable dissatisfaction.

Although most of these theorists are from the modernist period, they deviate from modernist assumptions about how the good can only be found in private, including in the family. Some of the problems with families today—divorce, abandonment, conflict, latchkey children—reflect the expectation that families should redress all of the harm that people suffer in their public lives, especially in the realm of work. Feminist scholars (Fraser 1989) argue that political and social theory has tended to ignore private life, including the family, because these are realms traditionally tended by women. Inasmuch as women have been viewed, until recently, as less-than-full citizens, theorists of

---

*Macpherson's (1962) term for a conception of the self that is highly materialistic and defines needs in terms of acquisition of goods.

modernity have tended to assume, perhaps contradictorily, that people can only have their needs met in private life (shopping, love, spiritual development) but that the realm of privacy, including the family, does not need to be theorized or addressed politically.

This is the line of argument of thinkers who embrace the image of family as a safe haven. On the one hand, women's and children's roles in the family are quite invisible, unproblematic. On the other hand, family is the place where needy selves can find solace and comfort, restoring themselves after work and school. Both the Victorians and Parsonians embrace this contradiction, in effect idealizing women as eternal caregivers who can heal the wounds inflicted by the world. Although in many ways this has been true, those who endorse the family as a haven in a heartless world did not take this a step further and recognize women's roles and contributions, awarding them economic and political value.

Radical and socialist feminists lament this devaluation of women's unpaid activity, noticing that such domestic labor (and, we would add, schoolwork) adds value to capitalism by reproducing male workers and preparing children for their eventual roles in the labor force. The recognition that good things happen in the family needs to be linked, they argue, to economic and political gains for women who are compensated for performing all of this domestic and emotional labor. Parsonians would respond that women are *by nature* giving and loving, fulfilling their destinies by providing comfort and warm meals. Feminists and Marxists counter that women and men are not by nature anything but instead are slotted into roles by capitalism and patriarchy that they internalize as parts of their identity. Men could become nurturing if they were restricted, or given access, to the home and family.

Underlying this discussion is the relationship between the family and the self. Where the self is assumed to be alienated in the public world of work and politics, as it has been for most of the modern period, the family and home buffer the self. Most modern theorists have assumed that this work is not work at all but women's destiny, their predilection to hug, hold, help, harbor. Feminists question that assumption, even if they do not often reject the family as a solution to society's problems. But it is not a solution that can be achieved apart from other important social changes that go beyond even the emancipation of women in public and private spheres to include the emancipation of everyone, including children. One of the most important things from which people would be emancipated, in the world we envisage, is *gender*, sex-typed behavior of all kinds rooted in the view of men and women as opposites.

What does the needy self really require to be happy and free? There are many answers, all the way from liberalism* and Platonism† to Marxism‡ and feminism. The Frankfurt School argues that people have certain "true" needs that can be discovered through human reason. At present, their needs are "false" not so much because they have the wrong content—rap versus opera—but because people are not free to choose their needs, which are instead imposed on them by the media and advertising. People are needy, and kept needy, because of capitalism, which, after World War II, requires people to shop endlessly, far beyond their basic needs for food, shelter, and clothing (Lavigne 2005). The culture industries§ stimulate endless consumption so that there will be a match between what people's labor produces and what they, with their wages and assisted by credit, consume. Without this match, as Marx well understood back in the mid-nineteenth century, capitalism will grind to a halt, having too much inventory that cannot be converted into profit.

The distinction between public and private life assumes that it is likelier that people's needs will be met in private (home, shopping, leisure) than in public. For most of human history, it was simply unimaginable that life would not be nasty, brutish, and short, as Thomas Hobbes (1950) characterized it in 1660. With abundance, though, we can reconfigure the public/private relationship, even if this is a hard sell to people, bred within modernity, who assume that work and public life will be unfulfilling and that they can find solace only in the private sphere. Marcuse (1955) draws on the early Marx** (1964), who

---

*A variety of democratic theory that stresses the importance of individual choice and assumes that people can clearly understand their best interests (unlike the false consciousness perspective).

†A philosophy based on the work of Plato from ancient Athens that grounds knowledge in armchair speculation and rules out empirical research.

‡A social theory grounded in the work of Marx that views capitalism as a struggle between business owners and workers; projects the end of capitalism and a society free of class conflicts.

§The Frankfurt School's term for how entertainment, such as movies, television, radio, and the Internet, become big businesses.

**As a young man developing his political ideas (at about the same time that Charles Dickens was writing his novels), Marx portrayed the good society as one in which people would enjoy their work and not be pitted against each other in economic competition and conflict.

first posited an end to alienation within the public sphere,* in arguing that today we have the technological potential to liberate people from backbreaking toil. Achieving this requires that we transform our political and economic priorities away from profit and toward the satisfaction of human needs (see Leiss 1976).

The needy self can now, at least potentially, fulfill its needs in work, politics, education, or science. Needs "need" no longer be privatized, especially where we retain from early Marx the insight that people are sociable and need to have communities of like-minded souls in which to become fully human. This is not to deny that people also require quiet time and time alone, as well as intimacy, nurturance, children, parenting, and siblings—family, by another name. We are simply attempting to view the boundary between public and private, or work and family, as permeable and the two realms as overlapping.

The problem with satisfying people's needs only in private life is that we then burden weekends, leisure, vacations, and family life with too many expectations. How many people actually experience deep-seated fulfillment in a weekend? Are evenings entirely carefree, especially if one's children are burdened with homework? Do most people return from a two-week vacation renewed? One of our main contentions is that an overburdened family life erodes the utopian promise of family as life-sustaining intimacy. Living for the weekend never works because the rest of the week is so de-energizing.

We question whether needs can be fulfilled only in private, at home, on the weekends, or on vacation. Early Marx understood that for life to be worth living, all of existence must change—work as well as leisure. One of the reasons that private life is so impoverished is that work takes such a toll on energy, creativity, and autonomy; work wastes people, who waste their time in burdensome toil. This raises another question about whether work can change without transforming capitalism, a meaty issue in its own right. Capitalism, with its insatiable thirst for profit, simply cannot afford to allow people rest; it compels them to spend idle hours shopping, soaking up the commodities that their own work produces. Work overwhelms family and private life because we have organized work in such a way that its logic of profit knows no boundaries, whether international, temporal, or psychic.

---

*The walks of life in which people encounter each other, such as work, politics, movie theaters, coffee shops, even the cybersphere; counterposed to the private sphere, including family life.

Work's demands on our private lives, which are not so private after all, thwart our efforts to restore ourselves and achieve intimacy. Family is but a pale substitute for community as we have presently structured the work/family relationship. However, family might *transform* work, a topic pursued below; work might be "familized," humanized, and in turn family would no longer be experienced as a respite from toil. This is already beginning to happen as workers, especially women, perform family-related tasks using the various electronic prostheses of fast capitalism while they are on the job, which is increasingly unhinged from the physical office cubicle but can be performed nearly anytime/anywhere (Grantham and Tsekouras 2004).

At stake in these reconfigurations of work/family/home/self are needs, which, as they have been for over two thousand years, are often thwarted by discipline and domination. These are not just slogans but descriptions of what Parsons, translating Weber's word *Herrschaft,* termed imperative coordination—having to do something, now, because somebody told you to do so. Workers are unfree; middle managers are unfree; housewives are unfree; women who do the double shift of paid labor and domestic labor are unfree; children are unfree, especially where their fast lives are dictated by rigid and often irrational school curricula and the expectations of parents, teachers, coaches, and politicians.

If family is where you get your needs met, we are falling short. We contend that family is not the only place where this should happen, but it is certainly one of the places. Rather than viewing the family simply as a site of oppression, projected onto people by corporate capitalism and Fordist rhythms of command and control, we view the family dialectically, in terms of its potential for bringing about change. To view something dialectically means to examine its hidden conflicts and to imagine how these conflicts can be resolved in a positive direction. This is exactly what the women's movement has begun to do. The fact that the personal is political suggests that people can change politics and social structures by making changes in their own lives. In the end, if we conceptualize and work toward social change with useful insights about the impenetrability of the personal and the political, it may be difficult in our perfect world to identify where family leaves off and the rest of the world begins. Social relations will have become familylike, based on intimacy, trust, and mutuality, which is what the New Left and feminists have wanted all along.

The problem is that feminists and Marxists have been locked into debate about the priority or primacy of gender and class, family and economy. This is a fruitless debate if we understand gender and class as aspects of the same overarching social structure based on a series of interpenetrating and overlapping hierarchies of valued over devalued or even valueless activities. To be woman, mother, or child, on this understanding, is to be deprived of economic and political value. To be a worker is to have less value than one's employer. To be a person of color is to be "othered" with respect to the dominant group. Seen this way, gender and class are not only moments or aspects of the same totality; they are *identical* aspects of devalued experience—devalued by the practices and discourses of the dominant groups.

Family is connected to work by virtue of the public/private split, which devalues family activity so that women, not to mention children, will not receive a wage. This split is really a hierarchy, in the sense of the preceding paragraph, with public activity having priority over private activity, even though apologists for patriarchal capitalism such as Parsons and Becker (1981) well understand that the public sphere would crumble unless overlaid onto the foundation of the private sphere, the Greek *oikos,* or household. In doing reproductive work, women produce—men, children, meals, comfort. Their production is necessary for capitalism and the male-dominated family, but it is denied the central "signifier" of value in our society—payment. Women are the only adults working for free, which tips the balance of power in the family away from them.

Feminists have rightly argued for a revaluation of the supposedly private sphere of family and childhood, noticing that this is not private at all but a crucial region for the production and reproduction of workers, consumers, children, and citizens. But it is less common to find family treated both as a site of struggle and as a utopian image of a decent society. Family provides a model of all human relations, between and among adults, adults and children, children themselves, and all of its members and the outside world. To "familize" or make familylike work, politics, education, and entertainment might be a worthy goal once we view family simultaneously as a site of women's and children's oppression *and* as a model of humane social relations that extend beyond one's own four walls. This is especially pertinent now that the boundaries between work and family have blurred, enabling, indeed requiring, women to "do family" while they are in their cubicles, in their cars, at the mall, and at Starbucks.

Since early Marx, images of humane social relationships have been drawn primarily from work. Early Marx argues that people are creatures of self-creative "praxis"* who imprint themselves on nature and in the public world by "externalizing" (Hegel's word) themselves, making the inner outer. In other words, people find themselves in work that they enjoy. He argued that a good society would enable people to pick and choose their vocations, over which they would have control and property rights. This is a transforming image because it flies in the face of nearly two thousand years of philosophizing and social theorizing that located work in Kant's realm of necessity (1987)—a burden that cannot be avoided. This utilitarian conception of work prevented radicals from remaking work as a venue for self-expression and democracy. However, Marx did not consider the family as an equivalent site of struggle, probably because as a pre–women's movement male he tended to ignore issues of the exploitation of women and children as somehow less important than the male class struggle.

Many feminists have tried to blend Marx's concern with work and feminists' concern with family and gender. We locate ourselves within that tradition of rethinking, but we take the position that a useful way to reimagine early Marx is to notice that family, household, parenting, and childhood are always/already utopian sites of personality formation, intimacy, sharing, democracy, and creative activities. Perhaps this is to say nothing more than that early Marx's image of creative work is perfectly consistent with images of family/families that allow social change to flow back and forth between the realms of work and family, especially now that those realms have become nearly indistinguishable in early-twenty-first-century capitalism.

In other words, the family is a site not simply of reproduction but also of production, of people, kids, meals, homework. This risks being a conservative posture only if we equate the patriarchal family of the nineteenth century with all possible arrangements that go by the name of family. As we said at the outset of this chapter, family is how you do intimacy; it is not an official Parsonian category designating inflexible roles and positions. Empirical work on family demonstrates that there are a multitude of such intimacies. The variety of families today, what Judith Stacey (1990) evocatively calls "brave new families," empowers our analysis where we learn from it that people do not feel bound, as perhaps they once did, to do only one kind of family—heterosexual, married, biological offspring, domesticated woman.

---

*Early Marx's term for human work that is both productive and creative, such as the work of a master craftsperson who would perform his work even if he was not paid.

We think that people crave "family" because their work lives are not particularly fulfilling, even though people may increasingly find "family" at work, as Arlie Hochschild argues in *The Time Bind* (1997). This is largely because they have so much time pressure and so many extra demands at home, especially because most households now have two busy adults who work outside the home. By contrast, the workplace seems almost idyllic, although it has its unique pressures and it is not totally insulated from family, especially where people are tethered to the home via the rapid information and communication technologies that are at once our salvation and downfall. In a curious reversal, people tend to work from home (which becomes a job site), just as they do family from the job site. For example, they might organize the Friday office lunch while making dinner and overseeing kids' homework at home. They will enjoy the lunch as a familylike event, especially in comparison with their usual fast-food (or just plain fast) dinners at home. All of this blurs, leaving people with insufficient satisfactions derived from either activity. Indeed, it is difficult, in postmodern times, to identify where family ends and work begins.

GOOD OR EVIL? GENERATIVITY VERSUS DETERRENCE

Underlying these discussions about family, work, and needs are fundamental disagreements about human nature. In the rest of this book, we counterpose democratic and authoritarian perspectives on family, parenting, and schooling. In his work on political attitudes and discourse, George Lakoff (2002) has theorized that there are two opposing models of human nature informing one's later political beliefs. Those who believe that people are basically good tend to be liberal and even libertarian, allowing children to grow up relatively unencumbered and to have democratic dialogue with parents. Those who believe that people are basically bad tend to be conservative, requiring parents and schools to punish children when they get out of line. It is tempting to believe that the best way to raise kids lies somewhere in the middle. Even people who view kids as basically or potentially good generally agree that punishment is sometimes necessary as a deterrent. And even people who view children as basically bad will give them rewards on occasion.

At some local elementary schools in our area, kids who misbehave are made to stand along a fence while the other kids have recess. The theory is that the children on the fence will be shamed into behaving.

An alternative perspective on this theory of crime and punishment—or deterrence,* as it were—is that kids, mainly boys, would be better served by having recess. The deterrence perspective on childhood crime and punishment derives from the view of people as evil; punishment is what they have coming to them and, in some cases, it might even rectify them.

What would the other perspective, based on human goodness, do or say about childhood misbehavior? If the fence, detention hall, Saturday school, or off-campus suspension should not be used as punishment, how should we get kids to toe the line? Is it even clear what "the line" is and how we should conceptualize it? Call this other perspective, in contrast to the deterrence perspective, the generative† perspective, using misconduct and mistakes as examples with which to reorient future behavior and also reinforce a democratic polity and society in which people are accountable to each other.

Let's say that the child's crime was to push another child while waiting in line. Viewing that child as good and not evil, the generative perspective would involve the teacher talking with (not to) the child, teasing out what was wrong and how it could be fixed. A second step would probably involve reconciliation with the pushed child, an apology, perhaps, and even restitution if necessary. The harried teacher might respond that she cannot do this every time there is an infraction of the rules because there are simply too many children in the class. Warehousing criminals and treating their punishments inflexibly, with rigid sentencing guidelines, only guarantees recidivism (repeat offenses) after the prison term has been completed. Similarly, kids always or often "on the fence" fail to learn how to function productively within the group and remain alienated, angry, and without hope. One of our contentions is that schools are increasingly modeled on prisons, with students viewed and treated as offenders.

Complicating this picture are the discretionary perspectives of the police officer (teacher) and the courts (also the teacher and perhaps also the school administration). Certain teachers may be more lenient than others. As a result, the same behaviors may be allowed by some teachers and punished by others. Schools increasingly grade "behavior"

---

*A strategy for correcting the behavior of children and would-be criminals based on punishment.

†A strategy of correcting the behavior of children and adults that stresses people's compassion and capacity for empathy and forgiveness.

or comportment in a formal way. A student's behavior is evaluated as unsatisfactory on the report cards if he or she has had more than a certain number of infractions during the grading period. In the meantime, they may miss recess altogether or have to sit at a segregated lunch table. In one elementary school in our area, academic issues bleed over into behavioral issues as students are deprived of recess if they fail to follow written instructions on classroom and homework assignments. Not following instructions is a paramount issue for the authoritarian defenders of the hidden curriculum, which includes a component of obedience and subordination. Children are being prepared for participation in a future workforce in which subordination is prized. They are always already in that workforce, and they are being judged by adult standards of behavior.

It can be extremely frustrating for kids to contend with some teachers who view them as good and others who view them as evil. Our kids have had both kinds of teachers. In some grades, their behavior has been evaluated positively and in other grades (and sometimes within the same grade) they have been given the occasional demerit for misbehavior. In more authoritarian school settings, there is a code of public silence, much as in a monastery or in the early Auburn prisons. This code exists not only to keep the hallways quiet but to teach kids to be seen and not heard, to be self-disciplined, and not to engage in confident self-expression. Many of our kids' teachers seem to value silence and obedience more than they value self-expression and creativity. Although we have solidarity with them as underpaid public-school teachers, we often lament their rule-bound ritualism and authoritarianism.

The deterrence perspective argues that you must lean heavily on miscreants so that they learn the consequences of disobedience—punishment. Because people are basically evil, they need continual reminders of the strong arm of the law and school. The generative perspective argues that people can be reformed and educated and that they need to be involved in their own redirection and in restitution. It is normal for kids to "act out" in public settings, not automatically respecting the absolute power of teachers and school administrators. They can and should learn respect for others, but not necessarily respect for authority. It is important for the generative perspective on criminality and children to emphasize that authority is not a divine right but a circumstance of convenience that can be changed. Everyone can become a teacher, and can teach, just as everyone is a student and has something to learn.

Freud* (1958) initiated this conversation when he argued that people contain warring impulses. There is a struggle transpiring within the self between the id and superego. By *id* Freud meant our primal instincts and appetites, and not only for sex. By *superego* he meant conscience, the feelings of guilt and prohibition that prevent us from giving full vent to our impulses. If the superego is successful in taming (and repressing) the id, what emerges is the *ego,* the rational adult self. Freud understood well, as do developmental psychologists, that growing or establishing an ego is a process and occurs gradually over time, with starts, stops, and backsliding. This occurs from earliest infancy through adolescence and even beyond it, as adults, too, learn and relearn. The process of developing an ego or self is termed primary socialization by social psychologists; the process of redeveloping the self once one enters adulthood (such as learning a second language) is termed secondary socialization.

There has been interesting discussion within Freudian psychoanalysis about how harsh superego restraints need to be. Herbert Marcuse argues that we can blend Freud and Marx (1955). In particular, we can view the superego not as a source of harsh constraint and punishment but as a civilizing impulse that does not shut down the id completely but, through nonalienating and democratic social arrangements, allows the id to flourish. We can release a "rationality of gratification" that expresses Eros, the life instinct. This will not result in free love as much as in erotized—in our terms familized—social relations that allow the person to express himself creatively but always within the democratic context of mutuality and reciprocity. Marcuse reinterpreted Freud, who was still quite nonlibertarian in his views about sexuality, to be a secret utopian, deploying the concept of Eros as a dynamic for transforming all human relations into sensuous, caring, and democratic ones. Marcuse read Freud as a critic of overrepressed late-nineteenth-century Viennese society.

This appropriation of Freud for our argument about family/families and schools as democratic projects has significance for our discussion in this chapter of varying political styles of parenting and teaching. People who view children as bad take the view that the superego (conscience, parental authority, the criminal justice system) must be strengthened in

---

*The founder of psychoanalysis, who argued that people are bundles of warring impulses; the id is our infantile desires, the superego is our conscience, and the ego is the rational adult who learns to channel his inner desires for sex and food into productive work activity.

order to check the unruly impulses of the id, the child within us who cannot take "no" for an answer. People who view children as good take the view that the superego is too strong, causing people to feel counterproductive guilt about their secret yearnings. They also take the view, as we do here, that the id can be harnessed to progressive social movements if we interpret these libidinal impulses not as purely sexual but as impulses toward freedom, democracy, and sensuousness. In many ways, this is really a debate about Puritanism, which, as Weber (1958) recognized, is a central feature of capitalism.

Weber argued that Luther and Calvin paved the way for capitalism by encouraging people to be thrifty, disciplined, and abstemious. People's ability to delay gratification (contra the id's impulse for immediate gratification) would allow them to save enough to start their own businesses, becoming successful entrepreneurs. But Marcuse (1955) argues that in post–World War II capitalism we now have the technological means to absolve people of much labor because we are able to provide for everyone's basic needs. He also recognizes that capitalism has produced "false needs"* for commodities and services beyond what is required to be happy. These false needs take us into debt, are frequently unhealthy for us, and prevent us from shifting sufficient capital† (productive wealth) to help industrialize and modernize the vast parts of the world that still lie in preindustrial poverty and have dangerously premodern political systems.

Marcuse maintains that sexual and social "repression," in Freud's terms, has been intensified since World War II in order to divert people from the technological possibility of their own liberation. Puritanism has been strengthened, which is certainly evidenced by the radical Right's attacks on wanton permissiveness, for which they usually blame the 1960s generation. The Right blames the alleged excesses of the 1960s, especially the women's movement, civil rights, and now gay rights, on permissive 1960s parents who did not make their kids toe the line, spawning a generation of youthful slackers and misfits. This demonizing of the 1960s fits perfectly with the agenda of the Right, which embraces "family values" and "faith" just as they take antifamily, antiwomen, and antichildren postures on matters of policy. The Right simply does not

---

*Marcuse's term, building on Marx's false consciousness, for how consumers in post–World War II capitalism must be stimulated by advertising to spend beyond their means (using credit) to purchase commodities they don't really need in order to keep the economy humming.

†Productive wealth that, unlike money you put in a savings account, tends to create more capital through profitable investment.

appreciate that many moms are working women who believe in equal pay for equal work, reproductive rights, and tolerance of gays and lesbians, extending all the way to gay marriage.

But just as sexual repression has been intensified, especially among supporters of the Christian Right, it has also been relaxed. Our media culture* (Kellner 1995) is awash in sexuality, which even creeps into prime-time television. Marcuse terms the easing of Puritanism within an essentially Puritanical culture "repressive desublimation." This concept describes how people for whom sexuality is taboo occasionally release their sexual natures, perhaps by watching pornography or going to strip clubs. And now, of course, we have the example of right-wing religious spokespeople and politicians who lead secret, "shameful" lives in which they, too, engage in repressive desublimation.

To view teachers and parents who endorse strict codes of student discipline and mountains of homework as authoritarian personalities like the followers of wartime Germany is admittedly controversial. But there is an authoritarianism afoot that manifests itself on several overlapping levels—national and state politics, the growing attack on universities and faculty, the movement to return to basics in K–12 curricula and teaching. A boy who was awarded student of the year in our son's class last year was praised by the principal as obedient to authority, a central value in Baptist Texas, which reelected Bush in 2004 with a nearly 70/30 majority. This same obedience was found in Germany in the early twentieth century and made way for the "Final Solution," as Hannah Arendt documents in her powerful study, *Eichmann in Jerusalem* (1964). Arendt observed and wrote about the trial of Adolf Eichmann, the architect of the Final Solution, which sent many millions of Jews and other enemies of the German state to their deaths in extermination camps. This bureaucratically organized carnage makes the 9/11 attacks, although horrific in their own right, seem like a flyspeck compared with the Holocaust's immensity of terror and death, its chilling pseudomedical methodology, and its state sanction. Arendt makes the argument, which is still controversial, that Eichmann was not a monster, not innately evil. He was just an ordinary bureaucrat who knew that what he was doing was wrong but compartmentalized his guilt in order to organize the many logistical details of the death camps, such as procuring large quantities of poison gas and requisitioning enough trains during wartime to transport the human victims to the camps.

---

*Douglas Kellner's (1995) term for everyday life dominated by media influences that frame what we know and want.

Arendt called this the "banality of evil," striking by its everydayness. By implication, and this was a finding certainly supported by Adorno's study of the authoritarian personality, anyone can be authoritarian in the sense of blindly following leaders gone mad in the interests of dubious vengeance. There was nothing inherent in the German national character that predestined the Holocaust; according to Arendt and Adorno, it could have happened anywhere that we find personalities weakened by declining families, economic and social inequality, and the deflection of the lower strata's angst toward even weaker and more marginal people. In this context, the admixture in twenty-first-century America of Homeland Security and so-called family values requires us to look carefully at the displacement of authority from parents to schools and its implications for a new authoritarianism. We pursue these issues as we examine schooling in later chapters.

In the following chapter, we consider the relationship between work and family more fully. The boundary between the two institutions has become fuzzy as people work off-site and perform family-related chores at work using electronic technologies such as the Internet, laptops, and cell phones. In a curious reversal, many people, especially women, now experience the workplace as a haven in a heartless world, with work colleagues becoming a surrogate family of sorts. The traditionally boundaried family is the site of tension, pressure, and conflict as family members lead increasingly hurried lives.

2

Implosion I

The Work/Family Boundary

In fast times, you rush around trying to get everything done—kids picked up and fed; work projects completed and voice mail messages answered; shopping, laundry, and car maintenance accomplished; bills paid and personal e-mail managed. That last chore is becoming increasingly odious, with the flood of virtual communications—perhaps people's last-ditch attempts to find community (Wulfhorst 2006). We are virtual selves, inundated and infiltrated by the world, which is increasingly difficult to shut out and turn off. Many people simply succumb and give over their lives to surfing, chatting, and texting, abandoning their selfhood to the curious new subject positioning by information and communication technologies. This is reminiscent of Timothy Leary, the 1960s guru who preached "turn on, tune in, drop out." Leary had hallucinogenic drugs like LSD in mind as vehicles of virtuality; today the Internet is that drug, turning our worlds upside down and bending reality and even time into surprising new shapes.

THE AGE OF INSTANTANEITY

When the Internet first became available, during the late 1980s, it was trumpeted as the Next Big Thing. Skepticism was in order, given the grandiosity of those claims. But the Internet has come to rival the telephone and automobile as a life-changing technology, transforming the ways (and the pace) in which we communicate, learn, write, spend leisure time, do business, and conduct democracy. Critical theorists have begun to address the Internet (see Poster 2001), especially within the context of democratic theory. Being digital (Negroponte 1995) seems to lend itself to digital democracy, opening up power (often by way of knowledge) to all takers. And yet critical theorists have also pointed to the ways in which the Internet can be used to control and coerce, much as Foucault (1977) warned in his writings about discipline and domination in the modern period.

Our interest here is in the traditional distinction between work and family as sociologically distinctive spheres. This distinction has begun to fade as postmodernity implodes institutional boundaries and blurs activities heretofore regarded as distinct. Karl Marx spoke of this where he borrowed George Wilhelm Friedrich Hegel's* term for interrelatedness—totality—in arguing that capitalism cannot be viewed other than as a total social and economic system in which institutions, as Parsonians call them, are strongly tied together (Marx 1964; Hegel 1967; Parsons 1951). Talcott Parsons himself spoke of the "social system" as a functionally differentiated but highly integrated and coordinated set of institutions and activities—like work and family—that, he theorized, confront the same challenges in dealing with both internal issues and external threats and constraints. Marxism and structural functionalism each develop the concept of totality as a way of drawing attention to institutional interrelationships.

For example, Parsons maintains that home and work have integrated divisions of labor. In patriarchal capitalism, the industrial division of labor is duplicated (and reinforced) by rigid gender roles (Blau, Ferber, and Winkler 2006). Families, like workers, have managers, even though the husbands who "manage" women may themselves be managed at work. Marx and Friedrich Engels (1972) discussed the family as the site of the reproduction of workers and of commodity consumption, opening the way to later feminist understandings of the interpenetration of public and private spheres.

Perhaps it has never been the case that the home and work have been separate. The family and work were not separated before Victorianism,[†] and with postmodern capitalism they have been reconnected, largely as a response to the impact of rapid information and communication technologies on self, society, and culture. They were separate, to some extent, only during the late nineteenth century as women with sufficient

---

*A German philosopher who preceded Marx and influenced Marx's ideas about the importance of work for the development of people's identities; unlike Marx, Hegel felt that capitalism was permanent.

[†] During nineteenth-century capitalism, factories were becoming more efficient through the use of technology and Victorians argued that the proper place of women and children was no longer in the workplace but at home; the Victorians developed the modern sexual division of labor.

means removed themselves from factory labor. And family and work were reseparated during the boom period following World War II, as capitalists had to convince women for a second time to remove themselves from the factories and return to their homes, now located in the suburbs. The ideology of "the mom" (see Douglas and Michaels 2004) is relatively recent, and it is likely to be short-lived because "moms," almost by definition, are creatures who occupy the "havens in a heartless world" of hearth and home. This ideology reduces the woman to her domestic activities and especially to her status as a mother.

As Susan J. Douglas and Meredith W. Michaels, as well as Arlie Hochschild (1997), document, it is tough to be a "mom" if one is also working outside the home for wages. We should not exaggerate the extent to which women now work for money—fully a quarter of American adult women do not work for pay outside the home, although they perform domestic work, which is still work. And yet for those women who work outside the home, time and role pressures encourage them to at least transform the traditional concept of the mom by including a career component. A mom, almost by definition, leads a life somehow insulated from the outer world, which is dangerous both physically and emotionally. Moms are insulated because they are restricted to their role as nurturers and denied access to the public sphere. And even if they must work, they view themselves primarily as moms—mothers to their children and wives to their husbands.

This chapter is about boundaries, primarily the one separating work and family. For most of human history there was a permeable dividing line between work and home. A boundary was erected late in the Industrial Revolution to enclose women and their children in the seeming isolation of the household. Even then, the outer world would seep into the home and family, exposing women and their children to external influences. The father would leave for war; he would die or suffer a debilitating injury; he would lose his job. The family wage, supposedly paid to men in order to keep their women and children in relative comfort, was always a myth, as feminists have pointed out (Dill 1988; May 1982).

There are many time robbers out there, sucking up people's waking hours, depriving them of restorative sleep, burdening them with too much to do, causing contradictions in their priorities. As women have rapidly entered the labor force since the 1960s but remained responsible for the majority of child care and domestic work, time pressure has become especially acute for them. No working woman with kids fails to understand the blurring of public and private spheres. She manages her children's doctor's appointments and lessons while at work and, via her cell phone, while driving. She checks work-related e-mail from home. She brings her laptop to her kids' soccer games and to Starbucks (Blair-Loy 2003; Grantham and Tsekouras 2004).

The electronic prostheses characteristic of this accelerated Internet age—cell phone, laptop, PDA—are key players in all this. These rapid information and communication technologies, more than any other factor, accelerate the rate of life in the twenty-first century, increase the burden of expectations, and shatter the illusion that home and private life are safe havens. That heartless world, which is paradoxically a source of enrichment, too, cannot be kept outside except on the rare vacation when we turn off our cell phones and decide not to check our e-mail.

Cell phones and computers are not the first technologies to change lives and remove boundaries. The printing press, internal combustion engine, airplane, radio, and television all broke down barriers, especially of space and time. The Internet is not unique in this respect, nor are cell phones. We do not advocate a technological determinism in which technologies possess certain benign or demonic essences that predestine their usages, regardless of human intent and social context. We are simply noticing that the boundary between work and home has been particularly assailed by these recent rapid technologies. One might say that these technologies that rob us of time and compel us to work anytime/anywhere are "globalizing" in the sense that they open the world to us and allow for the infiltration of our worlds by others. They at once extend the self and imperil it.

This is perhaps why postmodernists talk not about selves but about subject positions, noting the dispersal of the self as it must cope with the many tasks and intrusions thrust upon it. Our university, the University of Texas at Arlington, is probably not alone in requiring faculty to check their e-mail regularly (Wright 2001). At an obvious level, this represents progress in that it cuts down on expensive and ecologically despoiling paper. But at another level the demand that we check our e-mail "colonizes" our existence and experience, forcing us to deploy the prosthetic computer. In doing this, we are forced indoors, exposed to postural problems, and privatized; and, of course, we then must wade through the flotsam and jetsam of spam, episodic messages, listservs, bad manners, and flaming.

Herbert Marcuse (1964) argues that the self has undergone a process of progressive (and sometimes regressive) diminishment since the Enlightenment began during the early seventeenth century. Scholars of the Frankfurt School (see, for example, Horkheimer 1974) talk about the "eclipse of reason" and about "one-dimensionality" to refer to the growing inability of people to think critically about their social environments. It is not so much that people are simply blinded by ideology, which produces false consciousness* in Marx's earlier terms (1964), but that they are so immersed in everyday life that they cannot step outside of it and speculate about a possibly different future—utopia, the good society. They equally ignore the past.

This "one-dimensional"[†] thinking is probably what Marx, too, had in mind when he discussed ideology,[‡] a systematic and falsifying worldview binding people to their supposed fate. He suggested that ideologies engender false consciousness, a state of mind oblivious to empirical reality that avoids scientific explanations and instead explains the world in terms of mythic forces such as gods, or God. Friedrich Nietzsche (2001) reformulated this false consciousness as the love of fate, *amor fati,* the mind-set of the modern sensibility. The critical theorists blend Marx and Nietzsche not to abandon Marx's notion of false consciousness, induced by ideology, but to render more contemporary the processes of domination and discipline, which frequently proceed through discourse (more fully illuminated by French postmodern theorists such as Derrida, Foucault, and Lyotard).

Unfortunately, most postmodernists reject the adjective *false* in Marx's notion of false consciousness, denouncing this as the conceit of a modernist objectivism that pretends that we can stand outside of the world and see it perfectly clearly. But there can be a situated objectivity[§] that does not pretend complete clairvoyance but, rather, acknowledges distance between subject and object. This distance does not fully overcome the embedding of subject in object and vice versa—for example, the inherent ambiguity of people studying people—but, rather, makes a more realistic objectivity (and science, too) possible.

---

*Marx's term for how, in capitalism, people do not clearly understand the world and their own real needs; Marx felt that false consciousness is created by ideologies such as religion and certain political and economic theories.

[†] Marcuse's term for a mind-set that does not dig beneath the surface appearance of reality but accepts what things appear to be at face value; tends to be ahistorical and focused only on the present.

[‡] A term for interrelated systems of ideas that heavily influence behavior; for Weber, all societies need these interrelated belief systems, whereas for Marx ideologies are essentially fictions designed to deter people from political participation; a central ideology to Marx was religion, which he likened to an opiate of the masses.

[§] The way in which the search for truth and knowledge is always influenced by your local environment, background, biases, and blind spots; opposes positivism, which believes that the scientist can fully step outside the world.

This is the difference between positivism and a dialectical concept of science and social science. Marcuse and his colleagues are not saying that people are programmed with false ideas in order to buttress the systems of power and wealth. Rather, people are distracted and diverted from the big picture in much the way that Marx characterized ideology as a camera obscura, turning things upside down. People are diverted from this big picture because they will then accept as duty (Kant 1987) their prescribed roles in work, family, politics, and schooling, both matching production with profitable consumption and acquiescing to the executive committee of the bourgeoisie, as Marx and Engels characterized the state or government.

We cannot understand the family and its relations with other social institutions without grasping the immersion of people in a hurried and harried everyday life in which there is no downtime and hence no ability to grasp the big picture, truth, or grand narrative of what is really happening. People, via their cell phones, computers, and big-screen televisions, are so tethered to the everyday world that they cannot gain the distance or time necessary for reflection. Everyday experience, even more than Marcuse knew in the mid-1960s, is instantaneous and immediate, preventing the kind of "mediation"* that both Hegel and Marx valued so highly. By mediation they mean the ability to "process" one's life reflexively—theoretically, if you will—without simply succumbing to it.

THE WORK-FAMILY BOUNDARY FADES

The social technologies of rapid information and communication technologies (ICTs) that render life instantaneous and immediate tend to fade and blur institutional boundaries. The blurring of boundaries and compression of space and time provoke the experience touted by champions of the information superhighway of being anytime/anywhere. This space/time compression is arguably the most fundamental experiential difference between modernity and postmodernity, even if we acknowledge that much of the world today is in only the early stages of modernity or not even there at all. For the Enlightenment, space and time were firmly anchored and immovable. By postmodernity we mean a

---

*Hegel's term for the way in which people must rationally observe and process the world; opposes the positivist idea of the mind as a blank slate on which sense experience simply imprints itself.

stage of civilization that relies heavily on information and communication technologies such as the Internet to connect people globally, making issues of "place" less important than before. Not until 1905, which could be considered the intellectual dawn of the postmodern moment, when Albert Einstein published his first papers on the special theory of relativity, did we begin to recognize the plasticity of space and time. Einstein's relativity theory changed the ways in which we see the world and live in it, and it also undercut Newton's positivism, which pretends that we can stand completely outside the world in order to know it clearly.

Einstein recognized that our experiences of space and time varied according to our perspectives, or as postmodernists term them, our subject positions. People moving very, very fast would experience a different sense of the body and time than people standing still. In our emerging postmodernity, people experience everyday life in ways heretofore unknown in modernity, although there are certain important continuities of experience and institutions. Our economic system is still capitalist and it has certain enduring elements; the family is still largely hinged around state-sanctioned heterosexual marriage; the capitalist first world continues to exploit third-world countries and cultures for economic and political gain. And yet the experiences of space and time are fundamentally different from what our parents and their parents knew.

There are several ways to characterize these new experiences of the postmodern and especially the postmodern family. A range of scholars (see Harvey 1989; Jameson 1991; Stacey 1990) have written about them. Acceleration, instantaneity, immediacy, fluidity, and the flux of boundaries are all important characteristics of contemporary life experience in the Sargasso Sea of cellular phones, instant messaging, courier services, laptops, leased cars, and extreme makeovers.

In this context of slippery definitions, deferred meanings, and the loss of a firm ground for our truth claims, it has become difficult even to identify, let alone compartmentalize, the separable social institutions originally named by Parsons in *The Social System* (1951) to be constitutive of modernity. If we can work at home and on the road, as well as in the office cubicle, where, then, is the job site? If "parenting" takes place in the workplace day-care center, from the office desk using instant messaging and e-mail, and while driving, using cellular phones, where exactly is the home? And if home is the place where we eat dinner together, one could conclude that home is the Golden Arches, which McDonald's has been arguing for over half a century!

So much for place and space. Work for Parsonians was the place where you toiled eight or nine hours a day, and home was where you spent most of the rest of the time. But many kids spend much of the day in school and then spend hours traveling to and from baseball practice, music lessons, tutoring, and fast-food restaurants (Brooks 1996; Keller 2001). For many children, home is now the place where they spend the fewest hours. Home is a hotel or motel, and the parents' mortgage payment is merely rent. Perhaps work has become home for parents because they spend so much time doing it, and school and after-school activities are home for their kids.

If we are to talk about separable social institutions at all, we should talk about where, and in what time, people "do" these activities of working, parenting, growing up, schooling, playing, learning, eating, driving, vacationing, and working out. Many of these activities have been disconnected from their traditional moorings in space and time and now occur in sites and during periods of time traditionally reserved for other institutionally separable activities. The woman who plans her children's summer activities from the office computer is only one of many examples. The man who pounds away on his laptop while watching his child's tennis lesson is doing work in a nontraditional site and in nontraditional time. The child who completes her homework late at night while returning home from a distant soccer practice is "doing" childhood and school, even if in nontraditional ways.

The decoupling of institutions from space and time is not the only symptom worth tracking. We must also note the compression of time. People are more hurried and scattered, always multitasking. The Windows operating system for personal computing is a metaphor for these times. People can open multiple windows and perform multiple tasks, from e-mail and instant messaging to composing a memo and checking the weather or the latest airline fares. Whether people actually have more to do imposed on them by powerful forces or whether they choose to fill their time with these many tasks is somewhat beside the point. We suspect that determinism and agency* are both involved, just as they were for Marx when he talked about false consciousness. Again, this perspective does not simply blame the social system for indoctrinating passive citizens. There is a degree of choice involved in overextending one's line of credit, drinking too much, spending too little time with the kids, assigning massive amounts of homework, and overburdening children with school and activities. Marx's intention was to harness this "agency," as philosophers call it, and turn it in the direction of organizing

---

*A philosophical term for the active self who makes important decisions about his or her life and does not blame his or her social condition on fate or oppression.

social movements such as the workers' movement and later the civil rights, antiwar, and women's movements in order to change the large social structures within which our seeming "choices" play out.

In other words, people hurry, and they are conditioned to hurry. Part of this, as we have been suggesting, is technological in nature, brought about by rapid information and communication technologies that make possible the performance and surveillance of work outside the workplace proper. The first great revolution in the social technology of work in the early twentieth century occurred when Henry Ford inaugurated the assembly line for the mass production of automobiles. Initially, the workers walked along the line to their various specialized work stations. Later, the line moved and brought the automobile under assemblage to them. This allowed many cars to be produced and thus the Ford Motor Company's margin of profit could afford to be more slender. Ford amassed huge profits by selling many more automobiles at these lower prices. This system, although initially counterintuitive because Ford willingly accepted small margins of profit, was genius because the small profit margin would not drive up the car's price to the extent that only the rich could afford it.

We call this system of mass production *Fordism,*[*] a term coined by the Italian Marxist Antonio Gramsci[†] (1971). Today, our economy in the West and the industrialized East is increasingly termed post-Fordist,[‡] facilitated by rapid information and communications technologies that take production out of downtown factories, remove the need for large inventory, and allow more specialized niche production to suit the refined taste of consumers in a highly segmented market (a market in which people want not just bread but whole wheat bread with raisins, sourdough bread, or perhaps even squishy Wonder Bread). Post-Fordist production is "just in time" because the manufacturer, such as Dell, is

---

[*]The stage of mass production in capitalism, stemming from the early 1920s to the Internet capitalism of today, that emphasizes the production of many commodities with slender profit margins that allow for the masses to purchase them; Ford used the assembly line in his factories to manufacture Model Ts and Model As that were affordable to the masses, including his own workers.

[†]An Italian Marxist who developed the concept of Fordism to refer to the era of mass production sited in urban factories; he also developed the concept of "hegemony" to refer to a suffocating ideology that permeates everyday life but cannot be easily detected and debated.

[‡]A stage of capitalism, beginning with the advent of the Internet during the 1980s and 1990s, in which our economy moves from the mass production of commodities in factories to flexible production of niche product lines in white-collar businesses found in suburbs and abroad.

able to respond quickly to the customer's order, perhaps transmitted over the Internet or via a toll-free telephone number, and then courier the product to her door. Other examples of post-Fordist companies are Amazon and Google. This post-Fordist era no longer requires the worker to be chained, in effect, to the assembly line or to be in his office cubicle at all. One can work anytime/anywhere and shop anytime/anywhere, changing the dynamics of work and family in nearly unrecognizable ways. The Internet, then, has brought about the second major modernist revolution in working, but this second new social technology of work has had further implications for other social institutions outside of the workplace proper. It has affected family, home, school, leisure, shopping, parenting, childhood, diet, and health.

Actually, these two industrial revolutions, first the Fordist assembly line and then the Internet and post-Fordism, are connected, suggesting that the boundary between these two eras is quite blurry. Fordism augured a "faster" world in which people began to spend leisure time outside of the home. And today traditional Fordist companies are using post-Fordist techniques and technologies such as online shopping in order to keep their market share of consumers. Ford's plan was to put America on wheels (see Kay 1997) not only to make his fortune but also to improve the quality of life for early-twentieth-century urban dwellers who lived in dingy and crowded eastern cities and took the streetcar to work. He imagined that people with Model Ts would drive to the countryside on the weekend for picnics, enjoying the national park system that Theodore Roosevelt created during his presidency. The car was initially a means of escape from crowded cities and only secondarily a means of travel to work. In 1932, General Motors, Firestone, Standard Oil, and Mack Truck purchased city streetcar systems and then closed them down, requiring urban workers to drive during the week and then, as a means of escape, on the weekend and during vacation.

During the 1940s one of the new automobile drivers' destinations was restaurants. Two brothers named McDonald started an inexpensive hamburger restaurant in the San Bernardino Valley in California during the late 1940s, a drive-up hamburger store that would capitalize on people's newfound penchant for driving. Soon, this store and concept was purchased by Ray Kroc, a World War I compatriot of Walt Disney, who was busy simulating small-town American life in the hugely famous and profitable theme parks bearing his name. Kroc franchised McDonald's and, like Ford before him, accepted slender profit margins on his burgers and fries in order to sell them to newly mobile Americans in large volumes. McDonald's Golden Arches symbolized a fast and efficient post–World War II life to be enjoyed by busy families on the move. It was the beginning of the fast-food era in America (see Schlosser 2002), which is an integral part of fast capitalism* (see Agger 1989, 2004a). The automobile, now mass-produced, made this possible, as did the national highway system President Dwight D. Eisenhower established during the 1950s.

By the early twenty-first century, it has become commonplace for people living busy lives to eat outside the home or bring in take-out food (Keystone Center 2006; Lin, Guthrie, and Frazio 1998). Just as we can now work almost anywhere, we can also eat almost anywhere, fundamentally changing the nature of the household in which families used to convene for an evening meal. High school kids drive to school and go off campus for lunch, followed by a hurried evening meal between homework, sports, music lessons, or perhaps an after-school job (National Sleep Foundation 2006a). Some families almost never gather for a meal; instead each person eats at a time that suits him or her, depending on work, school, and activity schedules. This affects all family members, not just hurried teenagers; they are denied both the friendly mutuality of the dinner table and much-needed downtime.

There are two underlying assumptions here that were never questioned by Ford, Eisenhower, or the engineers who developed the highway system. The first assumption is that it is acceptable to fuel cars with expensive, polluting, and nonrenewable fossil fuels such as gasoline. At this writing, the price of gas in the United States is nearly $3 a gallon. The second assumption is that it is healthful and wholesome for people to eat on the run, especially at fast-food franchises whose food is often high in fat, cholesterol, and salt. Initially, fast food, like chain motels, was glamorized as the epitome of a progressive modernity for people "on the go," which was framed as a good thing to be. During the 1950s and 1960s, large gas-guzzling cars were covered in chrome and glamorized as veritable vessels for launch on the high seas of the interstate highway system.

Only much later, by the end of the twentieth century and at the beginning of the twenty-first, has the bloom come off the rose and fast cars and fast food been revealed to be unhealthful and a step backward. Some states enter the fray as they issue graduated driver's licenses and impose stiffer penalties for speeding on teens than on more experienced

---

*A term for an Internet-era capitalism in which people derive their knowledge of the world from rapid information and communication technologies and in which they consume ceaselessly.

drivers. Cars sport crash-test ratings. And we are even on the verge of a new era of automobile locomotion fueled by electricity, ethanol, and hydrogen. People are buying hybrids, perhaps following the lead of eco-politically correct celebrities. However, this remains a mixed picture: many Americans purchase inefficient large SUVs and pickup trucks, and they glamorize NASCAR, which weds speed, risk, and energy inefficiency in one noisy package.

Many who question these assumptions do not go further and indict the whole system of post-Fordist capitalism, which despoils the environment, turns life into a rat race, and colonizes poor countries. But a critique of fast cars, fast food, fast bodies, and fast life (see Petrini 2003) can lead to a larger questioning about the dedifferentiating, deboundaried* worlds of hectic, harried moms, workers, and children, who are becoming a new proletariat or pre–labor force in their own right (producing not surplus value[†] but schoolwork and other activities that constitute a pre-economic surplus value). In other words, we can adapt to the blurring of work and home, perhaps improving our coping skills by consuming products from the self-help industry, or we can resist this blurring, and other blurrings such as the one between adulthood and childhood, in the name of a larger critique in which both the planet and selves are at risk. That is the direction of this book, which seeks to transform work, family, and school in ways that have implications for all social institutions. We cannot isolate what happens in one institution from what is happening in all the others, given both the institutional dedifferentiation that has taken place (making it difficult to identify exactly where one institution ends and another picks up) and globalization, which makes what happens in our backyard relevant to people in distant countries and cultures.

INVERSION: WORK BECOMES FAMILY, FAMILY BECOMES WORK

Arlie Hochschild (1997) argues that as women enter the paid labor force and life accelerates, an inversion occurs: the workplace becomes like a family, and the household becomes a chore, becomes worklike. This is

---

*Removing boundaries around social institutions such as work, family, education, and entertainment in a post-Fordist, postmodern stage of capitalism; especially important is the erosion of the boundary separating public and private life.

[†] Marx's term for how underpaid workers, by working, contribute a component of economic value to commodities that turn into profit for the business owner; Marx argued that all profit is owed to workers' labor.

precisely our argument, although we take the issue a step further as we discuss the process of what we term "familization,"* by which we mean that social relations outside of the household take on certain positive qualities often associated with idyllic, if mythic, families.

Let's put ourselves in someone else's shoes to examine this process of inversion more closely. You are a working mother who goes to work from 9 a.m. to 5 p.m., with occasional overtime. You have a professional job (for example, you're an architect) that allows for some flextime in case the kids get sick, but by the same token you are counted on for occasional evening and weekend work. It is Monday morning. Your husband has just left on an out-of-town business trip. You have to get your kids off to school after a weekend at home with them. The kids attend different schools, with different start times. By the time you get to your office at 9 a.m., you are already beat! But you are also looking forward to adult conversation and mature responsibilities. You love your kids and husband, but you are glad to be out of the maelstrom of their demands and needs for several hours.

There is absolutely nothing wrong with these feelings. The problem in the United States is the lack of a national child-care policy and adequate parental-leave programs. You are forced to juggle many things if you want to have a full life—kids, husband, home, job, travel, and leisure (Blair-Loy 2003). The list is long and growing for most people. And on top of normal school-year responsibilities, you must also figure out what to do with your kids during the summer, when they are home from school but you still have to work. Some women who want children decide to put their careers on hold and stay home for several years until the kids are in school or even until after they graduate from high school. It is easy for feminists to be judgmental about such women, but they are making a deliberate choice regarding what they consider to be in their and their children's best interests. Of course, most feminists would agree with us that it is very unfortunate that women often have to make this choice. It would be better if parents could work flexible hours, have child care at the job site, take more time off after birth or adoption, and share the responsibilities of childrearing with partners who participate equally. Even sharing responsibility for children is not always a solution, as time demands make even shared responsibility for children difficult to reconcile with full-time work.

---

*Transforming social relationships, including those found in the workplace, into relations based on caring, mutuality, and democracy, especially where the actual family ceases to nurture and satisfy people.

"Inversion," then, is a metaphor for the office or business viewed as a family, with strong friendships, intellectual stimulation, perhaps even romance. It is an open question whether the traditional family has ever provided women (who do not work outside the home) with these enticements. We doubt that the family has ever been a haven, except perhaps for men. We doubt that it has been wholly positive even for men, because men absent from the home and from childrearing are themselves not fully human. They are not "connected" in ways that women are, and they bear this scar for life (Kimmel 2000).

And yet there is no doubt that most jobs are alienating in the sense that their occupants are not paid a full measure of their contribution to profit and that most workers have little or no control of the working process. Although Marx and Max Weber disagree on the causes of alienation, they agree that alienation in the workplace is a serious problem that needs to be addressed by sociologists and those who make policy. For people in the early twenty-first century to introduce elements of "family" to the workplace, such as collegiality, trust, informality, and interdependence, improves the plight of workers. It also responds to pressures on the home front, with too much to do and too little time in which to do it.

The inversion of work and home, then, is a relatively recent phenomenon that actually mitigates the effects of workplace problems by "familizing" social relations at work. People have lunch, celebrate birthdays, and e-mail colleagues, who become not only friends but familylike intimates. We view this in part as a way to humanize the workplace, which has always possessed elements of alienation, and in part as a reaction to an overloaded and frantic family life, which now bears symptoms of alienation much as work has always done.

Why is family (the traditional kind) increasingly alienating? There are several reasons: women experience role overload because they now work outside the home and they continue to bear the burden of child care and domestic labor; the family as it has been idealized by traditionalists cannot meet all of people's expectations and thus family members experience a sense of deflation and disappointment; children's lives have become much more frantic, with adultlike performance expectations by teachers, tutors, and coaches; and, finally, the walls of the home are no longer impermeable now that people are electronically connected to the world, leading to disenchantment with family life, especially for children who spend hours in front of television and on the Internet (Brody 2006; Stockwell 2005).

Work is now being reconstructed to resemble a big happy family. Family, which was a safe harbor of sorts, is now exhibiting workplace-like symptoms such as stress, sleeplessness, role strain, and role conflict. This is what we mean by inversion, although there are certainly still ways in which many jobs are alienating and ways in which family is genuinely nurturing and restorative. Hochschild is correct to notice that adults crave work as an escape from the rigors of family life, taking a vacation from kids and chores for a precious eight hours a day, even when their jobs offer conviviality with other adults only during short breaks.

The haven in a heartless world idealized by *Leave It to Beaver, Reader's Digest,* and now the Christian Right has become a job, a chore, while work has familylike qualities. This is a strange picture for Marxists, but perhaps not as strange for feminists. Inversion, though, is not the end of the story, with work becoming family, and family work. This can be a subversive as well as inverting process that remakes work, and it can launch a critique of the family that raises serious questions about children, childhood, schooling, and the role of women. There are two versions of inversion, then. One preserves the status quo and simply allows people some respite once the kids have gone to school. The other, radicalizing version notices that unfulfilling work is mitigated by familial relations, which model improved human relations of all sorts. It takes this insight and runs with it, further transforming the workplace so that workers not only enjoy conviviality and intimacy but also take control of the working process and enjoy the economic fruits of their labor. It also reformulates family practices, including childrearing, childhood, and schooling, in ways that decelerate fast families and improve the quality of life for everyone, especially children.

TOO MUCH TO DO: TELEWORK, HOME/WORK, MEDIA CULTURE

The limitation of an analysis of inversion, as we are calling it, is that it tends to redifferentiate work and family even as it notices interesting changes in postmodern capitalism. We must avoid this risk of redifferentiation because it prevents us from fully understanding why the household has become so burdened with expectations it cannot meet. The firewall surrounding family and home has crumbled; this firewall has not kept the world out, and, as a result, there is too much to do in too little time, especially for women and children, who are the most alienated occupants of the family. After all, since the late nineteenth century, men have been gainfully employed in the division of paid labor, which has been overlaid by a gender division of labor.

As capitalism evolved, women retained their household role in the gender division of labor, but since the 1960s many of them have added an additional role as a paid worker outside the home, although they earn less than men and are less likely than men to have supervisory and executive positions (Padavic and Reskin 2002). In a way, the logic of capital has triumphed over the logic of patriarchy in that women have been "freed" to be alienated alongside men in the capitalist labor force. And yet patriarchy is still found in both the household and workplace, with women doing more than their share of domestic labor and child care and occupying lower and lesser positions than men in paid labor. One of the only changes in the division of domestic labor since women flooded the labor force after the 1960s is that women now do less housework, while men do a little more (Coltrane 2004; Sayer 2005). As a result, unless families can afford to hire outside help, the net impact of the women's movement on household labor is that houses are a little dirtier than they were when women stayed home.

The firewall protecting family has nearly disintegrated because rapid information and communication technologies have penetrated the shield of privacy. Again, we do not deny that the outside world invaded the family before the Internet and cell phones; our parents listened to radio, and we were weaned on television, and both of these technologies still exist. But the Internet and cell phone have intensified the colonization of everyday life by allowing people to reach into private life and private time, encroaching on our autonomy. Not all of this is bad: computers and cells can be convenient, even making way for community and democracy (see Agger 2004b). But people rarely use the computers and cell phones for such constructive purposes; instead, people are used by the technologies, responding to calls, texts, e-mails, and instant messages that soak up time, money, and affect.

Technology is best viewed within a social context. We do not believe that cell phones, instant or text messaging, and e-mail are inherently good or bad. It depends on how we use them—and on how they use us. Young people who call, text, IM, and e-mail tend to seek uncoerced instantaneity, which means they want to make quick connections but not necessarily to have to respond immediately. They also want to filter their calls and messages. Kids also use these electronic media to engage in what Goffman termed "impression management," manipulating the ways in which others view them. Finally, cells, texting, and e-mails tend to lead to a depthless discourse because messages are brief and quick. Perhaps young people, and some older people too, crave community and connection, but their technological interfaces somewhat hinder the ways in which they seek these things.

The firewall around family has given way: we are increasingly preoccupied with telework, homework, and media culture (Kellner 1995). Telework (Gurstein 2001) is work done off-site, away from the office cubicle. It can be performed at home, in an off-site facility (such as a prison), on the road while traveling, during recreation, even while waiting for kids at their practices or tutoring sessions. You return home after a long day at the office, make dinner, do some laundry, put the kids to bed, and check your e-mail. You might find several e-mails from colleagues or your boss demanding responses. E-mail has become exponential: each e-mail message provokes another and another and another, quickly reproducing itself. A study of e-mail's tendency to reproduce itself might find that every morning's or evening's batch of nonspam e-mails cubes itself within a day or two.

E-mail is not the only culprit. The cell phone (Rippin 2005) is used for doing family, dating, chatting, and working. Our college students leave class with cell phones glued to their ears. Like e-mail, cell phone messages reproduce themselves in calls to be returned and then returned again, as callers play what is popularly referred to as "telephone tag." Although, like e-mail, the cell can be used asynchronously (that is, without immediacy but on a delayed, deferred basis), especially with caller ID allowing users to screen their calls and answer only for certain callers, calls made and messages left possess a certain momentum that, like e-mail, may increase rapidly. Families so depend on their cell phones that some purchase several phones on a family plan and dispense with their traditional landline altogether.

During an earlier modernity, it was harder to perform work off-site and after hours. Many of us are old enough to remember the rotary telephone and a time when voice mail, caller ID, and call waiting did not exist. If someone was not home, the call went unnoticed and unanswered. Technology produces and is accompanied by certain social expectations of presence, immediacy, and reciprocity. In an earlier era of manual typewriters, network television, rotary telephones, downtown shopping, and the afternoon newspaper, it was much more difficult for the long arm of the workplace to invade the family and selfhood. Without the miniaturization of computers in order to land astronauts on the moon, we might still live in such times, which, on balance, seem like golden years. Life was lived more slowly, evoking Walden Pond and *The Waltons.* We are in a rush and our families are eroding because we have allowed these instantaneizing technological prostheses to set agendas for our working, sleeping, playing, schooling, and childrearing.

Rapid information and communication technologies almost automatically lead to the prevalence of telework—working off-site, after or before hours. We say "almost automatically" because, as we just noted, technology does not have an agenda of its own. However, as soon as bosses could track employees with computers and phones, they began to use these means to ensure accountability and boost productivity. In spite of the rhetoric of efficiency and time savings, these rapid information and communication technologies actually increase work. This has been the history of supposedly laborsaving devices such as the vacuum cleaner and washing machine since World War II (Cowan 1983). They do not save labor but in effect "demand" that they be used, thus generating tasks that were not there before. For example, the vacuum is intended to replace sweeping floors or beating rugs, which involves much harder labor than vacuuming. But we now vacuum our rugs much more frequently than people ever bothered to beat their rugs, so we have actually increased our labor. And because it is easy to wash clothes now, people wash their clothes much more frequently, rather than wearing them repeatedly until they are visibly dirty. These laborsaving technologies are actually time robbers.

During the 1950s, advertising portrayed images of the radiant housewife in her kitchen surrounded by the latest technologies for meal preparation and cleaning. She could accomplish these chores and then have time to pursue hobbies and devote herself to her children and husband. This is the world idealized in those notorious 1950s and 1960s situation comedies with homemaking heroines like June Cleaver and Harriet Nelson. Today, advertising pitched to women emphasizes that women's lives are hurried and harried, especially now that they have careers as well as families. In this context, they need smartphones, laptops, and microwaves in order to get chores (both work-related and home-related) done fast and faster.

The other side of telework is not primarily technological but psychological. Although it is clear that Hoover vacuum cleaners and Black-Berry devices create whole new categories of time use, telework can be appealing because it diverts people from more mundane tasks such as making dinner, cleaning up, and helping kids with homework. As early Marx understood, the desire to work answers a fundamental human need to express oneself and to leave a lasting mark on the world. Even though most work is alienating, whether by Marx's or Weber's standards, people still strive to perform it out of a sense of duty or to find inherent meaning in it. Indeed, it is through work that people mitigate their unhappiness—despite an overbearing boss, insufficient salary, and boring routine. They "find" themselves in their tasks, being challenged and perhaps helping others. The so-called workaholic is like the alcoholic who cannot live life without the help of the bottle; telework is made to order for such people, primarily men, who cannot put aside their work tasks but derive identity from them. Whether this is a dangerous addiction (workaholism) or a healthy creative outlet (what Marx called *praxis*) depends on perspective. And, realistically, technological and psychological aspects may be intertwined: the boss wants to tether you to the workplace, and you derive meaning and identity from being needed, even as you are being mistreated.

Telework is matched by homework and media as time robbers. By home/work we are referring not only to children's school-related assignments and projects but to all domestic activities performed by children or adults that suck up time, from cleaning and cooking to balancing the checkbook and planning vacations. As the home becomes a little factory, the people in it are busier than ever; in effect, they are producers—of schoolwork, meals, ironing. Left-wing feminists since Mariarosa Dalla Costa and Selma James (1975) have noticed that women's domestic labor, including childbearing and childrearing, produces profit for capitalists. Without this unwaged labor performed primarily by women, men would not get dinner or comfort and the labor force would not be replenished with would-be workers. The wages for housework movement urged that women be paid a salary for this unvalued but important activity.

By home/work for adults we mean activities traditionally assigned to women, such as running the household, managing children, planning vacations, and performing or subcontracting home maintenance. Many of these activities are now performed with the aid of computers and cell phones. For example, you can find a local plumber by surfing the Web instead of consulting the yellow pages. Housework, performed primarily by women, reproduces husbands and children. It is productive in that sense and produces economic value for capitalism. Children's homework, discussed more fully in chapter 4, produces value in three senses: it inculcates certain skills; it teaches self-discipline and obedience to authority; and it prevents children from having too much idle time, thus preparing them for adulthood. Samuel Bowles and Herbert Gintis (1976) authored a classic study of this phenomenon called *Schooling in a Capitalist America*. We add to their analysis the contention that schoolwork produces future adults and adultlike children in that it robs children of unstructured time, which could be spent in nonproductive and potentially subversive activities. And where schoolwork will not fill after-school time sufficiently, children are encouraged to play organized sports and take lessons that suck up even more time (Rosenfeld and Wise 2001). Lost are childhood, play, and exploration.

Idleness is the devil's workshop, and people, including kids, are kept busy so that they do not use idle time to reflect on their situation, theorize it, and become radicals. This is an argument about how domination has deepened in post–World War II capitalism. People must be kept busy, and on task, so that they consume all the products their labor produces and so that they are diverted from the big picture, which would reveal the meaninglessness of lives as they are presently structured. Americans work for nearly fifty weeks a year, for forty or more hours a week, at jobs that do not have inherent meaning, are not particularly essential, and are undercompensated. If working people questioned this situation, they might either drop out or become politically energized. Hence, their time must be filled with telework, homework, and media.

Finally, information and communication technologies stream the world into our homes. This closes the circuit between production and consumption via advertising. Marcuse (1964) suggests that capitalists in an affluent society can only produce profit by in effect producing false needs for goods and services beyond what is required for the good life. Media culture also diverts people from the real causes of their un-happiness, serving as a balm for the soul. Television, movies, and the Internet consume a great deal of time devoted to leisure and relaxation. Americans watch television at night and spend other time, even when at work, surfing the Net (Harris Interactive 2004). This diverts them from their true needs, which can only be fathomed beyond the reach of marketing.

Jeremiads against television (e.g., Postman 1985) are by now com-monplace. We are not for or against television or the Internet as much as we are convinced that these often suck up time and divert us from more substantive projects. We are encouraged to spend our time this way both to expose us to advertising and to keep us away from troubling books and disturbing thoughts. In Ray Bradbury's *Fahrenheit 451* (1967), an allegory about a book-burning dystopia, people are forbidden to pos-sess books, let alone read them. We do not need an anti-intellectual fire brigade when we have laptops, plasma televisions, DVD players, iPods, video games, and TiVo DVRs for recording our favorite shows. These prevent us from reading and then writing. Thought control proceeds via time robbery, a process in which the media play a major role.

FROM FAMILY VALUES TO FAMILY/FAMILIES/FAMILIZATION

The Christian Right, which dominates the American political agenda today, argues for a return to the traditional family, which worshiped God and subordinated women and children. "Family values," a phrase first used during the 1980s, are regressive in the sense that they would remove women from careers and even colleges, turning back the clock to a time when women stayed at home, raised children, and obeyed their husbands.

It is a mistake to view social history as smoothly linear, with progress proceeding unchecked. The project of modernity,* as Habermas (1987a) termed it, or rationalization† in Weber's (1958) terms, contains moments of both progress and regress. Reason is under assault from fundamentalists of many cultures who would replace reason with revealed truth. "Family values" is code for an anti-feminist and homophobic political agenda inconsistent with the project of modernity.

This is not to deny that there are problems with "family" as it is presently constituted. Indeed, as we have been arguing, family has lost the relative autonomy that has allowed it to shelter damaged selves. Workplace imperatives subject families to the same performance expectations and obligations as work. Family has been accelerated as people within it do too much telework and consume too much electronic culture. By the same token, the hurts people suffer in the public sphere, especially at work, cannot be made good within the family, given its limited capacity for sheltering and nurturing people. And so family is burdened with expectations that it cannot meet, which has always been the problem with normative families since women left the labor force in the nineteenth century. Families are unable to make whole men, women, and children, given the preponderant weight of inescapable public institutions. And in any case families have succumbed to many of the same tendencies of acceleration, intensification, dedifferentiation, and loss of autonomy as found in public life.

In this context, *familization* is, at best, a utopian project, a way of conceptualizing all decent human relationships governed by norms of community and reciprocity. Habermas terms this the ideal speech

---

*Habermas's term for the Enlightenment's goal of a world society based on reason, science, democracy, literacy, and the absence of armed conflict.

†Weber's term for the tendency of societies to move from religious and mythological stages (before the Enlightenment) to a modern stage in which the world can be studied scientifically, manipulated, and predicted.

situation,* modeling democracy on the ability of speakers to engage in unhindered dialogue with the mutual intent of producing consensus. Although in some respects Habermas (1971) regresses behind early Marx by seemingly ignoring work, the body, and subjectivity and focusing instead on interpersonal speech, Habermas is saying much the same thing as we are about ideal speech or what we prefer to call familization as aims to be sought, if never fully attained. As actual families have become job sites, people seek "family" (community, reciprocity, identity, mutuality, Habermas's ideal speech) in the public sphere, notably at work. The inversion of family and work suggests the utopian agenda of familizing work relations so that they are governed by these essentially democratic norms of unencumbered self-expression, dialogical reciprocity, and community—what a left-feminist might mean by family values.

The Victorians did not intend this utopian notion of family, because for them family meant patriarchy, gender inequality, and hierarchy. So-called traditional family values, appropriated by the New Right as a code for the oppression of women, gays, and lesbians, were never intended to create community but simply to reproduce the hierarchical division of labor found in capitalist society at large. In *The Division of Labor in Society* (1947), Durkheim makes this clear where he conflates the industrial and gendered divisions of labor, preparing the way for Parsons's later defense of distinctive gender roles on grounds of utilitarian expedience (see Lehmann 1994): Durkheim uses the authoritarian workplace as a model for family relationships that reproduce adult male workers and their women helpmates.

And so "family" has never meant what we are calling family/families, the utopian transformation of all social relationships into familylike bonds of community and mutuality. We rely on images of family, whereas Habermas used the metaphor of democratic speech and Marcuse used the metaphor of a rationality of gratification stemming from his merger of Marx and Freud. All of these metaphors are important and noncontradictory. We deploy *familization* because work and family have become inverted, with people seeking missing familylike social relationships on the job and elsewhere in the public sphere (e.g., in communitarian voluntary associations and affinity groups), allowing the as-yet-unfulfilled utopian aim of family conceptualized as community to become a

_____

*Habermas's term for democracy, which he reformulates as a conversation among people that proceeds according to certain implicit rules such as turn taking, refusing to lie or browbeat others, and the commitment to be swayed by the power of the strongest argument.

universal project that transforms not only work but also all social relationships, including, ironically enough, families themselves.

These would be families in which people watch less TV, turn off their computers and cell phones, and minimize homework and other children's activities in favor of the purposive purposelessness* of spontaneous play. Families can be familized once we accept family or better families as a universal human desire, played out wherever people find conviviality, cooperation, and community, even (again ironically, for this is capitalism) in the workplace. The inversion that Hochschild and we are describing is quite extraordinary, given the tendency for work to be alienating and impervious to radical transformations. Again, we are not equating casual Friday or bowling on a team with colleagues from the workplace with a full-blown transformation of work and life. Capitalist workplaces are still hierarchical and bureaucratic, as Marx and Weber well understood. Rather, people are signaling a desire to be fully human within the community where they seek respite from the hothouse of the family in the eight hours they spend on the job, with other adults.

The fact that people seek intimacy, community, and democracy within their work relations suggests that there is a universal desire for these attributes of the good society. We believe it also suggests that family is falling short of people's expectations, which they attempt to meet elsewhere. Ideally, nurturing family and nonalienated work would not be disjunctive alternatives. Marcuse (1955) speculated that we could rebuild our society by informing every human action and decision with life-enhancing energy, transforming Freud's life instinct (Eros) into a drive for political and economic liberation (and the death instinct, Thanatos, into a drive for freedom from unhappiness and injustice, not death).

This is a compelling imagery, which made a great deal of sense as it played out during the 1960s, a decade theorized, appreciated, and criticized by Marcuse in *An Essay on Liberation* (1969a) and then in *Counterrevolution and Revolt* (1972). The first book was more hopeful than the second, which took stock of Nixon's counterrevolution against the New Left, antiwar, and civil rights movements. We are seeking a somewhat different imagery of liberation—family/families—because it builds on what Russell Jacoby (1975) called the politics of subjectivity or personal life. Although subjectivity is not totally political, and politics is

---

*Kant's term for play, free activity such as art, music, or sports that has no ulterior or utilitarian purpose; synonymous with Huizinga's and Marcuse's concept of the play impulse or instinct.

not totally subjective and personal, feminists have shown persuasively that we cannot ignore the politics of sexuality, housework, childrearing, schooling, and time use as we plot a better society. The family is just such a site of political subjectivities and intersubjectivities, bringing together parents, children, friends, peers, teachers, and mentors. Just as Marcuse, politicizing Freud via Marx, identified a universal desire to be gratified, issuing in the play impulse and new sensibility, so we are identifying a drive to be ensconced in familylike relations of trust, cooperation, community, intimacy, and democracy. And we also have Mill's (2003) marketplace of ideas* and Habermas's ideal speech situation as progressive models.

This is not a battle over utopian imageries but a way to locate political energy in activities ordinarily viewed as purely personal and prepolitical. People seek family—and thus extend family/families into work and also into leisure and play activities—because they reject and resent their unhappiness and powerlessness.

One of the major contradictions in the family is that people overburden it with expectations of how it can make them happy. When our work is not going well, we can retreat into the bosom of the family where we can be healed. But this was always an artificial view of the family, neglecting to notice that the family is firmly situated in history and is an outcome of power, struggle, and inequality, such as the inequality between men and women. Family, in a society in which work has primacy, cannot heal all wounds, such as poverty. Family has always been "colonized" by external forces. Think of Charles Dickens's *A Christmas Carol,* in which Scrooge's greed led directly to the Cratchits' penury. Once Scrooge saw the light, haunted by the ghosts of Christmas past, present, and future, not only did the Cratchit family receive a huge Christmas turkey but also Bob's salary was increased, improving the financial situation of the family and addressing Tiny Tim's medical condition.

Idealizing family and childhood in these ways gives women something to do when not employed in the factory. But by the 1970s, and partly because of the women's movement, American families could not afford to have only one earner. Women returned to the labor force they had left during an earlier stage of capitalism, and this changed family dynamics considerably. Now women did the double shift of cleaning

---

*John Stuart Mill's term for a democracy in which people float all sorts of ideas, including intellectual ones, in the hope that the best ones will survive and persuade others.

and cooking, on the one hand, and working for a salary on the other, albeit a salary significantly lower than a man's. This caused stress within the family; Blumstein and Schwartz (1983) show that marital conflict is heightened when the woman expects the man to do more around the house. Indeed, in households with an egalitarian household division of labor there is more conflict than in households where the wife does most or all of the household labor.

As well, families are more stressed because kids are now increasingly left to their own devices, especially if both parents work until after school lets out. Latchkey children are left alone until parents return in the evening. This fundamentally changes the nature of childhood and makes kids grow up more quickly than before. The prevalence of divorce reflects more liberal divorce laws, to be sure; but it also reflects the intrusion of the world and its strains into family life, imperiling the stability of families and causing many American children to grow up in homes with only one parent. And in most states where gay and lesbian couples are not allowed to marry, it is difficult for these couples to attain the kind of stability that helps insulate them against the dissolution of their informal unions.

Familization, thus, responds to deficits in family life thrust upon family from the outside. It is an attempt to create familylike human relationships, beginning in the workplace and other cultural spheres but perhaps ending in the family. There is no reason that families cannot fulfill the ideals of community and intimacy, especially where we acknowledge the permeability of the boundaries surrounding families and other social institutions in an age where boundaries can be pierced electronically. The problem with family is that family has been isolated as the only utopian site, which leads to it being the least utopian site of stress, struggle, and survival. If we expect less from family and more from the public sphere, while simultaneously recognizing that family is always already public and political, we can reconstruct all social relationships as, in effect, "families," a genuinely radical agenda.

IN LOCO PARENTIS: TEACHER AS PARENT IN A LATCHKEY AGE

Latchkey kids are kids at home alone while their parents are at work or elsewhere. The term "latchkey" stems from the nineteenth century. Some researchers substitute the term "self-care" to describe these kids left home alone, preferring the less pejorative sound of that term. These kids can be elementary age. As many as 10 percent of children aged six

to twelve spend some time in self-care each week, and the figures are
higher for children of higher-earning dual-career parents (Sonenstein,
Gates, Schmidt, and Bolshun 2002). Sometimes they stay at home alone
for long periods of time while parents work. Approximately 75 percent
of U.S. women between ages twenty-five and fifty-five now work outside the home for wages (U.S. Department of Labor 2005). And most
men work. Day care is expensive and not always the answer, especially
for after-school care. Although the latchkey existence can be defended
as a fairly harmless expedient that can teach independence, it can
be dangerous for kids in a crisis and it takes away time they could be
spending with parents.

This latchkey solution is especially prevalent during the summer,
when school is out but both parents (or a single parent) still work.
Although we are identifying a trend for children to be viewed as workers—homeworkers—paralleling the workplace productivity of their
parents, there is as yet imperfect sequencing of children's school year
and the adult work year in that kids are released from school during the
summer but most parents work all twelve months of the year. No one
is available to care for kids during the summer months. Some school
districts are moving to year-round schooling, but many parents rely
on a patchwork of organized activities (sports camp, music camp) and
self-care during the summer.

American adults neglect kids because they are themselves neglected, expected to work to the exclusion of nearly all else. In Europe,
workers routinely enjoy a month or more of vacation, compared with
the average of two weeks in the United States, as well as a shorter
workweek than their U.S. peers. And the two thousand annual hours
of work that American adults average do not include the informal,
unpaid hours of work that people perform remotely, from their cars,
their homes, and coffee shops. We have actually moved to a society of
more, not less, work, which is exactly the opposite of what prophets
of a postindustrial society* such as Daniel Bell (1973) predicted. We
fill people's time with work both because capital must be fed and because there is a deep-seated cultural assumption that people should
not be idle. This deprives children of parents who are "present" in
their lives, especially during the summer months, when children and
their parents need to restore and recover from the rigorous regimen of
the academic year. And, as we discussed earlier, one can be physically

---

*Daniel Bell's 1970s concept of a society so advanced that machines will take over
human labor, all needs will be met, and class conflicts will cease.

present and still be absent, especially if one is taking and making calls and working on job-related projects.

In this context, teachers become parents of sorts. They are responsible not only for the formal school curriculum but for moral and personal development. Kids in Texas attend school 180 days a year, for about seven hours a day. Their teachers are present for them during those many hours. They come to know them, if only imperfectly, and they not only teach them and evaluate their work but also evaluate their behavior and other aspects of their performance. In sociological parlance, schools "socialize" kids; they make them interpersonally aware and dexterous, and they expose them to the parentlike authority of teachers, who become their surrogate parents.

The best of all possible worlds for kids is to have both teachers and parents who care about them. Teachers resent pushy, intrusive parents, but the better teachers relish parental involvement in their kids' academic lives and in the classroom as volunteers. Strapped school districts rely on parent volunteers for both time and money. Increasingly, though, teachers replace parents as "parents"—those who deliver education, authority, and guidance. The much-ballyhooed decline of the family has really meant the decline of parental authority. Parents have absented themselves, not usually by choice, and they have been replaced, if unsuccessfully, by other agents and agencies of socialization such as teachers, the media, and peers.

This is not a happy transition for anyone. Parents suffer when they are away from their kids. Having children buffers parents' mortal aloneness and their lack of fulfillment in work. Kids suffer when their best friend is the television and when they learn the wrong lessons from out-of-control peers. Teachers, underpaid to begin with, are already overburdened, having to teach, grade papers, and now prepare students for frequent standardized tests, but now they must nurture their students, even when they have their own kids at home. This overloading of teachers is an impossible and unsatisfactory outcome, driving good college students away from the teaching profession. And it creates unrealistic pressures on schools to provide emotional sustenance for kids who lack real parenting and may lack stable homes altogether.

The displacement of authority from parents to teachers, schools, the media, and peer groups is entirely unsatisfactory. It breeds authoritarianism, the inflexible and punitive application of rules and sanctions; harried teachers understandably do not have time to evaluate context in correcting behavior and so they fall back on mechanical,

rote punishments that disserve the student. This inflexibility teaches
children to hate and fear authority and to experience school as a
prison, not a family. Although kids can be kids at recess, unless they
are being punished for earlier transgressions and miss recess, these are
brief interludes of freedom in a structured, rigid day. Even lunch can be
an ordeal. At our son's elementary school, lunchroom monitors stalked
the lunchroom, "grading" the kids on their noise level; too much noise
would earn them silent lunch or perhaps lunch at a table for repeat offenders and might even cause them to miss recess. And a new adminis-
trator installed a traffic light–like meter that actually displays the noise
level as it moves from green to yellow to red. Kids can look forward
only to in-class holiday parties and vacations and the occasional weekend when they do not have homework.

Our analysis is not meant to sound functionalist. We are not suggesting that social institutions such as schools and families have predetermined purposes. Because parental authority is on the wane,
schools and teachers consciously pick up the slack—in loco parentis.
Teachers become parents only by default, as kids look to whichever
adults are present in their lives—these could be coaches, too—for
guidance, discipline, and authority. Child psychologists well understand that kids seek limits and transgress them in order to check that
they are there and to see just what they involve. Kids may "act out" in
school because their parents neglect them and, perhaps subconscious-
ly, they want teachers to become their parental surrogates. Teachers
may either not understand this or reject it as an unwanted burden.
Kids, by nature perhaps, take what they can get—love, nurturance,
limits, boundaries. And they derive this from peers, too, with the ca-
veat that peers do not set limits and respond with love and nurturance
in the way that adults can. Peers might be viewed as siblings at a time
when family is less a destination than a hollow shell of its former or
idealized self.

We prefer to narrow the concept of the decline of the family to the
decline and dispersal of parental authority. Indeed, we are arguing that
"family" and familylike activities now take place in a variety of settings,
including work and school. People find love in all the wrong places,
or at least in unusual places from the perspective of the nuclear family in an earlier capitalism. In a world with blurred boundaries, what
counts as family is up for grabs, just as "the workplace" has many new
meanings now that people can work anywhere and anytime (reflecting
a happy capitalism in which people are always productive). There is
nothing inherently wrong with teachers becoming parent substitutes

as long as we understand that they are neither trained nor paid to do that. In addition, it would make more sense to create synchronicity between parental authority and teacher authority so that we do not have only one or only the other. Parents, especially younger and single ones, need help in childrearing from knowledgeable and caring adults, here teachers and also coaches, especially now that "childhood" is a complex and hurried process with all sorts of unprecedented outside influences.

The problem, then, is threefold: parents are increasingly absent from their kids' lives and cannot serve as loving and modeling beacons; teachers are overburdened with expectations and cannot be adequate parental surrogates without help from the real parents; and too often the type of authority meted out by teachers and schools is authoritarian, deriving its model not from loving family mutuality but from prisons and the military. Although individual teachers may not view kids as inherently bad, many of the rules and sanctions in place in schools, from strict dress codes to codes of silence and truncated recesses, suggest that we have moved too far in the direction of a model of authority found in the prison system. Prisons in America have been premised on the assumption that prisoners are evil but educable, not a great leap forward in humanitarianism from Lombroso's (2006) earlier biologistic and phrenological theories of atavism—criminals are born, not made. The Auburn, New York, prison, opened in 1821, began a new chapter in American penology (see Meskell 1999). Prisoners were now to be rehabilitated and reformed. They were housed in private cells, cut off from corrupting influences, schooled in morality, and severely disciplined. In many respects, we believe that this model has been transplanted to schools today, as students become, in effect, the prison population. Added to this Auburn model* of schooling is the analogy of schools to workhouses in which youngsters toil over workbenches in return for very modest rewards.

Alternative and free schools from the 1960s, and even some Montessori schools today, provide very different models of authority and mutuality. Here, students are viewed as good, if sometimes misguided, and are valuable members of a democratic community of learners. Teachers lead and teach Socratically and not with rigid curricula that involve teaching to the test. Dialogue replaces punishment as a way to correct and elevate behavior. Indeed, the very category of student behavior is abandoned

---

*An early American prison in which prisoners were forced to maintain a code of silence and engage in hard labor in order to rehabilitate themselves.

as students are conceptualized as willful agents who belong to a social contract—the very essence of democracy. These are not crazy or hippie ideas; good teachers in our current penal and productivist school system understand that authority is best imposed gently and through dialogue and modeling. They do not yell, nor do they punish. They are calm, not dictatorial. They are democratic personalities, not authoritarians. Such teachers exist and must be cherished for their efforts.

In the following chapter, we address the acceleration of childhood and the ways in which children become adultlike before their time. When family and home lose their boundaries, pierced electronically, kids are at risk as their parents leave them to fend for themselves. The outside world invades them, turning them into a pre-labor force of busy, multitasking underworkers. Schools now become a point of production as kids "produce" homework, extracurricular activities, and themselves as future members of the adult workforce. Kids resist these pressures as they desperately crave downtime, much like their parents.

3

Implosion II

Accelerated Childhood

Fast families breed virtual children, kids who nearly miss childhood altogether. The implosion of the boundary between family and the world, especially work and school (which is a kind of factory), imperils children perhaps even more than their parents. It short-circuits their development, imposing on them adultlike expectations about performance and productivity. This is an ironic turn of events. The Victorians invented the category of the child, where before, during the Middle Ages, children were viewed simply as small adults whose needs were no different from those of adults. The construction of the category of childhood required a corresponding concept of motherhood. Children cried out for maternal care, hence giving women who retreated from industrial labor an important role to play. Today, we are returning to the Middle Age conception of childhood. Children work very hard in school producing homework, which should be viewed as a commodity* whose value will be realized only later once kids move from the pre–labor force to the paid labor force. Although child labor laws prevent kids from taking on adult jobs, many from the age of sixteen perform jobs—or as Douglas Coupland (1991) aptly calls them, McJobs—in the service sector, earning minimum wage and having no benefits.

---

*Anything, whether goods or services, bought and sold in the open market; Marx noticed that under capitalism human labor becomes a commodity.

NOT PREPARATION FOR ADULTHOOD
BUT SUBSTITUTION FOR CHILDHOOD

Samuel Bowles and Herbert Gintis (1976) argue that there is a hidden curriculum* in our schools lying underneath the explicit curriculum of science, math, social studies, and English. This hidden curriculum stresses obedience to authority, punctuality, timeliness, and self-discipline. Mastering the hidden curriculum prepares kids for eventual adult roles in the workforce. We are also interested in another, even deeper, curriculum, underneath the official curriculum and hidden curriculum. This involves learning about how to become adultlike during childhood, actually substituting adulthood for childhood and adolescence. In particular, kids and teenagers are held to standards that in effect replace childhood altogether with adultlike production and performance requirements.

From the late nineteenth century until the 1990s, the notion of childhood and adolescence as distinctive phases of development was well entrenched. Why are we moving away from it, back to essentially feudal concepts of the child as a latent or even actual, albeit small, adult?

As we recall from the first chapter, Sigmund Freud (1958) maintained that repression is the sublimation and disciplining of basic antisocial urges (love, sex, food, etc.) in order to allow us to live peaceably with others. This is not a bad thing but one that is necessary for people to coexist without engaging in what Thomas Hobbes (1950) earlier called the war of all against all, like the characters in *Lord of the Flies* (Golding 1954). Herbert Marcuse argues that affluence and the rise of the middle class are actually threatening to capitalism because they allow people to taste freedom, which might lead them to question the very social, economic, and political system that has them working forty hours a week for fifty weeks a year in often unfulfilling and hierarchically organized jobs. Having more money and ample leisure time tempts people to become hippies, slackers, and perhaps even revolutionaries. As a response, capitalism must find ways to increase people's repression so that they are not diverted from their assigned tasks, in both public and

---

*Bowles and Gintis's (1976) term for the things that children learn in schools, such as obedience and punctuality, that may not be explicitly found in the written curriculum of science, math, geography, and so on.

private spheres. This extra repression is termed "surplus repression"*
by Marcuse. This amounts to toeing the line beyond the basic minimum
of self-restraint required for civilized social life.

We maintain that childhood is also threatening to an adult capitalism, in which parents are already surplus-repressed. Once post–World
War II capitalism successfully coordinated and accelerated all adult
activity via television, the Internet, and telework—all the social forces
we have been discussing in earlier chapters—it had to remove every
vestige of purposive purposelessness or play. Adults who participate in
playful activities such as sports are organized into leagues, which succumb to bureaucracy. Children may be viewed as defiant if they have
not yet been bent to the rule of surplus-repressive discipline and self-
discipline. Kids fidget until they get recess; this fidgeting is medicalized
as attention deficit disorder (ADD) and attention deficit hyperactivity
disorder (ADHD) and treated with drugs. Kids seek unstructured play
and are thus organized into highly bureaucratized and stratified leagues
(Sappenfield 2001). And, perhaps most important, they are subject to
surveillance, productivity, and performativity even when they are at
home, after formal school hours and organized-sports hours have ended
(Simplico 2005). Some are crushed beneath mountains of homework,
which advance what we call a rote culture. They become homework
machines that produce anticipatory surplus value—anticipating its
adult production.

We use the terms *productivity*† and *performativity*‡ often in this
book. Let's be clear about what they mean in the context of schooling and childhood. By *productivity* we are referring to the amount of
time and effort claimed by daily homework and school assignments.
By *performativity* we refer to the tendency to subject all childhood
activity to evaluation, from lunchroom decorum to sports and musical
performances. Performance could be said to encompass production in
that school performances do not exhaust the myriad ways in which kids
are evaluated. We contend that children constitute a pre–labor force
that not only prepares them for the adult labor force but also produces

---

*Marcuse's term for how post–World War II capitalism can satisfy people's material
needs but still persuades them to work hard and play essentially powerless roles in work
and political life; it is repression that one imposes on oneself, similar to Puritanism.

†The evaluation of children in terms of a prodigious production of homework and
other school-related tasks; this activity is often graded.

‡The tendency for all children's activities, from school to play, to be evaluated by
adults.

a certain "value" in its own right, notably the eclipse of childhood by adultlike performances.

The point of this is not simply training and regimentation of the kinds discussed by Bowles and Gintis (1976). Instead, productivity and performativity rob children of that precious time called childhood in which kids experiment, express, and exist outside of the adult world regulated by the clock and duty. Kids are implicitly time rebels; they come in from outside late, even after they have been called. They daydream and dally. They organize themselves and form secret clubs. They disdain the adult world of teachers, coaches, and parents. They have clandestine solidarity, which adults view as threatening to their own surplus-repressed routines. Kids are overscheduled and expected to live up to adultlike standards of production and performance by resentful adults who have lost their own freedom. Max Scheler (1961) argues that resentment is a typical response to deprivation and devaluation, a symptom of a society in which most people are envious of the few who benefit from their work. This concept is central to the Frankfurt School's critique of post–World War II capitalism.

This resentment leads to time robbery, which amounts to putting kids on adult clocks. Kids are overburdened by compulsive parents who want them to play soccer and baseball in the best ("select") leagues, for which they pay hundreds and even thousands of dollars per season (Rosenfeld and Wise 2001). Kids are kept up too late by teachers who assign hours of homework. Kids have to be pried out of bed in the morning in order to begin another day in the homework archipelago. Parents dissatisfied with this Promethean load may decide to homeschool their children or send them to schools with less productivist expectations.

By the time kids are in junior high school, their spirits are crushed, or nearly so. Adults hector them, admonish them, supervise them, regiment them. Parents, teachers, and coaches alike are the enemy. Depression among kids and especially teens is epidemic (Cutler, Glaeser, and Norberg 2000). Kids act out, destructively and self-destructively, when the load becomes too great. Academic expectations are compounded by parental expectations about their children's participation in sports leagues, music competitions, and spelling and history bees, all of which exist to reward middle- and upper-middle-class parents for their investment in augmenting their children's cultural stock of knowledge (cultural capital) (Bourdieu and Passeron 1990). Kids understand that parents are screaming like maniacs at their games because the games are for the parents. Parents even injure and kill each other at practices and games in their fanaticism (*NewsHour* 2001).

But few care about children's rights. There is no civil rights movement for kids, even though there is for animals and trees. In our concluding chapter, we outline such a movement and what we feel should be its desiderata. It is useless to retheorize and reconstruct families without viewing children as citizens, especially now that we have stolen their childhoods from them.

Interestingly, the denial of children's rights comes from both the Right and the Left. Liberals bemoan anti-intellectualism and lament the hours children waste on video games and television. Conservatives criticize public education and the supposedly leftist agendas of teachers and academics and urge a return to basics—fact-based education reinforced by standardized testing (General Accounting Office 2003). There is another possible critique of children's development grounded in the criticism of a rote culture, as we develop in chapter 4. This critique does not take the stance that anything goes in childrearing and schooling but, rather, that independent thought is too often disallowed. We, too, are troubled by an anti-intellectualism at large that stupefies children as well as their parents. Kids too easily become addicted to video games and television to the exclusion of creative work and exercise. This is a nuanced issue because we endorse play, too, especially conceived as an antidote to productivism, which we criticize in this and the next chapter. And a certain amount of electronic play is valuable and not to be rejected in the way that neo-Luddites reject television categorically (*Harvard Health Letter* 2006).

Indeed, kids' penchant for electronic entertainments, some of which are quite interactive, may be a response to time robbers such as schoolwork, music lessons, college-entrance-exam prep courses, and organized sports. And for children in religious families add hours spent in church and church-related activities. Kids need downtime, too. After a long week at school, kids need to unwind and indulge their fantasies, many of which are tied to their lives on the screen and in front of the video monitor. The culprit is not television or video games but a society in which neither adults nor kids are encouraged to play, by which we mean develop themselves outside of the grids of production and performance.

Kids' preference for television and video games, then, may be seen as a cry for help; their lives are too fast and cluttered, much as their parents' lives are. The time kids spend with information and communication technologies is symptomatic, not the cause, of alienation. Kids are alienated in many of the same ways their parents are, but their alienation is *at the hands of* their parents and teachers. Kids must produce and perform in ways that are very damaging to young beings; they do not have time for serendipitous learning, self-expression, and play. Adults, suspicious of kids' free time, regiment it, rationalizing that time must be "invested" productively, thus producing better grades, higher SAT scores, admission to better colleges, and entry into a lucrative career.

The motives of parents and teachers are complex. They want to help, and they realize that this is a rat race in which only the strong—and swift—survive. But parents and teachers are also jealous of their kids, who are not wage slaves and who sleep in on weekends. Our daughter's high school begins at 7:35 a.m., with frequent "before school" activities at impossibly early times for any adolescent. This is, we are convinced, born of adult resentment. Parents love their kids but envy their freedom and so cooperate in the restriction of children's freedom.

The key to understanding the acceleration of childhood and preparation of kids for a "preworkforce" is parents' simultaneous resentment of and yearning for children's freedoms. In this, children are not only victims but also utopian figures leading carefree lives. Early childhood is a metaphor, a destination as well as a point of departure, a time of purposive purposelessness in which the days are long and basic needs are met. Adults attenuate childhood precisely because they want to return to that earlier stage, which is Freud's basic insight. Radical social theories have not plumbed childhood for utopian energy and imagery because for nearly all social theorists, on both the left and the right, children are not yet citizens and, thus, do not matter. Radicals need children both because kids are people, too, and because children's lives are well worth emulating, at least until they are subjected to the disciplining routines of school, which is the anti-utopia.

Nostalgia: Radical Remembrance or Surplus Repression?

What to do with one's childhood once one is grown is a fascinating and often troubling existential and political question. Movies and novels abound in which youth is idealized; *Stand by Me* is just one example. Others depict childhood as hell; *Mean Girls* is a good example. For many of us, childhood was both; nothing can ease the awkwardness of growing up, and yet it is difficult to repress—why would we want to?—the sheer pleasure of time spent going to the park, playing sports and house, and just hanging out. Complicating this picture is school.

We may remember a caring elementary school teacher, but we may also remember one who was so strict or scary we threw up before school. One ninth-grade English teacher may have worn shorts and made Shakespeare come to life, but a later English teacher may have been authoritarian to the point of meanness. We remember sweet friendships and first loves but also useless schoolwork and pressure to succeed—although the pressure we faced was nothing by today's standards.

How we remember childhood influences how we view childhood once we are parents and, from that, how we bring up our children. If we are teachers, our view of our childhood frames the ways we teach and mete out punishment. How we view our own childhoods influences our parenting and teaching styles and suggests to us not only a view of childhood as a developmental stage but a perspective on production and performance. One of our main theses is that fast families in fast capitalism put a premium on children meeting adultlike standards of production and performance, and this largely flows from the ways in which we remember our childhoods.

This is not to say that the memory of childhood necessarily matches the facts of it. We could have been blissfully happy and remember ourselves as miserable. We could have been miserable but remember childhood as a utopian time. At issue here is how we reconstruct our earlier lives and whether we derive from that remembrance key insights about both children and adults today.

Our childhood and adolescent pasts can be a resource either for radicalizing recollection that provides the basis for a critique of fast childhood or an occasion of regret, repression, and rejection. If it is the latter, we are likely to want "more" and "better" for our own children—more discipline, greater achievement, noses pressed harder to the grindstone. If it is the former, we are likely to recall with nostalgia childhoods spent in leisurely play and self-exploration, with minimal acceleration by rapid technologies and fewer expectations about grades and behavior.

It is difficult, but necessary, to distinguish between the natural delight of learning about life and experiencing one's own mind and body and the social context in which these experiences take place. Many people recall their childhoods with affectionate nostalgia but do not use this memory as a radicalizing resource for theorizing and transforming contemporary ways of doing family and schooling. If one inserts one's autobiography into a sociobiography of one's generation, it is possible to view one's past and one's own family, especially one's parents, as having been a chapter in social history that is now closed. By contrast, today's families and schools occupy a later, and faster, chapter, especially when one considers phenomena associated with what we are calling acceleration.

The movie *Stand by Me* does not treat the actual reality of the Eisenhower years or the ways in which those years were giving way to a more tumultuous decade and generation. The movie yearns for yesteryear, a time before time when kids grew up unaffected by the social world around them. *Catcher in the Rye,* J. D. Salinger's 1951 novel, is more socially situating, presenting growing up not so much as a natural process but as a matter of choices made, which opens his account to a political reading. For those of us from the 1960s—what Gitlin (1987) terms years of hope and rage—it is difficult to ignore the political intrusions and inflections in our childhoods, making a radicalizing recollection of good (and bad) times possible.

But there is another account of one's past that lends itself well to surplus-repressive versions of parenting, schooling, and childrearing. Such versions that pretend innocence make for good stories and are equally ready for debunking: fundamentalist politicians who had wild pasts (and sometimes presents) now rail against permissiveness in the home and school. The New Right opposes giving condoms to high school kids and they pretend that kids will just abstain from sexual experimentation. These postures reflect sanitized memories of childhood because, if Freud is correct, all adolescents want to have sex. And these are the same evangelical zealots who as adults rail against libertine sexuality, drinking, and drugs and then get caught with their proverbial pants down. Congressman Mark Foley from Florida recently resigned after it was revealed that he sent suggestive e-mails to congressional aides. Foley spearheaded congressional opposition to child pornography. These sanitizing versions of their own pasts buttress ideologies of renunciation and abstinence that are betrayed by their own behavior. There is another possible version of childhood. The "boys will be boys" posture excuses overindulgence in alcohol and violence against women on the part of adolescent would-be frat boys even as those who adopt this posture also maintain surplus-repressed values of production and performance that apply equally to kids and adults. Kids and college students are supposed to "work hard and play hard," falling back on a strict differentiation of public and private behavior. This reformulates the Protestant ethic to allow for a disciplined approach to undisciplined behavior such as fraternity hazing, binge drinking, and the collective degradation of women. Here, fathers play a major role in reproducing themselves in their sons, citing their own adolescent and college escapades as the recipe for success in the business world (via networking in the form of golf and drinking).

Those who either shun or idealize their childhoods tend to enshrine discipline and legitimize the unchallenged authority of parents and teacher. Those who recall childhood as the best of times for its freedoms of expression and exploration, always acknowledging that children (and their parents) must make mistakes in order to grow, tend to be democratic in their approaches to family and school. They also slow down the process of growing up. The acceleration of childhood prevents children from learning how to be civilized and successful adults. This knowledge cannot be injected or memorized, as we too often suppose when we deploy standardized fact-based testing. In a rote culture, parents and teachers prevent kids from thinking for themselves, reproducing a society where few have the ability to imagine alternatives.

MEDIA CULTURE

We contend that the family was never a world apart, unsullied by social, political, and economic influences. One of the Frankfurt School critical theorists' major empirical and theoretical studies begun during the 1930s was a study of authority and the family, which led to a larger project called studies in prejudice (see Wiggershaus 1994). The most famous outcome of this second series of investigations was the 1950 book by Theodor Adorno and his California colleagues on authoritarianism* (Adorno et al. 1950).

Authoritarian personalities are bred in families without strong boundaries and positive adult role models. When children learn values from the media and their equally misguided peers, they do not develop ego autonomy, a Freudian concept describing the ability to think and act independently. Clearly, according to leftist psychoanalytically oriented theorists such as Marcuse and Wilhelm Reich, Nazi atrocities in the 1930s and 1940s were a result of group psychopathology, which was itself mediated through individual pathologies of true belief and blind devotion. The self was joined to society through the group, which was

---

*The tendency of strong leaders to impose their wills on people who identify with these authority figures, especially as they are mobilized by leaders to vent their anger about being powerless on visible minorities, such as Jews during World War II and gays and lesbians today.

mobilized in "the Final Solution" by Adolf Hitler's and Joseph Goebbel's charismatic leadership.

After World War II, authoritarianism in Western capitalist countries, including the countries that rebuffed the Nazi threat, was prolonged by weakening people's egos so that they became sieves of cultural and political commands, much of the sort that Eichmann received from Hitler and that he then passed on to his underlings. These commands—to consume and conform—stem from what Max Horkheimer and Theodor Adorno (1972) call the culture industry, a configuration of media, both electronic and print, that puts a price on culture and encodes certain important messages about the "goods" society. They characterize "enlightenment" at the hands of the culture industry, such as reading the morning paper or getting news from television, as "mass deception," addressing in their own way the extraordinary and horrible fact that Germans were mobilized to either commit or ignore the Final Solution. German Jewish intellectuals, the critical theorists were writing just after World War II ended and about a decade before Hannah Arendt conducted her study of the Eichmann trial (1964).

One of critical theory's main concerns was to determine how capitalism has outlived Marx's nineteenth-century expectation of its demise. They had two answers. First, Marx could not have anticipated the extent to which the state would intervene in the economic system in order to protect it from its seemingly natural swings between boom and bust. It did so, beginning during Franklin Roosevelt's presidency in the 1930s, by investing in job creation, managing the money supply, collecting federal taxes, providing welfare, and engaging in military adventurism and other hugely expensive and pump-priming national military and technological endeavors. State intervention in the economy would salvage capitalism, which, as Marx recognized, was highly prone to crisis, as manifested in the worldwide Great Depression.

Second, Marx did not foresee the extent to which popular culture would intervene to manage psychic crises of anomie and lack of motivation. Horkheimer and Adorno, living and writing in America during and shortly after World War II, immediately recognized the ideological and economic impact of radio, television, journalism, and the Hollywood movie studios. And, of course, now we would add the Internet to that list. Cultural creations are turned into commodities for rent and purchase at Blockbuster. Not only does this produce profit for cultural producers; it also diverts and distracts people from their workaday malaise, poverty, and powerlessness. After a stressful day at work, people veg out in front of the TV, watching broadcast television shows or rented or purchased movies. They listen to music, paying for radio broadcasts using the Sirius or XM satellite services, or download music onto their iPods. They shop, prompted by omnipresent advertising. You nearly have to live on a desert island to avoid the influences and temptations of the electronic and material worlds.

There is nothing wrong with the entertainment technologies per se. The issue for Marxists is that they divert people from the causes of their disempowerment—capitalism. They are, as religion was for Marx and is again today, merely Band-Aids, "opiates of the masses" that promise salvation in an afterlife or entertainment in the here and now in exchange for having to endure what Immanuel Kant (1987) called duty in work, at home, and during leisure.

The culture industry is a total environment that enmeshes us from morning to night. It is nearly global. It informs and influences us through multiple media reinforcing the power of its messages, which become inescapable. Management types now talk about "branding" to refer to the old-fashioned notion of putting brand names on products. Branding draws upon French theorist Jean Baudrillard's* (1983) insight that even more important than the product is the "simulation" of the product in the advertising and packaging imagery surrounding it. And so our Nike shoes might be cheaply manufactured in a third-world country by cheap labor in unprotected sweat shops, but we desire them for their "sign value,"[†] which energizes us to purchase them and thus augments Nike's profit. This is why kids walk around with branded clothing, which would be quite undistinguished without the brand logo. Abercrombie "signifies" a set of meanings that helps kids read each other and formulate their own identities. Nike might signify a somewhat different meaning involving athleticism and race. To Baudrillard, less important than the product itself is the signage encasing it, which becomes the real commodity: You are not really buying the shoes for their utility but to "become" a Nike, Reebok, or Vans person, whatever those signs and brands might signify (see Debord 1973; Goldman and Papson 1995).

This is very cynical, as capitalists well understand. Recently, scholars have published books on "bullshit," a colloquial term for purposeful deception. Harry G. Frankfurt (2005) and Laura Penny (2005) follow Russell Jacoby (1987), who wrote about the decline of intellectuality much as one of us has written about the decline of discourse (Agger

---

*A French theorist who stresses the importance of advertising and media for understanding human behavior, arguing that reality is increasingly "simulated" for us by the media.

[†] Baudrillard's term for the status value attached to commodities, nowadays referred to as "branding"; he argues that people don't want the shoes as much as they want the Nike logo identifying the shoes.

1990). These perspectives help us understand the pervasive effects of a media culture and the ways in which discourse and reality become inverted so that people—especially young people—lose all ability to differentiate the two.

Young people are especially susceptible to a media culture because they ingest electronic media and are adept at manipulating electronic cultural technologies and because they are already alienated, like their parents, and need release and respite. The many hours of television watched each day in the United States reflect this. This preoccupation with electronic media on the part of children and adolescents provides them with images of fast life and particularly fast adolescence that are unhealthy and avoidable. A media culture freezes the present—a world in which Paris Hilton is heroized, albeit for only fifteen minutes, and, more seriously, President George W. Bush is reelected even after he lied about the presence of weapons of mass destruction in Iraq. Freezing the present into unalterable fate—everyone shopping relentlessly, wearing porn-star fashions, and voting hard-right Republican—is dangerous because it misrepresents the diversity of the existing world and makes it seem unalterable.

This freezing of the present into fate has always been the project of ideologists. In Marx's time, and even until the 1960s when electronic media came to replace considered texts, ideology was purveyed through writings such as the Bible and economic treatises defending capitalism. These texts could be considered carefully; indeed, they had to be, given how dense they were. A media culture characteristic of a fast capitalism blurs the boundary between text and world so that, in effect, books ooze out of their covers and into the world, commanding their enactment by unwitting "readers" who thus forget (or never knew) how to read critically.

This is a hallmark of the decline of discourse: texts no longer stand at one remove from the world but become immersed in it, simply imitating it as if by rote. *People* magazine, *The Bachelor* television show, and MTV freeze the world they depict. Young people come to believe that everyone acts (or should act) like Brad Pitt and Jennifer Aniston, tries to capture Mr. Right with feminine wiles, and pimps their rides. A cyberculture is not distant from the world in the way that old-fashioned books were, even if those were books of ideology. It takes little effort to consume media; indeed, they are not consumed but rather inhabited, much in the way that some people leave on their televisions throughout the day in order to have companionship and not miss anything. Culture is background noise, not an edifying challenge to common sense, as it has been in the past from Plato to Picasso.

Media culture becomes a virtual ontology* (with *virtual* meant in both senses of the word). By ontology we mean a whole theory of being, an enclosed universe in which everyone acts like people on *American Idol* and commercials for Gap. This is an America drained of color and class. Everyone seems well-off and materialistic. Debates rage over whether Jessica Simpson is really smart and acts stupid as a ploy. The past is last year's reruns and fashions. The war in Vietnam and the civil rights movement are ancient history. Irony and cool trump passion and commitment.

You cannot blame generations X, Y, and Z for inhabiting this culture, which portrays them as frozen in time. Libraries are now computer labs, and newspapers, like our local Dallas one, come in "quick," easy-read editions. The point is not to affix blame but, rather, to understand the structural effects of culture—how it persuades people by its example to reproduce the quotidian. And role models for young people, judging, for example, by the former WB television network or MTV and VH1, are already highly sexualized, scheming, and strategic—like adults. Adults have to explain and undo, demystifying this programming and letting them know that not all teenagers have sex and drink. Our kids turn on television in the early evening and are regaled by advertisements for drugs that address sexual dysfunction (Linn 2005).

Media remove the boundary between reality and fantasy, or, to use a synonym, theory. One is immersed in the electronic world and loses sight of other realities and possible realities. This thwarts the imagination necessary to build a better life and a better world. The term *reality television* captures this idea nicely. By definition, television is not real, although it represents various realities. The term *reality television* pretends that television is real, but it also acknowledges a deficit in television that must be corrected by "reality," which means that we watch "real" people like us in various throes of crisis and decision. This has a utopian element, because we can imagine ourselves living lives rich with experience, whether gulping down hairy insects or competing for the man or woman of our dreams. And the "winner" receives big money and enjoys a respite from alienated labor, perhaps even early retirement. Televised sports fulfill much the same function as we are immersed in a world in which each play counts. The difference is that our sports heroes are frequently steroidal junkies bulked up far beyond what is "real" or normal.

Television was originally regarded as liberating and enlightening, bringing the world into our homes. It enriched reality, acquainting

---

*A philosophical term for a theory of being, of the whole universe.

people with the Kennedy assassination, the Beatles, and the 1969 moon walk. Now it is a substitute for reality or, better, a substitute reality. Yet like other technologies, it is diverse. There are good channels and shows that stimulate the imagination and compel people to turn off the television and search for the rich realities it describes. The Discovery Channel, the History Channel, Animal Planet, and PBS are all enlightening. And television screens movies that are worth watching, albeit usually interspersed with advertising, the signature discourse of our time because it blurs reality and fiction. And so the issue is not the technologies per se, nor even the claim that they make on kids' time, but the ways in which they exhaust or enrich "reality" and depress or stimulate the imagination.

Television clutters kids' lives and presents an impenetrable, omnipresent metaphysic of cool people, bodies, clothing, cars, and celebrities. This "reality" exhausts all possible realities and mires kids in an eternal present. Television's great crime in this sense is to short-circuit the imagination, although there are liberating versions of television that enlighten and entertain. Any adolescent learning about World War II, for instance, would do well to start with the hours of grainy black-and-white footage of the siege of Stalingrad, D-day, and the concentration camps broadcast on the History Channel.

ICTs: Internet and Cell

Kids are perhaps more naturally technology addicts than are adults, especially as they are taught at an early age to be adept at computer-related activities. They are thus prone to use information and communication technologies (ICTs) to the exclusion of other activities, physical play, and academic work (although we are cautioning about too much of that, too). Kids are also perhaps more adept than adults at finding community through ICTs, which instant messaging, e-mailing, and texting all facilitate. But these technologies—television, theInternet, cell phones—have three untoward consequences for children.

1. ICTs allow the world to stream through children, exposing kids to adultlike realities too early and setting adultlike agendas of work, homework, shopping, and sexuality.
2. ICTs freeze the world, defining its horizons in ways that preclude personal and social change.
3. ICTs rob kids of time and sleep, given their addictive nature.

Other rapid information and communication technologies do the same things, but in more accelerated and intensified ways. The Internet is this generation's version of television. Indeed, you can now watch television and movies on your laptop. The Internet trumps television because it is interactive, seducing people with the promise of chat and thus community. Again, all of this can be a great boon to the scholar, the independent artist, the political activist seeking to create a new public sphere—a version of cyberdemocracy (but see Kann 2005a). But the Internet is also a time robber, an advertising engine, a sinkhole of virtual selves without adequate ego boundaries, a placebo for damaged and alienated human relationships. The Internet, in its contemporary nature, tends to blur the boundary between science and fiction in that every Web posting seems authoritative. The Internet encyclopedia Wikipedia accepts entries from anyone, amateurs as well as scholars. Both good and shoddy research are posted, misleading young people to place their trust in the world flowing across their screens.

Kids come home from school and "IM" (instant message) their friends. They type brief and emoticon-laden bits of text in a discourse perhaps best described as computer quick. Upon inspection, this is fairly episodic and superficial stuff, where form is often as important as content—our kids are just making connections with other kids. Too shy to talk in the junior high school hallway or cafeteria, kids explore relationships virtually, in real time. They use their cell phones to do the same thing, texting other kids and thus avoiding voice-to-voice interactions and even the process of leaving a voice message.

The Internet is also, of course, a forum for e-mail, the stock-in-trade of early-twenty-first-century communication. People are increasingly snowed under by the volume of Internet traffic—work-related, personal, spam, listserv, and group messages and responses to responses ad infinitum. Who has not mistakenly sent a message to an unintended recipient, causing embarrassment or worse? Who does not gossip over e-mail? Who strictly obeys the workplace strictures about use of company computers and e-mail systems? As we discussed earlier, the sheer volume of e-mail constitutes a prime example of time robbery today, no less for kids than their parents. And much e-mail, like instant messaging, is composed quickly and without attention to the niceties of spelling and grammar, arguably causing the rate of social intelligence to decline further.

On the upside, IMing, texting, and e-mailing are giving vent to frustrated writers who compose not only texts but themselves. Their lives on the screen (Turkle 1995) are rich with textuality, reading, writing, and interpretation. They can also post their work and thoughts on the

Web for all the world to see, if only people are looking. MySpace and Facebook are hugely popular among kids for this reason. The Internet is rapidly changing the nature of publishing and libraries, making pulp seem old-fashioned and expensive. For critics of corporate publishing and mainstream media, the Internet is inherently edgy, open, and democratic, even if debates still rage over copyright, fair use, and "open source."

Cell phones are similar and yet different. We have touched on the ability of kids to text message each other. Cell phones, though, are generally more synchronous than the Internet in that communication takes place directly, voice to voice, in real time. You can always answer today's e-mail tomorrow, or the next day, or never. There is more instantaneity involved in cell phone calls than with the Internet, which, again, has an upside and a downside: you can achieve instant communion with another person, and you can pester her, too. Caller ID allows one to ignore the call, which affords control over time, but the caller can leave a message (which can also be ignored, but at the cost of losing a friend). The beauty of the cell phone is that you can be, and can stay, in touch while you are mobile, making the traditional landline seem old-fashioned.

This mobility, like the laptop that has Internet capability, is the downfall of fast selves and fast families today, even though, again, there are upsides. The upside is that you can juggle and multitask, which is even more important for women than men inasmuch as women work outside the home and are still primarily responsible for child care. You never miss an important call with the cell phone, unless your service fades out. But you never miss *any* call, which is the cell phone's downside. You are always in the public sphere (as long as others have your number).

SEX, ALCOHOL, DRUGS

The dismantling of the boundary between work and family, hastened by media and ICTs, sets an adultlike agenda of work, schoolwork, shopping, sexuality, alcohol, and drugs. We are interested in these last three issues, sexuality, alcohol, and drugs, not because we agree with the Right that children should be protected from knowledge about such things but because premature sexuality is an example of the negative consequences of accelerated childhood. Kids have sex too early, losing their childhood, because ICTs expose them to an adultlike world in which kids become adultlike. Kids own cars; they surf the Internet;

they e-mail, chat, text, and talk; they grow up too quickly, and some have sex in junior high, and a handful even earlier.

Imploding the work/family boundary breaks down the firewall between world and home. Kids watch network television and learn about sex from seemingly innocuous situation comedies and talk shows. Pornography sites pop up on their computer screens. They enter chat rooms with pedophiles. They watch movies with sex and violence. Their peers talk about, and have, sex, sometimes at school. The tremendous irony in all this is that the religious Right opposes giving kids birth control and knowledge about sex, yet their children, swimming in the mainstream, are at risk of pregnancy, STDs, and rape. These are worldly children who know too much too early. They are not insulated against adultlike behavior.

This worldliness is not restricted to children. There is far more sex and violence on television and in the movies than when we grew up during the supposedly liberated 1960s and 1970s (Pardon and Forde 2005). That supposed sexual revolution was a period of veritable abstinence compared with today, when kids have oral sex in junior high and high school bathrooms, in movie theaters, and at parties (Remez 2000; Stepp 1999).

Kids also drink, sometimes copiously. Teenage and college alcohol use is rampant and viewed as normal (Gatins 2005). Binge drinking has entered the vernacular on college campuses. Although teen and college drinking is not new, drinking during high school and even junior high school prepares the way for college and adult indulgence. In some cases parents provide the alcohol, either wanting to be cool or believing that they will have more control over their kids and their friends if they oversee these activities. Perhaps the drug revolution of the 1960s played a role in normalizing kids' drinking today, as boomer parents legitimize these behaviors on the part of their own children. Teenagers and college students also use drugs, sometimes of the designer kind. Party drugs such as Ecstasy abound; these are not drugs associated with transcendental, mind-expanding experiences but vehicles of sheer hedonism. That is not to say that the 1960s counterculture was philosophically elevated but only to notice that the counterculture, by its very positioning as "counter," attempted a political statement about productivism, performativism, work, the division of labor, the Protestant ethic, and the like. Alcohol and drugs today only facilitate "partying," the contemporary verb that refers to getting wasted, not being joyful.

None of this sets teenagers and college students apart. Their parents often consume Internet pornography, drink to excess, and use drugs.

Marx may have the best explanation for all this: opium (here not a meta-phor for religious bliss and disconnection but the real thing) sedates the masses, inuring them to their own suffering. It is no wonder that kids want to desensitize themselves to their overloaded, accelerated worlds—too much schoolwork, not enough parenting and community, little hope, possibly depression. Getting wasted or laid is balm for dam-aged young selves who have skipped over childhood and adolescence while their parents work too hard and are not home enough and their teachers are not worthy parental substitutes.

Young people negotiate these turbulent seas using technological prostheses that connect them to each other and use sex, drugs, and drink to numb themselves. It is not overreaching to view these modes of escape as resistance, not against capitalism per se but against fast life. The erosion of family and privacy leaves kids few alternatives to these technologies and stimulants with which to fill themselves with meaning and community, even if these are artificial and ultimately counterproductive methods. Again, it is difficult to escape the impres-sion that kids are adultlike in the solutions they have found for their troubles. Although the adult and adolescent worlds seem separate, they are remarkably parallel in their pathologies. This should come as no surprise: the collapse of boundaries affects everyone. Parents in a hurry sedate themselves and, by ignoring their kids, cause the kids to seek sedation, for which they use their parents as models.

SLEEPLESS IN SUBURBIA

This chapter is about both causes and effects. Erosion of the work/family boundary accelerates life, subjecting it to the Fordist and post-Fordist rhythms of the assembly line and the World Wide Web. Fast life accelerates geometrically, laying waste to children, teenagers, and their parents. Fast food leads to fast diets, feasting to fasting. Neither works; the body and psyche remain ravaged by the pressures of late modernity. Being plugged in (and turned on) has profound effects on the body and health. People do not eat right, they get too little exercise, and they get insufficient sleep. Our children are the first in memory to require stimulants in order to function. They stay up too late, messag-ing, texting, posting, and drinking, and they awaken too early in order to meet adultlike schedules set by adults.

Our argument is that once we remove the boundary between work and home, the pace of work sets the agenda for personal life. Everything must get done in a hurry. And there is too much to do. Juggling abounds. People, especially kids, are always plugged in—to cell phones, computers, and iPods. These technologies compel users to use them because they promise connection and escape, perhaps contradictorily. People lose the ability to reflect, react, and recuperate. They become, in Marcuse's apt terms, one-dimensional.

There are multiple, and often contradictory, motivations for using these rapid technologies. Employers thrust them upon their employees to keep them accountable, productive, and task-oriented. Adults (also employees, in most cases) use them to get organized in a busy, virtual world; this is especially true of women who both work and do child care. Kids and teenagers use rapid ICTs to entertain themselves and to build community, albeit of an electronic kind. There are pushes and pulls taking place, incursions and resistance. Too much schoolwork sends kids to video games, and too much e-mail to answer sends adults to watch television or pick up the phone to call a friend. Advertisers seize on all this and deluge us with their scripts and images (see Goldman, Papson, and Kersey 2005).

A casualty of fast lives lived on the electronic superhighway as well as the traditional asphalt highway (and sometimes both together) is time and especially sleep. Neither adults nor their children get enough sleep, according to many recent reports (Keller 2001; National Sleep Foundation 2006b). People wander around chronically deprived of sleep, which is perhaps the most necessary type of rest and relaxation, both of which are required for happiness and health. People need downtime, including deep REM sleep. But the acceleration of work, family, and childhood diminishes that downtime dangerously.

We are not alone in hearing horror stories from other parents and kids about their schedules. Kids attend school while parents work. Kids are picked up and driven to music lessons, sports practices, and tutoring sessions, doing homework on both legs of the commute and grabbing dinner at a fast-food restaurant on the way. But kids' games may start at 8 p.m. or even later on weeknights. They struggle into bed by 11 p.m. And this occurs several nights a week and then again on the weekend. In the midst of this, there may be other kids in the family who require attention and there are meals to be cooked, groceries to be purchased, and other errands to be performed—not to mention the parents' own needs to be met. Cars, cell phones, and the Internet are the glue holding these fast lives precariously together.

The overscheduled child is primarily middle-class and upper-middle-class. Class dynamics powerfully influence the extent to which kids are treated like members of a pre–labor force* by "helicopter" parents who hover over them and prepare them for adult life. Working-class children and especially poor children are less likely to have hovering, controlling parents who overbook their kids from morning to night. Poor children are less likely than middle-class kids to participate in extracurricular activities. Although they are not overscheduled for this reason, they may not have enriching experiences such as learning to play a musical instrument (Lareau 2003). As well, working-class and poor children are more likely than kids from economically comfortable families to participate in the "real" labor force (primarily in service-sector jobs) in order to augment their families' incomes. No pre–labor force for them; they are already adultlike workers.

Again, our portrait must be carefully painted. Financially strapped children may not have broadening experiences such as music and sports lessons, but they may well carry cell phones and even have access to the Internet. Perhaps these technological connections substitute for parental care, although it is clear that harried middle-class kids may also experience parental neglect, especially if they are latchkey children. It is possible, then, for middle-class children to be overbooked and also deprived of real parental concern, especially where other adults such as coaches and lesson teachers in effect replace parents during the many hours kids spend in these activities. Neither middle-class kids nor kids less well-off appear to be getting what they need.

The self is simply worn out by the technologically driven rhythms of post-Fordist everyday life. If you can be anytime/anywhere, you can be contacted anytime/anywhere and you can contact others. There is a glut of communication, although it is arguable that this is not often "real" communication between thoughtful and unhurried people. It is the hurried communication of computer texting and e-mail messages, often sent unsolicited in order to sell drugs, mortgages, or pornography. The information superhighway is becoming cluttered with time-consuming obstacles that vitiate the promise of a global public sphere in which people conduct democracy and express themselves creatively.

Skeptics might respond that one can always turn off the cell phone and the computer. But kids are enmeshed because they are so technologically versatile and because their use of electronic technologies is, in its way, an act of resistance. Adults are no less trapped by employers and by

---

*Children and adolescents who form, in effect, a working class, producing homework and other performances before they reach adulthood and enter the paid labor force.

their own busyness, which is redoubled by their technological access. It seems like ancient history when we just checked our mailboxes for letters and listened for the phone to ring. One was much more insulated then, and one had more downtime. Again, we are not simply blaming technology but noticing that the interaction of social institutions and the self gives rapid technologies a certain dynamic of their own that gathers momentum and overwhelms users, who are instead used by them.

Henry Ford understood, as did Marx before him, that business loves busyness. Without accelerated work and home lives, people would neither produce enough to make mass production feasible nor match this busy production with adequate consumption. Mass production makes way for, and requires, mass markets that soak up these commodities. Capitalism thrives both because labor markets and markets for commodities are now global and because there has been an intensification of production, consumption, and even childhood. McDonald's, for instance, stays afloat because it expands internationally and because it sells meals at all times of the day and even to people watching their waistlines and monitoring their intake of fat (but see Schlosser 2002 and Spurlock 2005).

Limits to capital include ill health and chronic fatigue. Sick and tired people overburden the health-care system. Add to this mix the extension of the working and school days into nighttime hours (during which people snack on unhealthy food) and you have a potentially incendiary situation for capitalism. Capital requires a certain minimal level of health, fitness, and rest. Capital's acceleration, abetted by globalization* and by fast technologies of working, information, and communication, threatens the self's body and thus the body politic (see O'Neill 1985). The minimal self (Lasch 1984) cannot be eclipsed without inviting a revolt of nature, here including the sleep-deprived, de-energized, overstressed bodies of the post-Fordist proletariat and their hardworking children.

This proletariat,[†] as we have been arguing, includes children, who miss childhood so that their parents and teachers do not expire of envy and, as ever, so that capitalism has markets for its products. A media culture sells media such as video games and DVDs through which people consume culture—a never-ending circuit of production and

---

*The tendency of communications networks, media, and economies during this century to become linked around the world, making "place" less important than it was in an earlier stage of modernity.

[†]Marx's term for the working class, in his day blue-collar and today largely white-collar.

reproduction (Stockwell 2005). It could be argued that "proletarianiza-tion" (Braverman 1974) has been extended to global labor pools and to pre–labor pools such as children, who produce adultlike schoolwork and perform to adultlike standards in their after-school activities. And teenagers and college students staff the service sector, doing less-than-full-time minimum-wage jobs, often without benefits. This is defended as a way to learn work discipline and to staff dead-end service jobs. We have a problem with youngsters doing dead-end, minimum-wage jobs and even with their working at all where hours spent in low-level paid labor rob them of time that they could better spend on growing up and finding their muse.

TIME ROBBERS, TIME REBELS

Marx's whole theory of radical social change rested on the dynamic relationship between alienation and rebellion. As the rate of profit fell and as workers lost their jobs, both of which he identified as natural outcomes of the logic of capital, people would be swept toward the revolutionary deed. This is the connection between his and Engels's arguments in *The Communist Manifesto* (Marx and Engels 1967) and his later *Capital* (Marx 1967). Although Marx failed to foresee the wel-fare state and culture industry that prolonged capitalism, he brilliantly understood the dynamic tension within capitalism between capital and labor, first world and third world.

. Writing in the mid-nineteenth century, during the era of the steam engine but before Fordism and long before the Internet (see Dyer-Witheford 1999), Marx tied resistance to absolute deprivation. In his world, losing your job would spell instant poverty. Revolution was to be forged in the crucible of class struggle on the shop floor, where labor and management/ownership were directly pitted against each other, and the stakes were very real and immediate. Since the separation of ownership and control (Berle and Means 1932), the embourgeoisement of the working class, and the spreading of false or one-dimensional consciousness, the struggle has lost its focus, if not its impetus. Alien-ation has not disappeared but is, if anything, even more intensive, as we have been arguing. But rebellion and resistance lose their apparent objects. Who are we to blame? Henry Ford? The Internet? Cell phones? Advertising? Teachers? Capitalism?

In this context, rebellion must be read carefully and detected through a microscopic, nuanced lens. Although people might not understand their resistance in these global and modernist terms, we view "time rebellion" as a crucial expression of a utopian urge. Parents and kids, in their own local worlds, rebel against and resist time robbery, sleeplessness, overtasking, telework, school assignments, short vacations, and hurried weekends. Even if they fail to theorize this rebellion politically (and they rarely do), they resist the ravaging of their psyches and bodies by slowing down the pace of their lives, changing their diets, getting exercise, being playful and self-expressive, building community, and perhaps even organizing politically.

Politically inarticulate and unaware of the connection between personal and public, kids push back when overloaded, hyped up, accelerated, and overcoordinated. Their bodies and spirits shut down; they sleep in, screw off, goof around, defy adult authority. These reactions need to be read symptomatically as cries for help and as protests. If orchestrated, kids' time rebellion—against what Marcuse, paraphrasing Freud who might have been paraphrasing Ford, called the performance principle—could be organized into a larger movement that resembles the New Left and counterculture of the 1960s. Kids are crying out to understand what is happening to them. Many are taught to view their overburdening and sleep deprivation as fate, a natural outcome of growing up in a hectic society. But something inside of them—perhaps their experiences of summer vacation, when they escape from the regimentation of the school year—tells them that things could be different. The most perceptive of them realize that their parents are in no better shape, running in place on the treadmill of fast capitalism.

What is being stolen from kids is their childhood. In this sense, they are worse off than their parents. We may not have inhabited the idealized world of yesteryear, but, like most kids who grew up in at least modest comfort during the 1950s and 1960s, our lives were unhurried; we were allowed to play after school; we were not exposed to a surround-sound, 24/7 media culture; our homework loads were manageable; and we ate few meals outside the home and even fewer at fast-food restaurants. We had the advantage of childhood, and this was possible because the family had not yet imploded under pressure from the world of work, which, via these hastening technologies of information, communication, and control, invades family life and even psychic space. The casualties of all this are time, sleep, reflection, recuperation, and reason. The solutions lie not only in reboundarying social institutions so that work does not claim time and space beyond the workday but also in "familizing" work, school, and other public institutions, a decidedly feminist and early Marxist agenda.

In the following chapter, we address schooling as it reinforces a "rote" culture, a culture of fact-worshipers. We consider kids' homework loads and the many curricular and extracurricular expectations of them. Compulsive parents, themselves caught up in the rat race, want "more" for their children but as a consequence attenuate their children's precious childhoods. In particular, we examine the norms of what we call productivity and performativity as they apply to virtual children.

4

Home/School

Toward a Rote Culture

Virtual children, robbed of their childhoods by the accelerating forces of fast society, are now sited in a worklike environment called school. They are expected to produce and perform in adultlike ways, ostensibly to prepare them for "real" work. In this environment, measurable progress is sought. This produces what we call a rote culture,* a culture in which fact fetishism, repetition, finite fill-in-the-blank answers and projects, and obedience to authority are hallmarks. Imperiled are imagination, creativity, risk taking, radicalism, and free thinking. Education remains mired in the Fordist era, even as the economy has surpassed the era of mass production and its reliance on heavy machinery and manual labor. To play roles in this economy, and perhaps to create a better, more human economy, people need to be able to think outside the box and not simply pass standardized tests.

PRODUCTIVITY AND SOCIAL CLASS

In this chapter, we focus on the dedifferentiation of work, home, and school. We argue that school has become an assembly line engendering adultlike productivity and performativity as well as future human capital. At issue are not only the hidden curricula of obedience to authority and timeliness but also the replacement of playful childhood with backbreaking schoolwork and other adultlike activities such as organized sports. In chapter 3 we argued that adults put kids on this accelerated program because they secretly resent kids' freedom of time, expression, and com-

---

*An everyday life, including schooling, dominated by formulaic thinking and fill-in-the-blank answers; inimical to creativity and thinking outside the box.

munity; they want to match their own unhappiness with that of their kids, somehow finding solace in the idea that misery loves company. In effect, they want their own childhoods back.

Schools are the new work sites in fast capitalism. They are little factories producing assignments, projects, and the adultlike beings we used to call children. They also produce obedience to authority, patriotism, and possessive individualism. They reproduce a fact-based version of the curriculum that is of little utility after school years are over. Few remember the fine-grained trivia learned in eighth-grade science. Although the curriculum is produced by politicians and educators, it is reproduced by children who perform within its constraints. What is most interesting about curriculum is what it excludes, such as theorizing (speculation beyond the facts) and respect for tolerance and diversity. Finally, the curriculum is reproduced in fact-based educational testing that allows school districts, teachers, and students to be evaluated.

The rhetoric about a knowledge-based economy aside (Bell 1973; Ellul 1964; Touraine 1971), schools are workplaces in which children's bodies are contorted over desks as they labor over preformed worksheets that often require fill-in-the-blank answers. This is certainly physical work; you have to sit still hour after hour. If you fidget or talk, let alone walk around, you are written up for a discipline-code violation. Even your fine motor movements involved in penmanship come under the sway of discipline, as we discuss later. Neatness is valorized as a component of self-discipline, the hallmark of a disciplinary society. School is corporal punishment for free-spirited and motoric children who learn by doing, not sitting still. Learning disabilities are diagnosed frequently by teachers frustrated by their students' apparent inability, or refusal, to stay on task.

More and more schoolwork is being done at home in order to fill children's time with worklike activities. We worked hard in school and got most of our work done in the classroom. Homework, even in high school, was mainly longer-term projects such as essays and papers. Our kids attend fairly average middle-class public schools in the Dallas area, and both are in the honors tracks. They do many hours of homework, both on weeknights and weekends. Our twelve-year-old son does at least two hours of homework a night, and he almost always has homework over the weekend. In addition, he is frequently tested, as often as two or three times a week in a particular class. He has seven classes in junior high, and he can easily take fifteen to twenty tests a week in total. Honors courses produce much of this busywork. Many of these honors courses are crowded not with elevating high-concept work but with dronelike copying and coloring. Some of our sons' courses are not designated as honors courses, and in these courses the homework load generally is lighter or nonexistent.

Homeschooling is also a growing phenomenon, especially in southern Bible Belt states in which parents mistrust the supposed liberalism of the public school curriculum (Princiotta and Bielick 2006). Estimates of the number of homeschooled children in the United States range from one million to more than two million. Parents purchase study guides and aids, often from religiously oriented bookstores, and work through them with their children. Kids usually spend fewer hours a day doing academic work than do kids in traditional schools. Homeschooling has become so prevalent that one can find sports teams and orchestras for kids who are going this route. Parental motives for homeschooling their children may be complex and even contradictory. The religious Right wants their kids to learn creationism and they want to avoid a multiculturalist political correctness. But they and other less conservative parents may also want their kids to be insulated from the prevalence of violence, drugs, and sexuality in organized schools. As well, parents with a sensibility like ours may want to avoid the spirit-deadening rote learning and the formulaic schoolwork that are standard fare in schools today. We choose to send our kids to public schools, however, because we think it is good for them to be around other kids, to have musical and sports opportunities, and to experience the occasional really motivating teacher.

We view homeschoolers as in fact responding to many of the same symptoms of decline and dysfunction in the school system that we have identified, such as rote learning and a penal environment. Homeschoolers are seeking solutions for their own malaise, solutions that they find in their own vital families. Homeschooling can be seen as the utopian expression of a desire for new and better schools, but it is a solution that actually isolates children and their parents even more. Homeschooling is the wrong solution to the right problem—schooling that has become ritualistic and uninspiring. The remarkable appeal of homeschooling attests to the sweeping criticism of public education that is spreading across America.

An interesting new addition to the homeschooling movement is called the "unschooling" movement. Spearheaded by the writings of Mary Griffith (1998), this perspective on schooling shares some of our concerns about rote learning in the traditional school system. Unschooling refers to learning at home and in the larger world driven by children themselves, who move serendipitously and in interdisciplinary ways from project to project, interest to interest. Unschooling is a utopian impulse within homeschooling grounded in a critique of traditional schooling that does not emphasize schools' secular liberalism but, rather, their stultifying character—a perspective that we certainly share, even if we have concerns about schooling that is not anchored in the public sphere.

The boundary between traditional school and homeschooling is beginning to blur as kids who are traditionally schooled bring home more homework. The extent to which parents are involved in helping their children complete their homework—explaining difficult concepts and checking it when they are finished—varies by social class (Kralovec and Buell 2000), as does the overall extent to which children from privileged homes are afforded more and better educational opportunities than poor kids, including such things as travel and Internet access.

We are not the only parents we know who are very involved in the kids' schooling and academic development. Indeed, we are relatively noncompulsive compared with the parents of some of our children's friends. These parents live and die by their children's grades and test scores. We are more laconic than many both because we do not obsess about grades—how many adults remember what grades they earned in junior high or high school anyway?—and because where our kids go to college and earn their first degrees matters much less to us than where they get their final degrees. Although there are certainly correlations among grades, test scores, college and graduate school entrance, and eventual career development, we feel strongly that childhood has become a job because parents and teachers want kids to form a pre-labor force, busily involved in production and performance.

Although the amount of time kids do homework varies from day to day and student to student, it is easy to calculate average homework time simply by talking with other students and their parents. Although some compulsive parents do not come clean about how long it takes their whiz kids to complete their homework, most parents of our acquaintance feel solidarity with each other and share the view that there is too much work being assigned, too much standardized testing, and too many rules regarding comportment in the schools. They tell the truth to other parents because they are mad at schools and state legislatures for mandating so much busywork and testing. In Texas we know all about this: when George Bush was governor of Texas, he legislated time-consuming fact-based standardized testing that he has now generalized on the federal level under the rubric of "No Child Left Behind." In Texas, all kids take the Texas Assessment of Knowledge and Skills (TAKS) tests in various subjects at most grade levels. If they fail the first time, they may try again. If they fail again, they must attend summer school. Ultimately, students may have to repeat an entire grade. Texas schools are rewarded financially on the basis of their students' performance on these tests.

It is by now well understood (e.g., Apple 2000, 2006; Bowles and Gintis 1976; Giroux 1988; Giroux et al. 1996; Wexler 1987) that schooling is thoroughly class-based. Wealthy school districts, with academically motivated parents, perform better than poorer school districts. This was already understood when debates were held during the 1960s about ending school segregation in the South and then later during the busing controversies in northern cities such as Boston. Kids at black and poor schools perform worse than kids at white middle- and upper-middle-class schools. Class is a "totality," a structure of experiences and opportunities that affects every aspect of a person's life. Although we take a Marxist view of class, Max Weber (1958) also understood the "hidden injuries" of class (Sennett and Cobb 1972) where he talked about people's differential "life chances" that depend on the class, status, and power position of one's family. Simply put, your life chances are diminished if you are from a poor home, poor school district, or poor neighborhood. Both opportunity and motivation are diminished as people experience their poverty as a treadmill that will not be relieved by cracking the books.

By the same token, sociologists also understand that class is not totally deterministic. Karl Marx (1964) himself realized that a few could ascend from the class position of their birth through hard work and sheer accident, just as others could drop beneath the social class of their parents. If there is a single characteristic that helps people move up and out of the class of their birth, it is education, measured as both total years of formal education and number of degrees attained. Students who earn BA or BS degrees average about $2.1 million in lifetime earnings. An MA or MS adds another $400,000 to that figure. And holders of advanced professional degrees such as JD or PhD earn upwards of $3.4 million over a lifetime (Day and Newburger 2002). These numbers reflect the role of credentials (see Collins 1979) in a knowledge-based post-Fordist economy. It is also true that children from professional families are much more likely than kids whose parents have blue-collar jobs to wind up with professional degrees themselves.

It is important to distinguish between aggregate-level information about social class and its effects on education and career outcomes and individual-level information about these interrelationships. Although the experiences and attainments of all the hundreds of millions of

Americans add up to average attainment (divided by the total population number), individual education and career paths may deviate from
the empirical norm. A standard example of this is used in methods and
statistics classes. Say a millionaire walks into a room of high school
teachers. If we calculate the average salary of people in the room and
include the millionaire's salary, the total will be much higher than if we
exclude him or her from the calculation. (We should instead calculate
the median income level, that is, the middle income level of people in
the room to control for the disproportionate impact of that huge salary on the mean or average salary.) And even among the high school
teachers, there will be telling variation. A female kindergarten teacher
in her first year of teaching may make around $40,000 (as they do in
our North Texas suburban school district), whereas a male (or even a
female) teacher who has thirty years of seniority and also coaches a
school team might earn upwards of $75,000.

And so, even if we adopt Marx's view that social class tends to
determine people's fortunes and failures in life, there is variation
among individuals that affords them some control, though certainly
not total control, over their life chances. Where you attend school
and whether, once enrolled, you take honors classes or regular classes
matter to your overall class position and life chances. How hard you
work in school and the quality of attention you pay to teachers and
assignments have impact on class outcomes. How you develop study
and intellectual skills that see you through not only college and graduate school but your future occupation has impact on your eventual
success and on lifetime earnings. A person is not totally captive to
her class, race, or gender.

And yet "productivity," understood as the amount of assignments
and projects completed, clearly varies by a family's social class, the
wealth of the school district, and whether the school is public or private
(Lareau 2003). This is very much in line with the related finding that
the people with the highest incomes in America tend to work more
hours than people with lower incomes (Jacobs and Gerson 1998). Not
only are wealthy people's hourly wages higher but also they work more
hours. Why do they work longer hours? Because they like being rich,
and because being rich is a burden of sorts, requiring one to pay many
bills and incur many expenses—the mortgage on a large house and the
costs of entertaining, travel, private school tuitions, and the latest cars
and entertainment technologies. In the case of academic productivity,
teachers and parents in affluent school districts think nothing of piling
on the work (and other childhood activities) that they believe correlates
with eventual economic success. As we noted earlier, they may fear that

if their kids do not spend all of their waking hours on school, lessons, and practices, they will be left behind in the competition for college admission.

Although we contend that the underlying penchant for heavy academic loads has to do with adults' resentment of their idle children, affluent parents who are not trained as sociologists tend to believe that the more homework their children are assigned, the more their kids will learn and the better prepared they will be for college and careers. Admittedly, there is some relationship between these two facts, although it may be largely spurious. That is, it is not the amount of homework that determines who will go to Harvard or the local community college but the fact that kids who tend to be assigned a lot of homework in exclusive private schools or affluent public schools are more likely for reasons of their parents' social class—involving educational aspiration and motivation, travel, educational resources, tutors, information technologies—to be academically and occupationally successful. In other words, it is not the compulsive homework that causes kids to be successful but their social-class characteristics that indirectly lead such schools to assign a lot of homework.

The issue of how much educational value homework adds to a student's intellectual portfolio has been addressed astutely in *The End of Homework* (Kralovec and Buell 2000). The authors argue that much homework is a waste of time and could be done in school if the school day were more efficiently organized. On a certain obvious level, homework is assigned in order to challenge students to use the concepts and techniques they learned in class. It is a way of extending the school day and teaching them to think and work independently, although some parental oversight is often requested by the school, even if it is only to check the completeness of the homework, or required by students who do not understand the assignment. We are not opposed to some homework. However, at issue in the acceleration—and abolition—of childhood are the many extra hours of schoolwork kids are expected to do. They are in effect producing value, much as Marx recognized that adult workers do. They are producing *themselves* as future adults. But they are doing it so intensively that they produce unnecessary value as they become adultlike in the amount of work they produce and in that they are being taught to delay gratification. This is unnecessary because children do not have to be adultlike; indeed, they should not be adultlike if they are to become actual adults. Only by experimenting, trying things on (including noncompliance with adult expectations), and searching for their muse can kids become citizens for democracy.

Marx suggested that workers labor for a portion of time each day so that they transfer enough value to the commodity that it can be sold at a price sufficient for the capitalist to break even—and they must work, in effect, overtime (for which they are not paid) in order to produce profit for the business owner. Similarly, children work sufficiently hard each school day, and after school doing homework, that they produce themselves as adequately developing elementary school–age children, teenagers, and then young adults. But things have changed since we were kids. Now kids work "overtime" to produce more value (measured as schoolwork productivity and gratification delayed) than is necessary for them to move smoothly along the developmental path. We are not saying that we should abolish schools or homework, but we are noting that children today produce and perform harder than is necessary for their well-being and the replenishing of the adult workforce.

One might go further and theorize that the surplus value kids produce manifests itself not as profit but as stress and lack of time for sleep, play, and recuperation. Learning disabilities or deficits, depression, obsessive-compulsive disorder, and plain old not wanting to get up in the morning are functions of too much stress and too little time for kids to be kids. After spending thirty-five hours a week in school, many kids put in far more than an additional five hours per week on assignments and projects, in effect working overtime. Just as time was central to Marx's analysis of the theft of workers' value (hence his close attention to the working day and the distinction between necessary and surplus labor time), so time is central to our analysis of kids' production and performance. Adults rob kids of time, and even of their childhoods. Perhaps ADD and ADHD are kids' protests against being so harried, tuning out the world of adults. Adults then push back, punishing and medicating their children and students. It is not far-fetched to view this as a new form of class conflict that goes largely unnoticed because social science neglects the children.

Adults may rationalize all this in utilitarian terms. Addressing their kids, they might tell them that they need to earn good grades and test scores to get into colleges and that they must get into good colleges in order to establish productive careers. Kids need mentorship as they learn how to set priorities and budget time and energy. But these utilitarian arguments conceal deeper drives for parental recognition and validation and a secret envy that leads parents and teachers to become time robbers. For Marx, profit, produced but lost by workers, would be reaped by the capitalist. It is not at all clear that adults gain materially by the loss of children's surplus value except in the sense that they are preparing future adult workers. Adults may also feel that they are preparing children for an easier life than they have had, which both is good for their children and may give them advantages as they outlive their pensions and Social Security benefits.

PERFORMATIVITY

In addition to doing schoolwork, kids these days must perform across the board, and not just academically. And even within the academic category, both comportment and schoolwork are evaluated. Although in-class work, assignments, and testing are a performance, they are more a daily grind, just like mining coal in the Appalachians or doing telemarketing. Performance includes the big test, game, cheerleading match, or choir competition. And the heart of performance is the ability to delay gratification—to practice, practice, practice. When kids are not busy with their homework, they are being driven to practices and lessons where they will do what athletes call repetitions, whether of kicking soccer balls or of bowing stringed instruments.

The production of schoolwork is a subset of the larger category of performativity. Both rob children of time and thus their childhoods. These two categories of activity stand opposed to the category of play (see Huizinga 1966; Sheehan 1978). Indeed, they are the opposite of play. The following items are all components of performance that is expected of children.

- schoolwork, especially tests
- practicing (sports, music, cheerleading)
- discipline, obedience to authority, timeliness
- dress codes and codes of silence
- penmanship and neatness
- public performances and their evaluation (music, sports, dance)
- multitasking
- résumé building
- working for money

Schoolwork and Tests

Children must produce assignments, often copious amounts, and turn them in on time. Points are subtracted for late work and/or work without the child's name written on the appropriate side of the page.

Frequently, the work is to be completed on photocopied worksheets that are illegible, faded, and even have grammatical and other errors. Tests are administered to evaluate students' retention of this material. From kindergarten through twelfth grade, these tests are almost always fact-based, forming a central value commitment of a rote culture. Memorization is often required to do well on these tests.

Practicing

Another important feature of the rote culture is the performance of many repetitions—math problems, gymnastics moves, baskets attempted. Children are taken to practice after school on weekdays and during the weekend. If kids do not practice enough, they do not make the best sports teams, dance squads, or orchestras. And regular practices in group activities such as teams are mandated by the coaches. Some exclusive or "select" teams require parents and kids to sign a contract not only committing a large sum of money to join the team but also committing to attend practice and not allow other sports to compete for the child's attention.

Discipline, Obedience to Authority, Timeliness

Discipline, obedience, and timeliness are taken so seriously in schools that children's report cards and daily evaluations have a category for such behavioral performances. In our local elementary school, code-of-silence infractions and missing work are recorded in students' daily "planners," which parents have to return to the teachers with their signatures. For parents to countersign these evaluations acknowledges that they are participants in the disciplinary grid, hence legitimizing it. Late work automatically receives a lower grade. In our children's not atypical junior high school, disciplinary violations including dress-code infractions such as a shirt not tucked in are viewed as insubordination and receive the humiliating punishment of a lunch "hour" spent copying the dictionary and then, in full view of other children, being marched into the cafeteria like convicts in order to eat a ten-minute lunch. This is called detention hall. More serious violations or repeated violations of minor rules may earn a student an on-campus suspension, the equivalent of a stint in a minimum-security prison with isolation from the other students and harsher work discipline. Students at this junior high are given a scant five minutes to move between classes. If students forget something in their lockers or need to use the bathroom, they are locked out of the classroom and have to attend "tardy school," a late afternoon with other troublemakers on campus. (We have learned that if teachers are late to their rotating supervision of tardy school, they are not punished, again demonstrating adults' secret envy of students' freedom that teachers and parents try to quash.)

Dress Code and Code of Silence

Many schools across America have moved to standardized school uniforms, such as a "spirit" T-shirt with the school's name or a polo shirt and khaki or blue pants or skirt (Sheeran 2006). Sometimes this is defended as a means of leveling class; poor kids cannot afford fashionable labels and supposedly will not feel relatively deprived in this uniform attire. Others suggest that uniforms bring discipline and obedience, undercutting gang and ghetto affiliations that teachers and parents fear as a threat to middle-class Anglo conformity (Deiner 2006; Lively 2006). And uniforms and strict dress codes may also address overly sexualized styles, especially among teenage and even preteen girls.

These uniform and dress codes are both martial and penal, following the model of prisoners in early America. These prisoners wore white or gray uniforms with horizontal stripes, setting them off from the rest of the population and conveying a visible stigma. Also taken from the Auburn model of prisoner reform is a code of silence, the better to concentrate the attention of prisoners/students on their tasks. In our son's former elementary school, children marched down the corridor in single file with a strict code of silence enforced. Violators were written up and punished. Kids who talked in class, even if quietly, were also written up. The assumption, of course, is that the accused students are guilty, even though they have been denied due process. All too often, teachers approach students and their minor transgressions of dress and speech with the attitude of "gotcha."

Penmanship and Neatness

In *Discipline and Punish* (1977), Michel Foucault notes that handwriting falls under the codes of discipline in a society of surveillance and conformity; he calls this the microphysics of power, noticing that even fine motor movements, with the fingers, are to be regulated. Foucault brilliantly links these daily dramas of power in the school to the prison system, blurring the boundary between citizens and their children, on the one hand, and prisoners on the other. In this day and age of word processing, which is taught to young children in school, penmanship is still taught and valued. Kids learn to write in cursive script. In our son's fifth-grade year, most of his written work had to be done in cursive even though, as we reassured him, nearly everything he writes during and after high school can be composed neatly and swiftly on a computer, which also has the tremendous advantage of allowing for revision.

Neatness is valued in other graphic tasks. One science teacher, a neat freak with perfect handwriting, lowers grades for sloppy figures. She is not alone. Checklists of gradable components (often called rubrics) of major projects such as stories and "books" contain a number of points (always too many) for neatness. The problem again is that kids without well-developed fine motor skills, especially boys, may not yet use computer graphics to produce nearly perfect copies. In some cases, schools do not allow children to use computer word processing programs to generate their texts because they want them to learn to write in cursive or because some children do not have access to computers. And so neatness becomes a metaphor for the underlying notion of self-control, which is a central feature of performativity in our fast society. Those who are neat make good workers and good adults.

Public Performances and Evaluation

Foucault (1977) discusses the importance of public punishment and execution during early phases of the criminal justice system. The latter-day pedagogical side of this is the expectation that children will perform well in public, especially in front of adults and parents. They have many staged events, all the way from drama and music in school to sports outside of school, in which they must perform with poise in front of spectators, mainly adults. And these children are almost always evaluated, whether in terms of winning and losing or in grades handed out by adult judges. Even music falls under this process of public performance and evaluation. In addition, there may be a focus on the public presentation of a child's academic work. It is not enough to have to create a poster on environmentalism, a model of a caterpillar, or a book report on Thomas Jefferson; students often have to present it to the class with points awarded for rhetorical skills such as speaking loudly, slowly, and clearly and making eye contact with the audience.

This puts tremendous pressure on kids, especially where parents heckle, exhort, and goad from the sidelines. Anyone familiar with Little League baseball and other children's sports knows that parents often behave like obnoxious children as they become intensely involved in the outcomes of these events. There is an element of vicarious experience and wish fulfillment in such dramas. There is also a message to children that parents expect them to perform, and perform well, because somehow a lot rides on these outcomes, whether in sports, music, or chess. Often accompanying such public performances and evaluations are trophies given out to the most worthy child participants, with progressively larger trophies for higher place finishers. Thus are children sorted into piles of losers and winners—and their parents, too.

Multitasking

Children are expected to juggle projects, assignments, and schedules, much as their parents juggle tasks at work and home. Even elementary school students, frequently beginning in fourth grade, move from teacher to teacher rather than staying in a single classroom. This requires them to carry backpacks with books and planners that they must organize and keep neat. As we just noted, their homeroom teacher signs the planners, with notes scribbled in the margins for parents, who must countersign before the planner is returned the next day. Kids are being taught to multitask, to keep science, math, and social studies straight, much as they must do on a higher level in junior high and high school. They must perform this balancing act each and every day, coordinating their many assignments and allocating their time wisely. If they have music in school, they must also bring their bundle of musical scores and instrument. In the morning, as they disembark from buses or their parents' cars, these small creatures plod along carrying the weight of the world on their shoulders.

Résumé Building

Striving parents believe that their children need an edge in the scramble for college admissions. Although baby boomers faced very stiff odds in this scramble, given the sheer size of their birth cohort, today there is renewed competition especially as parents believe (we think erroneously) that it makes all the difference in the world that their gifted children attend Stanford or Princeton rather than their local state university.

Parents recognize that good grades do not ensure their kids' admission to a prestigious college or university. Indeed, exceptionally successful kids who excel in grades and test scores are often rejected by elite universities for admission because they are "too" smart—that is, they are not well-rounded. This is subtle discrimination against children who may not have been elected to student council or made the basketball team.

Many parents pressure their kids to build their college résumés, their portfolios of high school activities. This is another source of time robbery for kids. In addition to schoolwork and activities, select sports teams, and music lessons, kids must now perform community service (many schools require a specific number of community service hours for graduation as the popularity of "service learning" grows) and engage in other extramural activities intended to make them look like future captains of industry, professionals, and members of the Junior League. In effect, they are competing for college entrance much as their parents compete for places in exclusive country clubs, based on a range of sociocultural characteristics that transcend grades and test scores.

Working for Money

The final category of youthful performance is working for money, adult-like behavior performed after school and in the summer. Although such jobs can certainly augment a child's résumé, they are for the most part designed to enhance the family budget and to accustom children to the drudgery of working, turning them into preadults who must bear up under a regime of alienated labor, imperative coordination, and time robbery. Finally, after-school jobs for students are a way for fast capitalism to staff the service sector, populating the minimum-wage jobs at McDonald's with willing takers. After having performed in school for thirty-five hours a week for nine months a year, kids with jobs spend their weekends and summers performing as wage slaves. In these activities, kids are now productive not only of schoolwork and activities but of real economic value.

FACTS VERSUS UTOPIA I: CURRICULUM AND EDUCATIONAL TESTING

For kids to be seen to produce a kind of preadult preeconomic value via school assignments and other performances, adults must have a metric to make comparisons and rank. The economy uses currency for this purpose. Today, increasingly, we use grades, standardized test scores, and class rankings to stratify our children into winners, losers, and those who fall in the middle. Today, this metric with which schools assess children's production and performance is grounded in a positivist notion of the acquisition and repetition of facts—untheorized pieces of information to be memorized and then regurgitated by rote. One hallmark of a rote culture is the reduction of knowledge to such information, and its casualty is what Hegel and Marx termed reason, notably the ability to imagine the world otherwise and to think globally.

Kids today are mired in immediacy, as are their parents. Positivism is no longer just a theory of knowledge but a cultural discourse, indeed a way of being in the world. Ludwig Wittgenstein (1953) called this a language game, for which there are certain rules. Herbert Marcuse characterized the dominant language game as one-dimensional consciousness, stressing the inability of citizens who have adopted positivism as their worldview* (*Weltanschauung*) to think or imagine the world differently. Facts triumph over utopia, the conjuring of different, better worlds. For Marx, unlike other more idealist utopians whom he criticizes, the imagining of utopia must be linked to the empirical reality of the present, which, by way of certain processes of negation, transcendence, and transformation, makes way for a qualitatively different future.

Today, we are training kids not to be utopians, dreamers, theorists, or intellectuals. Americans have always valued pragmatism (Dewey 1917; Rorty 1982), which is redoubled by positivism—a worship of the facts as they are. Positivism, an intellectual movement that began in early seventeenth-century Europe, allowed for the possibility of empirical, not just theological, knowledge. This allowed us to harness nature, making way for the industrial revolution, modern medicine, travel, and communication. The modern world would have been impossible without the age of reason, for which Immanuel Kant offered the vivid rallying cry "Dare to know."

The end of the Middle Ages ushered in an era of empiricism,[†] an open-minded approach to nature and society. René Descartes (1976) installed the knowing self at the center of a manipulable universe. It was not a great leap from empiricism (Isaac Newton [1931], Descartes, Kant [2003]) to democracy (Jean-Jacques Rousseau [1987], John Locke [2003], John Stuart Mill [2003]), which is a form of government in which rational and knowledgeable selves make decisions collectively, first through small town meetings (Tocqueville [1966] and Students for

---

*A concept owed to Karl Mannheim that describes one's total view of the world, a systematically interrelated set of beliefs such as religion or a political theory; it cannot be challenged piecemeal, only in total.

†A theory of knowledge owed to the seventeenth-century Enlightenment based on direct observation, experiments, and surveys in contrast to Catholic theology, which based knowledge on biblical interpretation; empiricists derive all knowledge from sense experience.

a Democratic Society) and then, as populations grew, through a system of representation (James Madison [Hamilton, Madison and Jay 1982], Thomas Jefferson [1944]).

But over time, empiricism narrowed into positivism,* an approach to knowledge that supposes that the knower can stand outside of time and place and know the world perfectly, without error. Following Newton's lead, positivists also ground knowledge in mathematics and scientific method, requiring knowledge to be built out of quantitative measurements. As Max Horkheimer and Theodor Adorno argue in *Dialectic of Enlightenment* (1972), positivism is highly dogmatic, rejecting nonquantitative approaches and adopting a posture toward the world that is inherently conservative. This worldview is conservative because it removes the self from the world and only allows that self to gaze at the world and then represent it as unalterable, thus freezing it into fate. For example, if one studies capitalism quantitatively using a positivist approach, it is understood that capitalism is an inevitable reality like nature that cannot be changed. Indeed, Newton modeled knowledge as lawful understandings of cause and effect.

Thomas S. Kuhn (1970), building on Einstein's less than fully deterministic model of the universe and of science (Einstein's model is a postmodern one, in fact), argued that scientific revolutions tend to occur in large paradigm† shifts, not through a piecemeal gathering of facts that accumulate into one big lawful answer. But social scientists, especially in the United States, have lagged behind this early-twentieth-century revolution in the philosophy of natural science, holding to Newton's model of a lawful universe and his implication about a positivist approach to science and method.

The tendency to worship facts, then, is a central feature of a culture that reproduces itself by mirroring and mimicking knowledge. The neoconservative turn in American politics since the early 1980s has ushered in curricular reforms, especially on the K–12 level, that worship facts, objective knowledge, and standardized testing. We have even seen this at the level of colleges and universities with the assault on postmodernism, critical theory, and leftism generally (Horowitz 2006). Architects of curriculum, especially in southern states such as our own Texas, not only soften the teaching of evolution, in violation of

---

*A theory of knowledge within empiricism that assumes that knowledge must be quantitative, that knowledge can be expressed in laws of cause and effect, and that the scientist can be completely free of biases and blind spots.

†Thomas Kuhn's term for a broad-based perspective or model such as the belief that the earth is flat (or round), within which scientists conduct their empirical research.

the Supreme Court's 1954 ruling on the separation of church and state, but also install factual rote learning, especially via memorization, at the center of K–12 curricula.

This reliance on rote learning not only inculcates a generation and eventually a nation of dullards but also banishes utopia, theory, and daydreaming as legitimate approaches to knowledge. Fact-based curricula and the accompanying educational testing are defended by their proponents as ways to improve public education. Indeed, President Bush's insistence that students must be able to pass certain benchmark tests is widely regarded as a much-needed measure of accountability curtailing freewheeling educational reform that began in the 1960s, when conventional wisdom taught from classical books was contested.

Students who must merely memorize do not theorize, speculating about the nature of the world. Rote learning is inherently conservative because it disqualifies the imagination required not only to dig beneath the surface of things but to conjure up new worlds and new realities—utopias, good societies of the future. Genealogies of the 1960s (e.g., Gitlin 1987; Hayden 1988; Miller 1987) reveal that the New Left was started by undergraduate students at the University of Michigan and University of California, Berkeley, frustrated by a fact-based mass education delivered by lecturers in large classrooms without dialogue. These students linked their critique of mass education with their emerging critique of American political adventurism in Southeast Asia and of racial segregation in the American South.

Ex–New Leftists such as Russell Jacoby (1999, 2005) and Christopher Lasch (1991) have written about the decline of theory and utopia since the 1960s. Jacoby identifies one of the causes of this as the "academization" of intellectual activity, which turns academic life into a career requiring organizational skills and intellectual conformity. Jacoby was not the first to look at this phenomenon. In *The Sociological Imagination* (1959) C. Wright Mills (drawing from early Marx) made many of the same points. His work was closely read by Tom Hayden and Dick Flacks, two of the main architects of the Students for a Democratic Society's Port Huron Statement* (Bloom and Breines 1995) criticizing universities for their bureaucratic conformity and stultifying

---

*Students for a Democratic Society (SDS), a group of young college students during the early 1960s based originally at the University of Michigan, started the New Left; they organized around issues of civil rights and stopping the war in Vietnam, and they had major impact on the direction of America during that turbulent decade. Issued in 1962, the Port Huron Statement, one of the founding documents of the SDS, established the New Left and stressed the importance of participatory democracy.

curricula and promoting participatory democracy in the country and universities. For Jacoby and ourselves, some of this story clearly has to do with the bureaucratization of intellectual imagination, and some of it has to do with the spread of positivism, which now becomes not a special theory of scientific knowledge but a generalized curriculum and culture.

American culture is deeply defined by positivism—a habit of mind characterized by an uncritical acceptance of the world as it appears to be. To this mind-set, the world is made up of discrete facts that can be objectively observed, and the present reality does not appear to be "contradictory," that is, in a process of fitful becoming. Positivism has become an ideology that strengthens the ideology of the market-place, which originated during the eighteenth century in the writings of Adam Smith (1998). This is in part because pure markets are now heavily regulated by the government, as John Maynard Keynes and Franklin Delano Roosevelt understood and promoted, and because it is in capitalism's best interests to deepen ideology, transforming it from falsifiable claims about the economic system (e.g., Smith's contention that in capitalism all boats rise, even those of the poor) to a generalized consciousness of reality that views "the facts" as static, ahistorical, and lacking depth.

This is a fact fetishism that contents itself with mere appearances. The world *is* as it is presented in the daily newspaper, television sound-bite news, and talk shows. People do not theorize and create images of a better society because a pragmatic culture discourages such speculation as going beyond the evidence. In addition, people, especially young people, are busily promoting themselves and advancing their education and careers. They adopt an instrumental rationality* (see Marcuse's [1969b] critique of Weber) that fits given means to preestablished ends—juggling school assignments, going to college and still making your car payments, getting into graduate or professional school. They abandon philosophy, theory, Reason with a capital R, because these activities do not pay off. Everyone knows that the philosophy job market is dismal, with unemployed philosophy PhDs swelling the ranks of cab drivers.

This positivist mind-set is learned from the very beginning of elementary school education, and it is reinforced through junior high, high school, and college. Students are taught to take notes, memorize,

---

*A Frankfurt School term, drawn from Weber, for a mind-set of narrow purposiveness that tends to ignore the large social implications of one's actions.

and study for objective tests on which they provide facts, dates, names, definitions, sums, formulae, and taxonomies (Tyre 2006). There are few essay tests, and fewer term papers assigned. Major projects are required in science, English, and social studies classes, but these are frequently accompanied by grading templates in which creativity and originality make up only a small fraction of the overall grade. As we indicated earlier, neatness often counts for a higher percentage of the grade than originality or quality of work, as does following the instructions for the project to the letter.

Many parents recognize that they, not only their children, are being evaluated. Many parents help guide their kids on the projects and play a major role in their final assemblage, but other parents work too many hours at too many jobs to help in these ways. The projects with obviously parental help earn better grades than those that have been (also obviously) completed by the student alone. Teachers who may not be well equipped intellectually to evaluate these projects make errors in judgment about the meaning of the scientific method, the demography of the state of Wisconsin, or the causes and consequences of the civil rights movement. Our daughter had a teacher who told the class that she was forced to teach evolution but did not believe in it; one can only wonder how well she taught it.

Curiously, parents, faced with unmotivated and overburdened teachers, may actually prefer objective tests and assignments where there is only one correct answer. But even in this type of grading there is never complete transparency. Word choice matters, as does one's interpretation of the textbook. Jacques Derrida (1978) reminds us that language is not a perfect mirror of nature but is full of inconsistencies, contradictions, and ellipses. "Objective" assignments and tests are never completely objective, and "the facts" are never transparent. One must theorize them, that is, place them in a larger context within which one can interpret the meanings of words and the world. But a hallmark of positivism is the banishment of theory as an ungrounded and noninstrumental activity. Positivists maintain the pretense that knowledge can be perfectly objective, especially if we replace language with quantitative measures and mathematical figures.

Hence, a positivist K–12 curriculum, which spills over into the college years, spawns an educational testing movement that (a) attempts to assign number grades or scores to quite subjective assignments and tests, and (b) seeks to standardize grades and scores across regions, cultures, and social classes through aptitude testing. By now there is a growing literature on the shortcomings of the SAT test and others of its ilk (Buchmann, Roscigno, and Condron 2006; Rothstein 2001). It is clear to most sociologists of education that such tests measure parents' social class and not children's innate ability, and the scores children receive on such tests have been shown to predict success only in the first year of college (Baron and Norman 1992). The predictive ability of such tests, taken during high school, falls during subsequent years of college. But given our intense fact fetishism and mistrust of theory, speculation, and subjectivity, we allow colleges and universities to make admissions decisions largely on the basis of these standardized test scores.

Kids are taught not only to retain and reproduce facts, often through memory drills, but to worship them. The region beyond sheer information is demonized as the preserve of eggheads and intellectuals. Whenever one hears or reads the adjective "fact-based" in matters of curriculum, one should immediately recognize the political agenda of the hard Right, which wants to drive out evolution, civil rights, affirmative action, and the legacies of the 1960s. Parents, even liberal ones, may unwittingly acquiesce to this because they fear incompetent teachers' subjectivities in evaluating their kids.

FACTS VERSUS UTOPIA II: WHAT'S MISSING FROM THE CURRICULUM

Positivism marches through the K–12 and college curricula. Facts and numbers are worshiped; theory and poetry are compartmentalized in a few semester-long classes. Missing from our traditional school curricula are studies in prejudice; class, race, and gender studies; and interdisciplinarity.

Studies in Prejudice

By now, the 1980s critique of secret liberalism in the curriculum has become second nature. The 1960s have been metabolized and reversed as Lynne Cheney (1995) and Allan Bloom (1987) have been institutionalized, their critiques of political bias on the left a segue to religious fundamentalism and what George Bush and Karl Rove call faith- and fact-based education. It is difficult to underestimate the conservative counterrevolution that began as soon as the Weather Underground townhouse in Manhattan blew up in 1970; that event put a symbolic end to the freedoms of inquiry, politics, and culture that had flourished during the 1960s. Although 1960s people (see Agger forthcoming) still exist, they wander in the wilderness, staffing marginal programs, departments, and universities in academia, having withstood the conservative counter-revolution within academia. The price of their purity is marginality.

It did not take the Bush regime to convince many school administrators, educators, and parents that elementary, secondary, and postsecondary education had swung too far to the left. It did not take even the courts' attacks on affirmative action. By the 1980s and certainly by the end of the Clinton years, the national pendulum had begun to swing back to the right as school boards, school administrators, and legislators began to purge the curriculum of alleged leftist biases remaining from the 1960s.

As a result, our children are almost never exposed to studies in prejudice. These are classes and lessons about, and against, stereotyping. Kids scapegoat gays and lesbians, the newest unprotected minority, by inserting a casual word into everyday discourse: gay. For something, such as a test or a teacher, to be "gay" means that it is bad. This word still, of course, refers to gays and lesbians, but now it has taken on a universal connotation of negativity. "That's really gay" is a commonplace derogation among America's young. Rare is the teacher who debunks this secret homophobia, and even rarer is the school curriculum that teaches children about the impact of racial, ethnic, gender, and sexual-orientation antilocution. Studies in prejudice are not taught because they would be viewed as subversive and because they would acknowledge the illiberalism of mainstream American culture.

Class, Race, and Gender Studies

Class, race, and gender are not named as axes of discrimination and inequality in most school curricula. Although one of our son's social studies teachers clearly taught a revisionist version of U.S. history, this kind of teaching is the exception, not the rule. The textbooks in use today omit serious consideration of class, and they address race and gender only in brief discussions of the civil rights movement and of suffrage and latter-day women's issues. Class, race, and gender do not march through the K–12 curriculum any more than they march through college curricula, in spite of conservative caricatures to the contrary. U.S. history is not taught as a history of oppression of minority groups by dominant groups, nor is the economic underpinning of domination recognized. Although protected classes such as blacks and women are mentioned, it is not at all clear to students that the United States was built on a foundation of slavery and of the oppression of women by men. Similarly, the economic basis of capitalism in the exploitation of labor is not made clear. Indeed, quite to the contrary, America, especially at Thanksgiving, is celebrated as a land of opportunity for all.

By the time students get to college, they are shocked to learn that millions of Americans are poor and that the average household income of the bottom fifth of Americans is around $10,000 per year. In the classes we teach, students rarely guess correctly the average American household income. They think it is in the six figures, given what they see on television. They are befuddled to learn that the average American household income is just $46,000 per year, a figure that includes households where both spouses or partners work outside the home. Some of our students know that George Washington and Thomas Jefferson were slaveholders, but virtually none of them knows that Washington and Jefferson fathered children with some of their women slaves. And although it is commonplace to inveigh against Arab cultures' veiling and mistreatment of women, few can explain why it took until the twentieth century for American women to be given the right to vote.

Interdisciplinarity

K–12 curricula are divided up neatly into homerooms, subjects, textbooks, and periods, with time reserved for lunch and a little bit of time for recess. Although college life affords kids more social latitude, the American university is still modeled on the departmentalized nineteenth-century German university, with knowledge pigeonholed into disciplinary niches. Our kids are taught a disciplined world, with clear boundaries around those disciplines. Interdisciplinarity (see Klein 1990) is nearly invisible except in some colleges as a dumping ground for students who cannot find a traditional major. All of this is defended as rigorous, and as a way to encourage specialized scholarship. The benefit would be rigor, perhaps at the expense of panoramic scope. Scholarship would proceed narrowly but dig deep.

This is not a brief against specialization or professionalism. Without specialization, we would not have cured polio or begun to exploit alternative energy sources. We would not have developed the Internet or made inroads in the fight against cancer. However, the disciplinary differentiations that our kids learn almost from the beginning of their education send a message that the world can be neatly divided up and that subjects do not overlap and intermingle, especially in this postmodern stage of capitalism. This is not only a critique of elementary, junior high, and high schools. College students have few opportunities to synthesize the knowledge gained in their course work and move freely across disciplinary boundaries.

Intellectual compartmentalization is less a considered stance than a bureaucratic response to potential chaos. K–12 administrators and curriculum planners have too much on their plates—budgets, publics, parents—to find the time to think deeply about intellectual serendipity and overlap. But the compartmentalization of subjects is entirely consistent with the view that knowledge consists of facts—English facts, social studies facts, math facts—that must be memorized and utilized. This approach to knowledge is made possible by the reduction of specialized knowledge to testable items.

Our children have never been asked to write an essay or examination answer assessing the causes and consequences of 9/11, the Vietnam War, or the suffrage movement.* Instead, they are tested on minutiae surrounding the events and activities of events and movements. The dominant epistemology of current K–12 curricula is less explicitly positivist than it is oriented to testability, which is one of the pillars of positivist scientific method.

Since the first Sputnik satellite was launched by the Soviets in 1957, American school and college curricula have been heavily weighted toward math and science. This emphasis continues today, although it is now matched by an emphasis on computer science and computer applications. Newton well understood that math could be viewed as a royal road to truth because it is seemingly objective and unambiguous; numbers do not lie. At least they did not until Einstein, who showed the relativity of mathematical and physical truths. Math occupies a central place not only in the curriculum but in educational testing, such as the SAT and GRE. Imagine that math had to share center stage with studies in prejudice or cultural studies. Just as all American high school students would confront algebra, now they would also confront a series of courses in stereotypes, cultural studies, women's studies, and interdisciplinary studies. Or perhaps they would take advanced placement courses on the history of ideas, philosophy, modernism, and postmodernism. Imagine that they would study media culture—and thus themselves—reflexively.

A good deal of the current curriculum involves learning and mastering what Basil Bernstein (1975) called restricted codes, such as calculus, French, and computer programming. Even English, a potential site of

---

*A movement of American feminists led by Susan B. Anthony and Elizabeth Cady Stanton to win the right to vote for women; finally, in 1919 Congress ratified the Nineteenth Amendment, allowing women to vote, and in 1920 the states ratified this amendment.

interdisciplinarity and politically and culturally relevant work on language, has been "scientized" by grammarians, who, in spite of their discrediting in linguistics decades ago, still perversely flourish in the public schools. Again, there is nothing wrong with restricted codes; one hopes that one's doctor has mastered internal medicine and has memorized the body parts depicted in *Gray's Anatomy*. But in our schools today, there is little premium placed on synthetic, broad-gauged public knowledge of the kind Jacoby defends in *The Last Intellectuals* (1987). Perhaps we are only saying that American schoolchildren are not taught to be intellectuals—who think, theorize, and synthesize across categories and boundaries. They are taught vocationally and on a model that has been out-of-date for the better part of a century.

MAKING THE GRADE IN A ROTE CULTURE

In American schools a great deal of emphasis is placed on grades, which requires that teachers be able to grade, to evaluate. Teachers feel that they need to grade nearly all performative activities of their students so that they can track their students' progress and report to inquisitive parents. Learning and intellectual exploration are reduced to mastering factual knowledge that can be readily evaluated. Few teachers are able to kindle students' excitement about learning in this context of compulsive evaluation. Indeed, as we have been arguing, everything kids do, in school and at play, falls under the regime of evaluation.

Kids experience ennui in school because they do boring, rote schoolwork and because they are constantly scrutinized and evaluated by teachers who have little verve for their subjects. The rare caring, compassionate teachers stand out; they make their subjects come alive and they do not fetishize grades. They are flexible, and they deal with kids on their own level. Of course, public school teachers are among the most underpaid of any professionals in America. They should earn as much as college professors, perhaps more, given the seriousness of their task. We are not blaming individual teachers but noticing that teachers, like anyone doing alienated labor, adapt to the structural constraints of their jobs. There is pressure to teach to the test, provide gradable assignments, emphasize recall, and otherwise instill in kids that education, like everything else in America, is a struggle for the survival of the fittest. Teachers are inmates, too.

Our kids receive not only six-week grades that go on their report cards but also progress reports every three weeks. And there is a final day of reckoning at the end of the school year, when students must attend an awards ceremony at which the best and most conscientious students are given plaques and certificates attesting to their merit. This begins as early as elementary school, where parents and students sit through lengthy ceremonies with printed programs and carefully engraved plaques and medals. The subtext is clear: achievement, albeit within the constraints of rote learning, is to be rewarded. Kids are being paid for their production of academic value, even if not in the currency of the realm. At our local elementary school, the fifth-grader who exhibits the most civic-mindedness (patriotism) receives a major award from the Daughters of the American Revolution. The Veterans of Foreign Wars awarded prizes to the best boy and best girl in the fourth grade. At these award ceremonies, kids even receive cash equivalents—tickets to the local amusement park and bowling alley to be redeemed over the summer.

Learning should be reward enough, or at least grades should be. These awards ceremonies become a public display of sorting and selection because the school system is committed to reproducing the class system, which involves both credentials and cultural capital. The awards are really for the parents, who bring their cultural capital to the table by having the Internet at home, taking their kids on stimulating vacations, and pushing them to succeed academically. At these ceremonies, the "best" parents take videos of their brilliant progeny earning these trophies, memorializing the parents' contribution to the reproduction of human and cultural capital. One imagines that parents in their dotage screen these videos for their grown children, hoping to be compensated for their sacrifices. Just as the awards are not really for the kids, neither are the videos for the kids. No kid in America wants to watch videotape of the tedious awards ceremony they have already endured in person. They know that this is for the parents.

By high school, grades have become so talismanic that kids live or die by their GPAs and class ranks. In local North Texas high schools, the valedictorian routinely has a GPA higher than 4.0 by virtue of having honors courses weighted more heavily. These GPAs are calculated to many decimal places in order to break ties. In 2003, parents of a Plano, Texas, high school student complained that their daughter was unfairly denied the honor of valedictorian (first in class rank), which went to another girl, because their daughter's GPA was miscalculated (Talbot 2005). The school district, in its Solomonic wisdom and worried about legal action, decided to award the title of covaledictorian to both girls; the GPAs were calculated to the *fifth* decimal place!

Again, grades and class rank are for the parents and their sublimated, envying egos. Parents also believe that the United States is an open-class system in which the cream rises to the top. Supposedly, colleges base their admissions decisions on strict, objective criteria such as GPA, class rank, and SAT scores. But, as we noted earlier, there is a great deal of subjectivity and selectivity in college and graduate school admissions, the better to reproduce an elite that is not totally dominated by Asians, Indians, and Jews but still has place for WASPs. This is finessed by suggesting that elite colleges look at the total portfolio of the applicant, leaving room for the weighting of extramural activities such as student council and athletic participation. In other words, colleges and universities may reproduce the American elite in ways that belie their own commitment to objective merit.

In fact, elites require a wide repertoire of skills, from the mastery of restricted codes to the demonstration of social skills such as networking, communicating, spinning, genuflecting, and manipulating. The television show *The Apprentice,* in which billionaire Donald Trump pits would-be junior executives against each other in the performance of collective projects and then picks a winner, demonstrates that what counts in business today is pragmatic problem solving and people handling, not sheer IQ or test scores. This story is as old as Elton Mayo and his human-relations approach to industrial management (see Bendix 1956).

Academic workaholism among kids is denigrated as an Asian and Indian cultural trait (Hwang 2005). Images abound of such children being denied childhoods as they slave away over their textbooks, musical instruments, and spelling-bee guides in order to earn the highest grades and the most career capital. Such exaggerating images have a semblance of truth. We do not endorse joyless childhoods devoid of play; indeed, that is the point of our story here. But such caricatures of the single-minded Asian workaholic miss the actual diversity among Asian kids and contain a sinister thread of anti-intellectualism. This anti-intellectualism (see Hofstadter 1963) crystallizes in the American veneration of the well-rounded person, supposedly prized by college admissions officers. Here being well-rounded means not to be bookish, introverted, geeky.

One of the problems with meritocracy* (Young 1959) is that elites need wiggle room in order to ensure their own reproduction. The

---

*Young's (1958) term for a society in which people's upward mobility and achievements are purely products of their demonstrated merit and not also products of who they know, networking, and cultural capital.

circulation of elites (see Pareto 1991; Schumpeter 1976) requires a certain amount of inbreeding. In the college admissions trade, this involves favoring "legacy" children, offspring of former students, especially those who have donated money to the university. Affirmative action, born of the social movements of the 1960s, counteracts this to some extent by placing underrepresented minorities, if not social classes (for whom there is no affirmative action), in colleges, universities, and certain occupations. It is recognized that institutional racism and sexism* over time, over generations, have made it difficult for minority kids to do well enough in terms of grades and standardized test scores to make them competitive with wealthy white kids who have had private school educations.

In Texas, which is part of the Fifth Circuit Court District, affirmative action was struck down in the 1992 *Hopwood* decision. In response to this ruling, the state decided that the top 10 percent of every high school graduating class would gain automatic admission to the state university of their choice, usually the University of Texas at Austin. This ensures that poor and minority schools would be allowed to send their best and brightest to the shining city on the hill in Austin. But that flagship branch of the University of Texas system has become so large that undergraduate enrollment has been nearly capped. Thus, at UT-Austin, fully two-thirds of undergraduate students admitted for fall 2005 were admitted under the top 10 percent rule.

Opponents of affirmative action also oppose the 10 percent rule, which has been reconsidered but not yet eliminated by the Texas legislature. Opponents argue that the policy is too inflexible and excludes well-rounded middle- and upper-middle-class kids from white school districts—kids driving their own late-model cars who want to join sororities and fraternities at UT-Austin but finish below the top 10 percent in their high school classes. In effect, then, if you attend a high-powered suburban high school in Austin, Southlake, Plano, or Arlington, Texas, some might regard you as a victim of reverse discrimination, which is exactly what Michael Bakke argued in his famous Supreme Court case regarding his denial of a seat in the entering class of the University of California at Davis Law School (see Ball 2000).

On the one hand, then, schools, parents, students, and colleges place great emphasis on grades and test scores. On the other hand, they want flexibility in admissions decisions so that their not-quite-super-bright kids

---

*The tendencies within organizations for dominant groups to promote themselves and keep minorities and women out of leadership positions; it does not require overt racism but, rather, the perpetuation of subtle forms of discrimination in hiring and promotion.

will not be excluded in favor of Hispanic and black students who are in the top tenth of their high-school classes or in favor of other students whose parents are severe taskmasters.

How might we configure college and graduate school admissions differently? We would de-emphasize grades, tests, and class rank, all of which reinforce fact retention and fill-in-the-blank answers, but without de-emphasizing academics. We would probably ask the student applicant simply to write a letter explaining why a particular university is a good fit for her, and we would invite applicants to submit samples of their work, whether writing samples or perhaps tapes of musical or theatrical performances. In these ways, we would make admissions less mechanical while accentuating creativity and imagination as prerequisites for admission. Our fundamental assumption underlying all this is that intelligence, imagination, and intuition do not vary by social class but are latent in all humans. Unfortunately, both K–12 and secondary education are flawed by class biases and protections that only reproduce class structure, including the children of elites and excluding those of the underclass. It is difficult to change this system of cultural and socioeconomic reproduction so long as capital, human capital, and cultural capital form an intimate connection.

In the next chapter, we examine the production of people, especially children, in K–12 and college classrooms. We look closely at the connection between the production of economic capital, on the one hand, and human and cultural capital on the other. Capital is productive wealth; human capital is your skill set and educational credentials; cultural capital is what and who you know that make you a versatile, worldly person capable of getting ahead. We also examine the college admissions process and the impact it has on parents' and teachers' expectations of children.

5

Class in Class

Capital, Human Capital, Cultural Capital

Postmodern theory helps us understand the power of discourse and media in early-twenty-first-century society. Michel Foucault (1977), Jacques Derrida (1994), and Jean Baudrillard (1983) supplement the critical theorists' analyses of culture and power in important ways, much as feminist theory enriches traditional Marxism by drawing attention to the boundary between private and public. Indeed, our study is indebted to this configuration of French, German, British, and American theoretical influences. Together, they help us understand the ways in which various types of class—economic, human, cultural—are reproduced "in class," during and after the school day.

POSTPONING THE POSTMODERN

The problem with postmodernism, however, is that it tends to obscure the salience of class. Although a left postmodernism (see Agger 1989, 1992, 2002; Best and Kellner 1991; Harvey 1989; Jameson 1991) is possible, Jean-François Lyotard's (1984) critique of Marxist grand narratives* remains the critique of record for many theorists and cultural critics who draw from European intellectual sources. It is our view that we inhabit a perhaps postmodern (late, fast) stage of capitalism but that we have not surpassed capitalism in the direction of a technological utopia (Bell 1973) or a decentered postmodernity (Baudrillard 1983; Huyssen 1986; Kroker 1994). We cannot understand fast families and their virtual

---

*A French postmodernist term for sweeping theories or stories about society, such as Marxism, that reduce social explanation to a few major variables and that tend to oversimplify the complexity of social life.

children without understanding the enduring significance of class (in class) and particularly the ways in which capital has been augmented by human capital (Coleman 1990) and cultural capital (Bourdieu 1977).

The culture industry puts a price on cultural works and practices (via the process of *commodification*, putting a price on something) and creates a seamless discourse and universe of domination nearly impenetrable by external critique. We lose touch with the possibility of other worlds. This approach to cultural studies deepens Marx's nineteenth-century concept of false consciousness by drawing attention to state intervention in the economy and mass culture's intervention in psychic life. Culture, as ever for Marxists and left feminists, remains political and economic.

In today's Internet capitalism, it is not difficult to make this argument persuasively. Cybercapitalism oozes into every nook and cranny of public and private experience, through advertising, the Internet, journalism, television, radio, music, and movies. The virtual self is nearly defenseless against these invasions and positionings. Our children are particularly vulnerable because they spend so much time plugged in (Linn 2005). The acceleration of the family leaves kids to their own devices and to technological devices wrapping them in the agendas of busy commercialism. This culture, which we consider rote, is steeped in immediacy as well as in a seemingly cosmopolitan maturity as kids gain access to formerly adult worlds of entertainment, sex, violence, and celebrity. Kids today, like their parents, know a great deal about cultural ephemera but very little about what is really going on in the world. Could they ace the following sociopolitical intelligence test?

- Has Iraq ever invaded the United States?
- What is Halliburton?
- Which countries have weapons of mass destruction?
- What happened in Jasper, Texas?
- Can you name a single contribution of W. E. B. Du Bois?
- What supposedly happened at the Gulf of Tonkin?

This indictment of young (and older) people's lack of social and cultural literacy risks becoming an elitist exercise. But we are simply noticing that factual knowledge promulgated and then tested by the traditional K–12 and college curricula does not necessarily add up to wisdom or critical insight. This is because, as Marx originally recognized, capitalism encourages people to exist in a state of "false" consciousness, failing to really understand the world around them, and within them, so that they do not correctly understand the deep mechanisms of domination, exclusion, profit, and exploitation enmeshing us in arbitrary social, political, and economic relationships. The greatest enemy of capitalism is utopian thinking, the ability to "think otherwise" and imagine the world differently. Capital mystifies its mechanisms of production and reproduction so that people will view capitalism as both good and necessary, as a piece of social nature or as naturelike.

Since Marx's time little has changed about capital's need for false consciousness, even if postmodernists and liberals alike reject the implication that only a few—socialist intellectuals—possess the "truth." The Frankfurt School anticipated this critique of their perspective by indicating that the truth of the world will only be known from the vantage point of Reason, the ability to think freely and deeply about the nature of things. A fact-worshiping culture, school curricula, standardized educational testing, and our surround-sound electronic culture are all enemies of Reason in this sense, substituting episodic entertainments such as sports, game shows, and music videos for real contemplation. It is difficult to disagree with Russell Jacoby that we are enduring a "falling rate of intelligence" (Jacoby 1976) even as we are witnessing an information explosion. Information dissemination that seemingly puts the world at our fingertips, or at least that portion of the world available to a Google search, is also the enemy of careful study and sustained reflection.

The Internet makes for fast scholarship. Our students drag and drop their term papers from sundry Web sites, using pastiche as their research method. Admittedly, the open-source implications of the Internet blur the boundary between original and derived authorship and put into play some thorny issues of copyright and intellectual property. But the drag-and-drop term paper skirts these more interesting issues and simply deploys the Internet much as one would deploy a term-paper service, although without the unwieldy expense. Again, costs and benefits abound. Search engines and googling are terrific resources for the young author to become acquainted quickly with Martin Luther King Jr., Ty Cobb, or the Mississippi River. Yet too often the Internet, in its haphazard and often superficial offerings, is an inadequate substitute for pulp resources—we used to call them books—that require studied and leisurely contemplation.

Ultimately, the Internet makes the world more the same, promoting fast capital, fast culture, and fast scholarship. Immediacy and instantaneity overwhelm attempts to think through the issues—to theorize. A postmodern capitalism* is still capitalism, ruled by private ownership of capital and requiring false consciousness in order to blunt intelligence and forestall revolt. The Internet perfectly serves a culture in which all that we know and are simply repeats what "is" already, making eternity out of the present or the past few years, when Web pages were posted. One of the main problems with the Internet is that it is difficult to reference sources before its advent, giving the impression that everything worth knowing happened recently. This promotes what Jacoby (1975) calls "social amnesia." The critical theorists (see Agger 1992) might have utilized postmodernism better to understand cultural discourses that become sites of power in their own right. What Foucault (1977) calls the microphysics of power in everyday life involves pixels. These sites (see Timothy Luke 1989) are now Web sites, centers of profit and diversions from what really matters. The Internet, CNN, courier services, and cell phones—all the accoutrements of a drag-and-drop culture—persuade people that this is a really distinctive moment of modernity, perhaps a postmodernity,[†] in which all that is solid melts into air, as Karl Marx and Friedrich Engels phrased it in *The Communist Manifesto* (1967). Yet this is still a world in which economic differences explain almost everything about our life circumstances, whether we live in Grosse Pointe or Pontiac or whether we live in middle-class suburban America or in desperate sub-Saharan Africa. The majority of the world's people do not have computers or access to the Internet. They are lucky not to starve and to avoid infection with the AIDS virus. One of the main projects of capitalism, now as before, is to divert attention from these stark economic differences and especially to mystify the fact that some people's comforts are won only at the expense of many people's suffering.

The Circuit of Capital–Human Capital– Cultural Capital–Capital

By *capital* Marx meant productive wealth, not the dollars and pennies that we might squirrel away in a shoe box or savings account. Capital is wealth that can make more wealth by profitable investments. By human

---

*A twenty-first-century stage of capitalism in which globalization and the Internet play major roles in production, consumption, and information flows.

†A stage of historical development believed by postmodernists to follow the stage of modernity; characterized by globalization, rapid information flows, the declining relevance of place, and the weakening of class conflict, similar to the concept of postindustrial society.

capital, economists and sociologists refer to the ensemble of skills, education, and actual work experience people possess in a knowledge- and science-based economy that allows them to move forward in their careers. By cultural capital, theorists deriving from Pierre Bourdieu* (1977) refer to the ensemble of knowledge about the world (current events, history, etiquette, popular and elite culture) people possess that allows them to appear knowledgeable and cosmopolitan, to impress other people. Social skills—manners, interviewing skills, interpersonal dexterity—might fall into either the human capital or cultural capital category, but they are probably most appropriately viewed as cultural capital.

Marx theorized that production and consumption form a "circuit." His argument is rather obvious: production must be matched by con- sumption for manufacturers and investors to extract a return on their investment out of the commodity. He also stressed the dual roles that workers play as both producers and consumers.

Marx profoundly disagreed with Adam Smith about whether the capi- talist has a right to the extra portion of price called profit. Smith (1998) believed that there must be some incentive for capitalists to take the desperate risk of investing their hard-earned fortune in a new business. Risk should bring economic reward. Marx countered this by suggesting that profit is actually created by the blood, sweat, and tears of laborers who in effect transfer economic value to the commodity by working for a portion of each day longer than is necessary for the capitalist to reap an adequate return on his investment. Marx also theorized that the relationship between capital and labor is not only unfair but likely to get worse as a few large capitalists crowd smaller manufacturers out of the marketplace because the larger companies are more efficient and can price their goods less expensively or at least dominate the market. Think of Microsoft or Wal-Mart in this regard.

As capitalism moved from an industrial to a postindustrial phase, although with industry obviously still remaining, capital in the original nineteenth-century sense of productive wealth was supplemented by human and cultural capital—expertise and credentials, on the one hand, and interpersonal savoir faire, on the other. Middle-class, middle-man- agement bureaucrats and office workers needed to be able to read, write, and do arithmetic. They also needed a modicum of cultural and social civility, the particular mission of the liberal arts (see Leavis 1933).

---

*A French anthropologist who identified the importance of cultural capital (tacit knowledge of the social world) to explain who gets ahead and who doesn't.

Early in the twentieth century, theorists such as Max Weber argued, with prescience, that work would become increasingly bureaucratized. Weber warned that bureaucratic conformity and rule-bound ritualism would stifle initiative. It would stifle more than that, imprisoning the human spirit. Weber termed that "the disenchantment of the world" (1958). On the other hand, though, he said that the rise of middle-class office work fundamentally disqualified Marx's blanket condemnation of wage labor as wage slavery. People with modest but regular incomes, with a car or two in their garages, capable of saving for their children's college education, and having two or three weeks of vacation a year, lived on Easy Street compared with the penury of Dickens's England during the mid- to late nineteenth century. Dickens's *A Christmas Carol,* with its dire living conditions and long working hours, was published in the same year that Marx wrote the economic and philosophical manuscripts in which he indicted capitalism in human terms for its theft of the very self.

And so theorists beginning with Weber tried to make a virtue of necessity, a process rapidly accelerated by Talcott Parsons (1951) during the 1950s. Parsons gilded Weber's iron cage, turning the Eisenhower (and early McDonald's) years into a postindustrial utopia. This was to be a perfect society with an economic horn of plenty that would see the abolition of all work. People with college degrees would enjoy managerial positions in science- and technology-intensive occupations, bringing home the bacon, with fringe benefits, to their wifely helpmates who, according to Parsons, were fulfilling their destiny by raising children and catering to the needs of their husbands.

People were now to be viewed as human capital, recognizing that as capitalism shifted from backbreaking industrial toil to creative mental work in sparkling modernist office buildings, "people" became capitalism's most vital resource. Not people in the sense of their unique individuality but people viewed as "skill sets," the ensemble of their degrees, other credentials, professional work experience, and their interpersonal, team-building capabilities. These changes were accompanied by a shift in managerial philosophy from Frederick Taylor's time and motion studies,* designed to maximize industrial-era efficiency by speeding up the industrial working process, to Elton Mayo's more humane approach that recognized that the happy worker, capable of making

---

*Studies undertaken by Frederick Taylor in the late nineteenth and early twentieth centuries designed to maximize workers' output in the industrial factory, later to become the basis of his "scientific management" approach.

his voice heard to upper management, would be more productive. This would not totally replace the experience and reality of subordination—of having a boss upon whom one's entire livelihood rested—but it would humanize work in ways that would make people, especially men but now women too, clamor to get out the door in the morning and leave the stresses of home life behind them. The bureaucratic office, as we discussed in earlier chapters, became a kind of utopia.

During the 1950s the home was also seen to be utopian for women, allowing them to fulfill their destinies as mothers, wives, and efficient operators of domestic laborsaving technologies. Only with the women's movement beginning in the 1960s, and out of sheer economic necessity during the 1970s to the present, did women begin to escape the hectic pace and interpersonal intensity of domestic labor and become office workers, too, with work and family transposing themselves in the ways we discussed earlier.

These transitions had an impact on the career trajectories of white-collar office and professional workers. One did not enter industrial labor directly after schooling ended but went to college for one and possibly two or more degrees. Thus, the worker was produced as human capital, the outcome of schooling. In addition, as one took required courses in the liberal arts core curriculum during college, the worker was reproduced not only as human capital (having a particular skill set) but as cultural capital, a worker capable of blending in, engaging in teamwork, working collaboratively, understanding the social and cultural context of work, dealing with external constituencies, and finding restorative ways to enjoy leisure time, especially by consuming media and the commodities purveyed through it.

Thus, cultural capital—the person possessing a modicum of familiarity with the latest trends, fashions, gossip, and product lines—was necessary as an overlay on human capital. It was necessary because, as Marx originally recognized, the person is both producer and consumer. One must not only know how to perform one's occupational duties but also develop a taste for owning a computer, a laptop, a BlackBerry, a cell phone, an upscale automobile, and the many other products advertised through electronic media. Cultural capital is certainly necessary to impress the boss and clients with an insincere savoir faire. It is also important in order to close the circuit of production and consumption in this postmodern stage of capitalism. Only in this way can we create new capital, new productive wealth.

Human capital has its analogue in children's homework, which reinforces certain skill sets. Having adequate cultural capital, such as a certain worldliness and interpersonal versatility (especially network-ing and sycophancy), allows one to be performative, which also has its analogue in childhood as participation in extracurricular activities. The high school student council member will be tomorrow's initiate into a junior management position. That kid will not necessarily be the sharpest tool in the shed; he should not be, given the importance of being well-rounded in an anti-intellectual culture. But his grades will be adequate, just as the junior management initiate will not be a geek or a grind. He will work and play hard, the two sides of the suc-cessful postmodern self. These will intermingle: people will go out after work to socialize with colleagues, trading anecdotes about the workplace and also discussing what they watched on television last night. The public and private sides of their identities blur to the point of near identity.

And, as we have been arguing, kids are also involved in acquiring human and cultural capital, in many of the same venues as their parents and other adults. Kids watch the same television, gossiping about what happened on *American Idol* or *Lost.* And they surf the Net, lighting on the same sites as their parents, perhaps even using their bookmarks to acquire the latest in gossip and ephemeral information. Kids aug-ment their stock of cultural capital in the process. Kids also do their schoolwork, which leads to human capital. In these ways, they produce themselves as would-be adults with the appropriate skills/education and social savvy relevant to the workplace. Perhaps the way to look at this is that everyone is now a child, even though childhood as a category is slipping away, whose parenting is done by a media culture that is more like Big Brother than paterfamilias.

The Skilled and Worldly Self

In a sense, then, we are produced, much as we produce memos, soft-ware, and automobiles. We produce ourselves, a process that might be called reproduction by Marxists and feminists. The social system enlists us in this production/reproduction now that we have moved from an extractive and industrial economy to an economy based in knowledge, science, technology, and service. Industry has been outsourced to the third world, out of sight and out of mind. The self is both producer and primary product. Indeed, a definition of family in postmodern capitalism might be one of the places, a kind of factory, where selves are produced (like, for feminists, a gender factory [see Berk 1985]). This is another way in which we are transposing work and family, with the real "factories" of the twenty-first century being the family, school, and media, which together produce selves.

Capital in the sense of productive wealth—mutual funds, real estate, stocks, and bonds—still exists, of course. It is now intermingled with human and cultural capital as selves become part of the production process itself. No, the self has always been implicated in production. Now *we are the commodity*, spewed forth by families, schools, teams, and media. The commodity we are is labor, as Marx originally understood. But in Marx's era, labor was unproblematic; people would starve unless they lent their physical power to the early industrial production process. Today, labor must be manufactured, educated, mentored, lessoned, civilized, entertained, and rendered worldly.

This labor—us—is produced as skill sets and worldly selves. We know how to do our jobs, and we are versatile with the ephemeral, superficial world so that we can negotiate life with others and respond productively to advertising, which induces us to close the circuit of production and consumption. This labor works to shop and shops to work. And this labor is produced and reproduced starting from our earliest exposure to television, when we learn rudimentary skills and morality from *Sesame Street* and *Barney & Friends.* The skilled and worldly self, capable of passing standardized tests and navigating the electronic grids of stimulation and exhortation, enters the production line even before kindergarten. This virtual self is produced by Disney and McDonald's as well as by television. It is also produced by preschool and day care. Mothers are replaced to some extent by "day-care providers," who are some of the most significant workers in the process of the assemblage of virtual selves.

This view of productive childhood is not unprecedented. In the eighteenth century, children labored alongside adults in the early factory system. There, children were directly involved in economic production. Today, they are involved in the economy as consumers. And they are also involved in the economic production process inasmuch as *they* are being produced as future workers and as a pre-labor force that skips a crucial stage of development. In this sense, perhaps there has never been a golden age for children except during the period between the end of child labor in the nineteenth century and the post-World War II period before television and the Internet. Childhood has always been colonized by producers of commodities and manufacturers of human and cultural capital. It is too late to start this production process during high school or even after. Children must be recruited into premature adulthood and the pre-labor force beginning in preschool and then in the elementary school years.

By the time kids get to junior high, as they approach their early teens, it is almost too late to restore their innocence, understood as human development of the autonomous and rational self. Once childhood is given over to the production of human and cultural capital—the post-modern capitalist work and consumer force—it is nearly impossible for these early teenagers to escape the disciplinary grid. They are so saturated with the world, including school assignments, testing, and media, that they lose distance from the ordinary and everyday. They lose themselves just as they produce themselves. As Theodor Adorno (1973) recognized, this distance is essential in order to take stock and think the world otherwise—to be utopian, in other terms.

The skilled and worldly self that we try to fabricate beginning in early childhood, in much the way that Henry Ford manufactured cars, can do well at the game of Trivial Pursuit and charm clients at a cocktail party. He or she can also impress an interviewer in the workplace and, once hired, can multitask and earn raises and promotions. But this self cannot criticize the existing social arrangements from the vantage of a larger theory, cannot start or participate in a social movement, cannot slow down life sufficiently to be a time rebel, let alone a political rebel. Immersion in the world and immediacy in communicating with others are not qualities that allow one to become an ideology critic, seeing beyond the given world to what might be. This postmodern self cannot bridge past, present, and future in a way that grounds utopia in reality, and in "reality's" self-negating possibilities. In these senses, the youthful human capital and cultural capital that we are creating actually stand in the way of a deeper understanding of the meaning of life and of its possibilities.

Much as Weber understood about bureaucracy,* when we teach people certain skills and afford them interpersonal dexterity in order to function effectively as producers and consumers, we also disable them from becoming original thinkers and thoughtful citizens. Weber (1958) recognized that bureaucracy is a trap in that it promotes rule-bound ritualism, genuflection to authority, and moral blindness. Sycophancy is framed as a team-building skill. Initially designed to help us move past the premodern into full modernity, with its global "rationalization," bureaucracy over time enmeshes us in pettiness and stupidity. Similarly, in seemingly surpassing old-fashioned productive capital grounded in

---

*Weber's term for a social organization based on a top-to-bottom chain of command and a high degree of task specialization, typically found in the modern world of work.

manual labor power, a fast postmodern capitalism that produces selves with human and cultural capital is actually blocking initiative and inno- vation by miring people in the everyday, a one-dimensional society. They cannot see beyond the latest fashions; the latest gossip; the class, race, and gender hierarchies as we have constructed them; the homogeneity of the political parties; the time robbery that fatigues and stresses us. These postmodern selves are the proverbial rats running in place on a treadmill, even if they are now running in place on a real treadmill as they turn play and athletics into a second job called "working out."

In this sense, the late modern or postmodern is constraining, block- ing developments that might seize on the transposition of work into family and family into work as a radicalizing opportunity. Our college students have given up on politics, if they were ever tempted by politi- cal movements and ideas. They almost all disavow feminism as archaic, out there, over the top. Mothers are more progressive than their daugh- ters, and teachers more than their students. Young people do not vote in huge numbers, and their music and films of choice are about the self, not social justice. Our contemporary culture of narcissism turns the self inward; self-orientation is the result, but not an orientation to self that would unpack the deep layers of power and culture bleeding into our psyches and bodies, positioning us as victims and agents. One of the great lies about our stage of capitalism is that people actually "make choices" destining them for success or failure. Although we do not deny the possibility of making fundamental decisions that free us from determination by external forces, this agency is not evident in superficial choices such as how to present ourselves to peers, dates, mates, and prospective employers. The presentation of self (Goffman 1959), although seemingly in our control, is limited to the few options available to us—the clothing offered for sale at Gap or Hollister, the vehicles on the Ford or Toyota dealership lots, the songs available at iTunes for downloading to our iPods. As Thorstein Veblen (1979) and Vance Packard (1957) have long known, advertising is not an exercise in philosophical agency but a shell game.

PRESENTATION AND PRODUCTION OF THE SELF I: CLASS, RACE, AND GENDER SCRIPTS

Having swallowed large enough doses of human and cultural capital— schoolwork, exposure to media, peer pressure, parental approval and disapproval—young teenagers and even preteens begin to select a public self much as one would choose a meal from a restaurant menu. The virtual self (see Turkle 1997), in its postmodern plasticity, is infinitely iterable and alterable largely because much youthful self-presentation occurs on the screen, through MySpace postings, instant messaging, texting, and e-mail. Screen names are disconnected from one's real name; they summarize, abbreviate, or deceive, depending on one's whim and context. And fashions in clothing, makeup, and hairstyle are by definition ephemeral, changing with the seasons and sometimes reaching back to the past for new substance. (Think of what girls in the 1950s and early 1960s used to call pedal pushers, which have returned to stores in recent years as capris, or the seemingly timeless flip, now almost always blonde in the wake of Marilyn Monroe.)

These affectations can be called scripts (see Goffman 1959) because they are given to the self and because they encode totalities of meaning. To be a "goth" who wears black and has many piercings is to take a value position and existential stance evoking the 1950s beats. Today's slackers are yesterday's hippies, protesting against prisonlike school, time robbery, and a rote culture. These affectations of identity disclose class, race, and gender. Preps wear clothes pasted over with logos; black hip-hop kids wear baggy jeans; girly girls wear low-rise pants with tattoos showing in the small of their backs. Clothing has always encoded these meanings, but today, with kids and their parents having more purchasing power and with such a surfeit of meaning, these self positionings signify more than ever. They must "mean" because there is so little meaning elsewhere.

These meanings can sometimes overlap and contradict each other. Middle-class white girls who wear low-rise jeans with visible thong underwear also sport wristbands with the acronym "WWJD," meaning "What would Jesus do?" Their display of sexuality blends with born-again religious values, although this is best seen as a contradiction. The postmodern self is branded, a double entendre suggesting that our identities are thrust upon us and that we wear our identities on our sleeves. Our adornments conceal who we really are, a finding consistent with the postmodern idea that there is no stable reality or identity.

Universities, understanding branding and Baudrillard, follow suit. Stores are stocked full of branded hats and shirts with nationally identifiable university logos on them. Even if you did not, or will not, attend the University of Michigan or the University of Texas, you can simulate this experience by wearing clothing bearing the schools' logos. Universities enjoy a cut of the profits from these items, and they thus advertise themselves to prospective students, who are often less concerned with a university's curricula or the quality of its faculty than with the currency of its brand—Duke for preps and basketball; Texas for parties, Greeks, and football; Brandeis for the socially aware. We live in a state with this "big state university" mentality; we can always find University of Texas at Austin and Texas A&M signage, and we can easily find the major national brands such as UCLA, USC, Michigan, Duke, Notre Dame. But it is nearly impossible to find the brand of our local utilitarian branch of the University of Texas, located in Arlington, which is midway between Dallas and Fort Worth and most visible for its professional sports teams and theme parks.

The internalization of brands as sources of identity begins early in a child's life. Initially, it is foisted upon the small child by the adult, who dresses her or him. Girls are gendered by their parents, mostly by their mothers. Boys are gendered, too. Both are placed in class- and gender-signifying apparel, with prominent brands. This produces the young self and its cultural capital. It sets up interactions with peers, parents, and teachers that reproduce identity, gender, class, and race. The self becomes a captive of these airtight compartments that mark them forever unless they make a concerted effort to become, in the case of privileged kids, slackers. It is possible to shift identity, but never completely and only after years of resistance and reflection. No elementary school child can mount this resistance; they accept the clothing and identity their parents lay out for them. Although as they age they refine and differentiate identity by observing peers, others will have treated them *as* their class (thus reproducing it) nearly from the beginning.

It is an adult illusion that kids just naturally congregate and aggregate themselves into cliques and factions. For the most part these decisions have been set in stone long before they are consciously made by children. Driving a Lexus SUV, the parents drop off their designer-appareled children in the carpool line at the local public or private school. (If there is a uniform code, the sartorial markers will be more subtle, but noticeable by fashion- and class-conscious parents.) Teachers and other parents take notice. The teachers expect that these parents could be trouble if Johnny or Sally has academic difficulty or behavioral issues. They steer a wide berth. Other parents position these already-positioned children on their children's invitation lists for parties and other events. Thus begins the production and presentation of the self, whose identity is enmeshed in these signifiers that form the basis of other people's attributions of cultural capital. Kids with expensive haircuts and early braces on their teeth are the ones who end up at Georgetown and Duke. There are few accidents here.

PRESENTATION AND PRODUCTION OF THE SELF II:
PLANNING THE ADULT SELF

Parents knowledgeable about the salience of human and cultural capital—even if they do not have degrees in critical sociology—proceed to
assemble the adult self as soon as their kids are born. They want to pass
along their class position and its gender and race ramifications. They
push their young daughters into soccer, adorned with pink ribbons and
nail polish; they send them to charm school to learn etiquette; they sign
them up for Advanced Placement courses in high school; they attend
the right summer sleepaway camp, with girls of the same or would-be
social class who will attend the same universities and rush the same
sororities.

Jacques Steinberg's *The Gatekeepers* (2002) examines the process
of application and admissions decisions at Wesleyan University, an elite
eastern liberal arts college. What he describes occurs at universities
around the country. His is a sobering account, both because competition for admission to a brand-name college is intense (again, brands that
substitute for the real thing, whatever that might be) and because objective academic criteria often take a backseat to subjective evaluations of
human and cultural capital. A college operating as a pure meritocracy
could just as well take the kids with the highest SAT or ACT scores,
going down the list until they had filled up their entering class. But as
we said earlier, the anti-intellectualism of American society militates
against this. Schools want well-rounded, but not necessarily the brightest, applicants, those who will perpetuate the class structure. As well,
schools are under pressure to ensure a measure of diversity and so they
use sociodemographic criteria such as race and ethnicity, but only at
the margin. Indeed, WASP applicants may be the new "protected class,"
given the academic portfolios presented by Asian Americans.

Steinberg documents how it is not enough, and probably never was,
to have good grades in honors courses, to play in the school orchestra,
and perhaps to be on the debating team. One needs a much stouter
portfolio of adultlike activities—community service, travel, perhaps an
entrepreneurial activity, sports involvement (sports is big in this process). These measured activities constitute the core of "performativity,"
as applied to the pre–labor force. Such schools want leaders because
they realize that they are training a future elite. In effect, kids are being
evaluated in terms of their productivity and performance in high school
and earlier, their academic "output," and their dedication and versatility
as community citizens and leaders. Especially important is to ensure

that the kids have "met their full potential," human resources jargon for never having had an idle moment. Students who take few or none of the honors or AP courses available in their high schools are downgraded, as are kids who are good at only one extracurricular activity, such as those who are "just" star violinists or cross-country runners.

At work here is the expectation that high school students have spent their precious high school years between about ages fourteen and eighteen producing an adult self. This production is preparation (for adulthood), and preparation is production—it takes time and energy. It is clear from Steinberg's account of college admissions decisions that kids with too much time on their hands (to daydream? create? play?) are viewed as underachievers, where, in fact, they may be just the sort of iconoclastic people who end up starting Apple and Amazon. We think back to our own childhoods and high school years and it is clear that virtually none of these pressures to produce the adult self were in play, even though, as baby boomers, we faced similar demographic pressure as we competed within a large birth cohort for college admission.

A student can profitably attend Western Michigan University for a BA and then make the leap to Michigan State University or University of Michigan for an MA and perhaps an additional professional degree. Parents who are not particularly familiar with academia believe the hype that an undergraduate degree at Dartmouth or Duke is qualitatively better than one from Western Michigan or University of Massachusetts at Boston. To be sure, one will have classmates with greater cultural capital and higher family income at these elite private universities. It is true that the adult-selves-in-training at University of Texas at Austin and Texas A&M, the "elite" public universities in Texas, are making productive interpersonal connections in a state that is rather parochial in the sense that few attend college outside the state and many remain in state after graduation. These networks certainly propel one's career. But in a mobile society in which people cross state and regional boundaries frequently, both for and after college, it is probably true that network building matters more at the postgraduate level.

As for the quality of faculty at the Dartmouths and Oberlins, it is unclear that they are for the most part better than faculty at Western Michigan and UMass-Boston. Generally, faculty at liberal arts colleges have heavier teaching loads than at colleges and universities with graduate programs and they are accordingly expected to publish less. However, it makes a significant difference for a college student to be taught by a professor who actually contributes to the research literature with her own publications than by one who merely has mastered the literature in her field but who does not publish. Of course, if the publishing faculty member is unexcited by teaching, then it does not matter whether she publishes. Although there are accomplished faculty at Oberlin, there are a larger number of productive faculty at Michigan State and Arizona State. There may even be a greater number of productive faculty at UMass-Boston, a secondary institution in the UMass system, than at Dartmouth or Oberlin. This is not simply because at many research-oriented universities teaching is devalued and undergraduate students are taught primarily by graduate students and adjunct faculty. The best of all worlds is to be taught by a publishing faculty member who is excited by interactions with students in a small-class setting.

Most parents do not know this; they are going with the brand and with published data about average freshman standardized test scores and rejection rates. As Steinberg points out, for all but about fifty of the two or three thousand American colleges and universities, the vast majority of applicants for admissions are accepted. It is only at elite schools that have become brands that one sees rejection rates of greater than 50 percent. And this is because the brand creates a market—high school applicants.

Academics know that the quality of one's education depends in large measure on who your professors are and to a lesser extent on who your classmates are. Ideally, you will get the best of both worlds. The problem is that many lower-division undergraduate students (in their first two years of college) take large-enrollment classes taught by teaching assistants or adjuncts. One might be taught by "real" full-time faculty at smaller liberal arts colleges, but these faculty might not conduct much, if any, research, thus not occupying the cutting edges of their fields. It is difficult to find smallish universities with research-oriented faculty who also care about students. One of the best examples of this kind of university is Rice, in Houston, Texas. Classes are small and many departments have PhD programs, which, for undergraduates, means that the faculty who teach them will be research leaders in their fields. Rice is not yet a national brand or much of a regional brand. As of this writing, the school is considering eliminating its football program, which will diminish its brand status even further but will produce newfound economic resources for its academic programs.

In *The Gatekeepers* Steinberg is in effect saying that elite colleges and universities are looking for students with good high school grades, test scores, and class rank, as well as leadership experiences, musical and sports activities, and community service. Parents help their kids build a résumé that captures these experiences, believing that the road to success begins and perhaps ends with the brand of one's child's college admission. Adulthood is thus being produced and performed early, before its time both psychologically and physically. One of the hallmarks of adulthood is independence, especially in decision making. But pushy parents are denying their children this capability when they overschedule them in order to assemble the résumé-level characteristics of achievement and comportment thought necessary for getting into elite schools (see Rosenfeld and Wise 2001). These parents are producing both their children's adulthood and their own in the sense that what it means to be a successful parent in their circles is to have one's child in an elite college or university. And, in this age of conspicuous consumption, parents display their success as parents by pasting their children's college decals on the back windshield of their Lexuses and BMWs. Thus, the university, child, and parents are branded—that is, their identities are made visible as "signs" or status symbols that, according to Baudrillard, become more important than the reality of what goes on in these colleges and afterward.

CONTRADICTIONS OF THE PRODUCTION OF ADULTHOOD: ALWAYS ALREADY ADULTS

These productions of adulthood before their time become a self-fulfilling prophecy, making adults of children, who become compulsive about production and performance for the purposes of building a résumé and thus a life. Colleges' statures, emerging from the currency of their brands, overtake the learning and living that take place in the four or five years of college. This is not to deny that important learning is going on after high school but to notice that the sign value of one's college is frequently more important to parents than the educational value accruing to those who matriculate. This is consistent with a culture in which facts overwhelm imagination and theory, making test scores, grades, and class rank desirable in their own right and not as proxies for the underlying issue of what one has learned, let alone how imaginative one is. At issue here is the phrase "what one has learned." As we have noted, for many parents and K–12 teachers, schooling is about acquiring facts rather than learning how to learn and create, hence the objective assignments and factual tests to which K–12 students must submit on almost every day of their school careers.

This emphasis on factual knowledge continues in college, where many professors teach to the test and expect students to reproduce what they have been taught and what they have read. This is an important issue in the philosophy of education: are we teaching "content" or are we teaching a method or theory of learning? To some extent, ideally, we are teaching both. Imagine the medical student who fails anatomy or the civil engineer who cannot pass calculus. But far too many teachers, from kindergarten through college and even some teaching graduate students, view learning as ingestion and not as the sparking of imagination. Teaching should set students free and help them find their calling. At the risk of using a pop psychological cliché from the 1990s, good teaching is "empowering." It empowers students to go beyond the syllabus and to take issue with learned authorities, or at least to enter into dialogue with them.

When we talk about the brand appeal of colleges we are acknowledging that who you know, and your social skills, may be as important as what you know in the way of content. In addition to possessing diplomas, those who get ahead network, drop names, and possess social intelligence. These attributes form cultural capital, which over time translates into real economic capital as people build careers. By cultural capital, Bourdieu (1977) was simply describing how tacit and informal but important cultural knowledge—about iconic philosophers and musicians, about history, both ancient and current, about fads and trends—helps people accumulate real economic capital. It advances their careers and makes them seem educated. It possesses a certain symbolic value that can be converted into career opportunities. However, looking more deeply at the concept, cultural capital is fundamentally contradictory in the sense that we might use the German word *Kultur* to stand opposed to the more conventional English world *civilization*. When Sigmund Freud titled one of his later works *Das Unbehagen in der Kultur*, the title was translated into English as *Civilization and Its Discontents*; the German word *Kultur* was translated as *civilization*. *Kultur* connotes a quality of intellect and sensibility that is expressive and cosmopolitan (as in "a cultured person") and civilization suggests the ensemble of modern advancements in technology, science, and even the arts (as in "the fruits of civilization").

Bourdieu, were he writing in English, would probably use the term *civilizational capital* because that is the sense of his term for the type of informal knowledge about the world that can be converted into the impression of savoir faire. *Kultur* and *capital* stand opposed to each other as expressive and spiritual sensibility versus a utilitarian attitude,

Weber's means-ends rationality. To have cultural capital in the sense of knowing the latest hit television show, who won the second presidential debate, and the site of the next summer Olympics signifies a person who is current with the ephemera of the moment. Now Bourdieu well understands that this type of ephemeral knowledge can be important, for example when one is being interviewed for a job over lunch and one's future boss tests one's knowledge of baseball. If one's masculinity is in play, then one had better know how to talk knowledgeably about the Red Sox and their heretofore tragic destiny. But if one was to really talk to the interviewer about deeper matters, such as the implied political metaphysic of rap music or the implications of the Internet for intellectual copyright and fair use, let alone about Bach's fugues, one would be shown the door, dismissed as an egghead or pretentious or both.

Cultural capital in an anti-intellectual culture betrays *Kultur,* substituting episodic knowledge for a deeper sensibility and passion. To call cultural knowledge capital already degrades it, turning it into the utilitarian. But much cultural knowledge is not actually of any practical use. Knowing the difference between the spleen and liver could save your life, but cultural capital is useful only in that it impresses others who know even less than you do about what really matters. The triumph of facts over theories already decides in favor of culture's utilitarianism. Knowledge of Hollywood movies, network television, and professional sports can be reduced to sheer data, answers to be supplied on game shows. American game show contestants who know so much trivia that they emerge victorious from week to week may be viewed as eccentric, taking trivia to another level and secretly discrediting the whole enterprise of acquiring "culture." This may also hold true for the driven children who win spelling bees. The only way to accomplish these prodigious acts of ingestion is by memorization, learning facts by rote.

Spelling bees for children are another venue in which the absurdities of having excessive cultural capital are played out. The 2002 documentary *Spellbound* reveals driven children and their driving parents poring over lists of esoteric words, committing them to memory. This occurs after all of their other academic work has been completed each day. Kids ordinarily learn how to spell by reading, a whole-language approach far superior to rote learning. Spelling bees are peculiarly American, blending the American penchant for making everything a competition, the more structured the better, and for the rote learning of facts—an anti-intellectual academic sport, at the risk of committing several oxymorons! The spelling bee is the height of meaninglessness: polysyllabic words never used in daily discourse or writing are memorized by children machinelike in their ability to retain the lists of words. Spelling bee participants are not idiot savants but simply workhorses.

The properly prepared adultlike child—who has produced herself by living an accelerated if superficial young life, sleep-deprived, and stressed—is always already an adult. What it means to be "adult" as opposed to "child" or "teenager" becomes ambiguous; the boundaries between the various stages of human development blur. Preparation for adulthood—the rituals of human and cultural capital acquisition, all the way to the absurdity of résumé building during and even before high school—becomes adulthood. Our teenagers are working forty or more hours each week, producing and performing to the point of exhaustion.

The contradiction of culture and capital is seen vividly in these preternaturally worldly young adults. They can plow through taxonomies and commit them to memory; they can stay up late to juggle and complete assignments after practice; they are well versed in popular culture; they can manipulate electronic communication technologies. But they are not "cultured" in the sense of having *Kultur*. They are not creative, independent, or inquisitive. For them, school is work, as are lessons and practices. Like their adult counterparts, kids relieve their stress and fatigue with shopping, viewing, vegetating, drugs, and drink. Kids are already alienated because they are no longer kids; they must produce and perform, and even the cultural capital they acquire is of the instrumental variety, memorized to pass tests and play along with the contestants on game shows.

A good benchmark of whether cultural capital promotes *Kultur* or a more utilitarian civilization is whether or not those who possess it read and write. Although e-mail and instant messaging are "texts" of sorts, their authorship is casual and not studied. Kids who IM each other do not intend their works to endure for posterity; indeed, they do not view their rapid-fire composition of greetings and responses as authorial work at all. Although some kids keep diaries and journals, most resist writing, both because the surround-sound electronic grid makes reading and writing seem painful and because the writing they do in school is drudgery. This school writing frequently involves grammar, a relic from half a century ago and certainly not an efficacious route to literary style, and formulaic "writing trees" and other templates for stories and essays. The best way to learn to write is to read copiously and then to write furiously and often, without much structure. Kids will develop an ear for language only if they use it frequently and without evaluations, constraints, and punishment.

This aversion to text could be defended as a characteristic of a "post-textual" age of images, graphics, and representations. But text and image are mutually reinforcing. Kids adept at creating Web pages and working in HTML are certainly doing important literary work, creating artifacts and themselves. But HTML is one of Bernstein's (1975) restricted codes; Web page designers are specialists, artists and authors at the highest level. Web design is not for the faint of heart, any more than is learning to play the violin or speak a second language.

Kids learn to read in early elementary school and quickly grow to love it. Then teachers and the curriculum kill their love of reading by requiring it, testing on books' details, and turning writing into a gram-mar-driven chore (Tyre 2006). In our school district, reading is even turned into a competition among schools: the Battle of the Books tests kids' minute factual knowledge of stories they have read, encouraging them to miss the big picture—meaning via configuration (*Gestalt* or pastiche). By the time kids finish high school, many hate books but love television and the Internet. This is easily fixed by refraining from turning reading and writing into formulaic architecture, and then test-ing on it.

When culture becomes utilitarian—simply a means to an end, capital—we lose the sense of *Kultur,* the intellectual, civilized person who is curious about the surrounding world. We have already ruined much of the skills-oriented curriculum, from math to social studies, converting it into preparation for career via human capital. We also ruin culture—reading, writing, poetry, interpretation, criticism—by transforming it into factoids and formulae. Our teenage daughter had to find and highlight her vocabulary words in a Mark Twain novel, whereas learning to spell them and know their meaning should be enough. After reading the novel, she pored over the text, combing carefully with a yel-low marker to unearth these cultural nuggets. A deeper understanding (really, any understanding) of Twain's work has no chance under these circumstances or when the student is tested once or twice a week on aspects of plot. In late elementary school, our son took computerized tests on books he had read—the Accelerated Reader program. Again, he had to remember who said what to whom in chapter 6 rather than grapple with bigger meanings. Our son loves to read, but it is in spite of these tests and not because of them.

The main contradiction of preparing for adulthood is that the prepa-ration itself ends childhood. Kids are expected by adults to become adultlike en route/rote to successful adulthood. Their parents impose brands, identities, and peer groups on them for utilitarian reasons, a process beginning in preschool. This is at first a fitful process, because kids obviously are playing roles. Think of little kids playing house or dress-up. They are simulating adult behavior. But by the time they get to high school, prematurely mature-looking sixteen-year-olds could pass for adults in their sexuality, makeup, clothing, drinking, and acquaintance with the adult world. By then it is too late. Where little children resist—by crying, pouting, sullenness—teenagers and even preteens gobble up adulthood, fantasizing about their first cars, first dates, first proms, first times living away from home. Their production of and preparation for adulthood bleed into the real thing, but many years too soon.

This acceleration has produced a dialectical negation,* so to speak, in the phenomenon of twixters—young adults in their twenties who, after college, move back in with Mom and Dad (Grossman 2005). Twixters are yearning and searching for a mate, a career, an identity. The world has rushed by too quickly, and their systems have shut down. Pushed out of the house too early, they return, filling up the empty nest. Economic downturn, especially after 9/11, hastens this process of returning to the parental home as twixters experience difficulty finding decent jobs in their chosen fields.

Social psychologists, dealing with families of alcoholics and drug users, talk of codependence, referring to people who cannot get their needs met and thus cause others close to them to share their pain. Parents with less-than-satisfying lives make their children codependent; these parents live vicariously through their children and also, as we have been saying, act out their resentment of childhood freedom and play. Although parents seem to be preparing their kids for adulthood simply because they recognize that it is a dog-eat-dog world and only the strong survive, parents are in fact involving their children in their own struggles for career success and the validation of their own identities, reproducing their career and developmental contingencies in their management of their kids' lives. The dad who plays on the company softball team in order to get ahead enrolls his son in an elite baseball league, stressing the kid with his own expectations and robbing his

---

*An idea, drawn by Marx from Hegel, suggesting that the world should not be viewed as static but as in a continual process of becoming and change; refers to the tendency of social arrangements to become dysfunctional, producing conflict, and then for those conflicts to be resolved, producing overall progress.

son of time perhaps better spent on unstructured play. Or the mother dealing with her own aging and graying sends her daughter to charm school and dance lessons, attempting to retrieve her vigor and femininity through her daughter. It is no wonder that kids return home after college, having failed to individuate themselves successfully during their school years.

The acceleration of childhood does not automatically mean that kids are given psychic independence and the resources to make important choices. Children left home while their parents work are not necessarily better off; indeed, the neglect they experience may sap their ego strength and thwart further development. One of our son's friends, an older boy, is often left home alone but he cannot do anything fun outside the home without checking in with his father, who is a stern disciplinarian. The father can rarely be reached, and so the son stays home alone, the worst outcome.

This young man and others of his ilk are neglected but rendered dependent. Left to their own devices, they lead fast lives, but they hurry back to the home once they founder in the adult world. Parents who have adultlike expectations of their children turn them into adults before their time, which never works. This boomerangs when the kids, finally grown, do not have the psychic or financial resources to go it alone. Some psychologists talk about the "enmeshed" family, the family that experiences too much blurring of roles and identities. Although the fast families of the early twenty-first century are frequently too anomic, they become enmeshed because grown children who have not successfully established autonomy live out their parents' expectations of them, which reflect their own inadequacies and disappointments.

The important thing to remember here is that everyone in the family is damaged, parents as well as kids. Parents lead hurried and harried lives, which they impress on their own children, who are at once smothered with adultlike expectations and neglected by absentee parents too busy working, commuting, and living to provide real guidance. This blend of smothering and neglect, approach and avoidance, is characteristic of our age, as people interact frenetically but do not have enduring relationships. Adorno (1978) termed this the damaged life, and he felt that everybody shares this fate in a society grounded in imitation or what we are calling rote.

And so to produce adulthood as a member of the pre–labor force is already to be an adult, or at least adultlike. Kids watching R-rated movies and surfing the Net for social contacts are behaving like their parents, who are probably in the other room doing the same thing. Kids plugged into their cell phones are most certainly not talking to their parents, who have their own busy schedules. People are intensely alone, which creates codependence: I bring home my problems, which become your problems, and together we suffer together in silence, unable to name the cause. The main problem of fast families is inadequate insulation from the external world, which floods the home, the self, the psyche, and time.

A good Marxist recognizes that contradictions bring the possibility of resolutions. Accordingly, Marx felt that the alienation of labor would spark class struggle that would bring about socialism* and then communism.† Here, we are noting the contradiction involved in preparing kids for adulthood in ways that are always already adult. Time robbery—theft of a whole stage of human development—brings time rebellion, kids who want to stay kids and who reject the acceleration of their lives. Although kids do not theorize their lives and experiences in these terms, they resist and rebel, providing the platform for more organized efforts on behalf of kids by sympathetic adults. This resistance and rebellion takes the form of sleeping in, absenteeism, not paying attention in class, refusing to complete assignments, loafing through lessons and sports practices, returning to the games and interests of early childhood, and developing peer groups of like-minded friends. It may also lead to Columbine. Kids' psyches and bodies can take only so much abuse.

These acts of resistance are childhood expressions of alienation. They are a symptom of fast families and virtual children in the early twenty-first century. Caring adults, both parents and teachers, need to recognize what is going on and let kids be kids, giving them time to recover and restore. Perhaps we need to rethink schooling and especially the articulation between school and career. It could be argued that the most important things kids can learn in school are what they like to do and are good at, how to get along with others, how to empathize and assist the less fortunate, and how to solve problems. At present, many parents feel that schools are accomplishing two things: helping their children get into college and extinguishing their love of learning.

---

*An intermediate stage of economic development between capitalism and communism in which there is a mix of private ownership of businesses and state ownership of business.

†An economic system in which all of the means of production are owned by "the people" and run by the government; according to Marx, this stage of development would eliminate class conflict and provide everyone with a living.

In our concluding chapter, we explore children's rights and parental responsibilities further as we consider parenting and schooling for democracy. We suggest pragmatic steps that parents and schools can take to slow down childhood and build democracy. Just as family/families can be a worthy progressive goal, we can position progressive schools as a new opening to the democratic public sphere. Schools today resemble prisons and factories, but they could be much more—gathering points for democracy, "families" of people who participate in a living and learning experience. Call these public "families" communities.

6

Children of Parents, Children of Democracy

In fast capitalism, parents become children in the sense that their needs come first and children become parents in the sense that they stay home alone and confront adultlike expectations. This is not good for anyone and needs to be addressed, as we have been doing in this book. This reversal of roles inhibits human development both for kids and adults. And, as we argue in this concluding chapter, it hinders democracy, which we tie to our earlier concept of family/families—basing all human relationships on intimacy and mutuality.

BRINGING BACK THE CHILDREN

Our analysis leads to the conclusion that children are being neglected, both in practice and in theory, which is strange because we are also noticing that children are being saturated by media and by schools that have taken over parenting. Parents have their own battles to fight. This is symptomatic of a world in which almost everyone is alienated (in early Marx's sense of being separated from their essence or project and from community). Parents are no less alienated than children. Indeed, they are children, too, especially if they are caring for their own aged parents. And in their expectation that their kids will raise themselves (using various electronic prostheses) they are affording their children a certain premature adulthood, which leads to the general perception, on both the left and the right, that "kids grow up too fast." The Right blames permissiveness and a sexualized culture, while the Left targets a "fast" society in which all of us are struggling to keep up with the dizzying pace of things.

Children are also being neglected by sociology and social theory, which tend to view childhood as invariant, a biological life stage portrayed in a static way by developmental psychology and sociology textbooks. Children are almost nowhere treated as subjects and objects of political and social theory, as we are doing here, which is another way of saying that they are not treated historically, in terms of continuities and discontinuities with the past. Either children are omitted entirely from social theory—by far the most common scenario—or else childhood is treated as smooth evolution from early childhood through the teenage years. In this chapter we seek to remedy this, and we suggest a children's bill of rights. First, we consider the need for sociology and social theory to consider children in the context of not only families but also the public sphere. Second, we suggest that a link between the public and private spheres is schooling, which crosses the boundary between both spheres. Finally, we suggest a children's bill of rights and accompanying parental responsibilities.

Children are prisms through which we see ourselves, adults, more clearly. They are a palimpsest, our better nature. They embody us, and we are imprinted on them. Of course, children imprint themselves on us, too. But children also reflect the larger society, especially schools and the media. We can look into their eyes and see the reflection of blackboards and televisions, billboards and video games. And children are irreducible to these impinging influences. They are always already agents, even if we do not acknowledge that or give them room to move. Children are utopian, not yet turned into robots or regimented. Children play and, hence, model playful society for all of us. Finally, children model democracy for adults who forget how to be flexible, share, and make decisions collectively and spontaneously.

The democratic and utopian modeling that children provide to adults is almost never noticed, partly because social theory assumes a world peopled by adults and because few theorists regard play as a political category. Play is for recess, which is becoming ever shorter. Or play is the avoidance of work. And, because this democratic and utopian modeling is rarely noticed and theorized, the attenuation of childhood is also disregarded as a social problem. This attenuation of childhood is a social problem both because kids are people, too, and because kids are a democratic and utopian resource at a time when there are few workable images of a better society. Childhood becomes a visible problem only when the child is so stressed out that he or she attempts suicide, abuses drugs and alcohol, threatens violence, or fidgets in class. Otherwise, parents and sociologists generally believe that children are doing fine even as their lives are hectic, the expectations of them adultlike, and their sleep inadequate. Teenage depression, like "attentional" issues, is addressed with medication or therapy and not real social and personal changes.

We need to bring children back into sociology in order to see ourselves better, develop empathy with our kids, and notice that children, in their best nature, are models of cooperation and purposive purposelessness or play. Ignoring children not only defeats them but robs us of images of a different, better order in which adults, too, behave like children and sometimes during downtime do things for their own sake, unconstrained by routine, duty, or the clock. We steal our kids' childhoods because we are not happy with our own adulthoods. We might rationalize this by saying that we are "preparing" kids for the tough road ahead, but in reality we resent them and we do not want them to have what we do not. It is difficult to interpret hours of homework, standardized testing, overscheduling, participation on select sports teams, and inadequate sleep any other way. These are symptoms of systematic and purposeful neglect, and they violate children's basic rights.

The absence of children from sociology and social theory is less and less notable as children's lives are accelerated and attenuated. Children wearing labeled clothes and makeup, having sex and watching violence, yearning to drive and date, are, seemingly by their own choice, fleeing this golden stage of insulation and experimentation for the serious adult world. A children's bill of rights seems unnecessary when children have their own phone lines and cell phones, their own televisions and computers, and their own eating schedules. Kids are always already mature when they can stay home alone, without parents or babysitters. We make a virtue of this necessity by believing that working parents allow their kids a maturing independence. Neglect is autonomy by another name.

Children are not the only ones losing developmental time. Parents, too, are losing their lives to the time robbers of work, commuting, media, and rapid information and communication technologies. No one has time, and thus a real life, in the 24/7 world made possible by rapid technologies and desired by people in marketing. It is not as if neglected kids have parents sitting on the beach in idle repose, although some parents vacation without their kids in order to have "their own time." Children "versus" parents is not simply the new form of class conflict. Nor are teachers to be demonized. They are often parents, too, and they are no less harried. Parents and teachers are positioned in a fast capitalism to be enforcers, even though they lack real and legitimate authority. No one has such authority; that is the problem.

Children have been missing from social theory out of condescension and because of the fleeting nature of childhood today. When four-year-olds play organized sports and attend tutoring sessions, it is easy to forget that they are not producers and performers. It is natural to ignore what is increasingly missing—childhood—under pressure of accelerated development.

Condescension is another matter. Women and people of color have been missing from sociology and policy, too, until relatively recently. This is partly because they have done the dirty, often invisible, work, which is kept quiet and secret lest it have to be politically recognized and, in the case of housework, waged. Children do dirty work, too, of a different sort. Schoolwork does not have exchange value,* but it prepares the way for it by developing human capital. More important, though, is the concealment of children's secret lives as utopian beings. Just as mainstream sociology has failed to link the circumstances of the very rich and very poor—a causal relationship—so too have we purposely ignored the utopian lives of children who do democracy and play collaboratively and thus overturn the performance principle of a utilitarian capitalism.

Parents, to provide their children with a better life than they had, emphasize career building and academic utilitarianism, thus hastening the arrival of adulthood. Kids are coached by parents to take honors and AP courses in junior high and high school in order to capitalize on grade-point-average formulae that weight these courses more heavily, thus pleasing college admissions officers.

Compulsive parents steal the precious interlude between the toddler stage and adult responsibilities. Parents' compulsions are bundles of good and bad motives. They want more for their kids than they had or have. They recognize that the world is competitive, especially inasmuch as other parents are also pushy. (This becomes a vicious circle leading to earlier and earlier preparation.) Parents are unfulfilled, and they project themselves onto their children, who reflect their glory. They are narcissistic and self-oriented in the ways that our culture teaches us to be. Christopher Lasch (1979) talks of the "culture of narcissism."[†]

Narcissists impose their own compulsions for success on their children, and they live through them. They are pitiable because they confuse the real and illusory: their kids become homework and test-taking machines and résumé builders without acquiring the gravitas that

---

*The cost of commodities, the value at which they are exchanged in the capitalist marketplace.

[†]An everyday life characterized by a high degree of self-absorption, in which people's appearances and their material possessions are more important than their interior or inherent characteristics.

characterizes people of distinction. Our schools mollify these parents by placing their children in classes for the "gifted and talented," as if every local elementary school and junior high had dozens of Einsteins in their midst.

Again, blame is ample and to be shared. Parents are at fault, as are schools, teachers, the media, and capitalism. The only innocents are the truly innocent: children. Ask any child with driven parents if she or he really enjoys traveling to practices and games or doing hours of work in order to earn straight As and it quickly becomes clear that they are doing this for their parents, who leave them little choice. Kids who do not measure up have their parents' affection withdrawn or worse—they are punished. Kids are scolded when they receive a semester grade in the low 90s, even though that is still an A. These kids and their parents are brainwashed into believing that life is all about plugging in the right answer. Of course, this is partly correct: The drones inherit, if not the earth, at least the middle-management positions. Supply the right answer, suck up to authority, and manage impressions and one can live on Easy Street, in a house with three thousand square feet, annual vacations, and a couple of cars. These adult outcomes will be preceded by college years spent in fraternities and sororities, making connections and learning middle-American social skills and values. These people are not gifted and talented but merely inhabitants of a rote culture in which they prosper.

Who are comfortable intellectuals to put down commercial art, television, fast food, suburban life, and consumerism? Actually, we are not prescribing values but noticing that no one is really free to choose values, given the power of advertising and media to reproduce themselves. Everything is salesmanship, of cars, food, entertainment, even personality itself. *Super Size Me,* Morgan Spurlock's 2004 documentary on the perils of eating fast food for a month, makes it clear that Americans are becoming ill, with clogged arteries, because they are duped into eating outsized portions of fatty "fast" food and because they do not exercise but, rather, drive and watch television. Popular culture is, after all, an industry and a marketing confidence game. McDonald's food is life-threatening, as Spurlock documents after eating a month's worth of the stuff. Indolence is life-threatening. Cars are life-threatening on several levels. False material needs plunge us into debt that can only be relieved by working overtime.

The only group for whom children have not been forgotten or neglected is the advertisers and retailers. Last year, fully $13 billion was spent on advertising directed at children for fast food alone. This is not a rational society by the standard of allowing people to make up their

own minds uncluttered by hidden persuaders. Kids are not free to ignore these surround-sound, omnipresent advertisements on television,
the Internet, and billboards and in the print media. They are not free
to ignore "branding" on clothing, especially where such brands signify
status and identity. They are not free to ignore the fast food sold in school
cafeterias. They are not free to ignore arresting advertisements with
hip music for iPods. Kids are a captive audience ignored by sociology
but targeted by marketers.

Media culture encodes social theory if one can read it correctly (see
Goldman, Papson, and Kersey 2006). Media culture *becomes* social
theory in that it helps us map people's subject positions. We identify
kids, their parents, other authority figures, the people who work behind
the counter at fast-food outlets, teenagers wearing the latest clothing,
guys who work in auto repair franchises, and so on. In this posttextual
age, such positioning can be read for what it tells us about normative
expectations—how people are supposed to behave. And, given the
absence of children in sociology, this is one of the only places to look
for the kids, even if the affluent kids in advertising for Gap do not necessarily resemble kids across our class, gender, and race maps.

We suppose that the kids have been missing from social theory for
the same reason women and people of color have been missing. For
much of history, these groups have been exploited, and their plight has
not changed much from generation to generation. However, women
and black Americans struggled against their invisibility and joined
social movements that remedied some of this. There are no social
movements for kids, even though kids' lives have arguably been getting
worse—faster. Kids are the hidden—but huge—minority, defined as a
visible group less powerful and more likely to be the target of discrimination than the dominant group, which is more powerful and likely
to be doing the targeting. But what are we supposed to liberate kids
from, exactly? From stress, sleeplessness, attenuated development, sex,
violence, overwhelming and rote schoolwork, parental performance
expectations, résumé building, materialism, gender, class, and race—this
list is very long indeed. We pursue this discussion in the final section
of this chapter.

PARENTING DEMOCRACY

We view the main problem of the early twenty-first century as the lack
of strong-willed, democratic personalities capable of standing up to

corrupt authority and working for local and global change. People parrot answers instead of wondering whether the questions are meaningful in the first place. To be sure, kids need to know information, such as the nation's capital, the value of pi, and the geological source of petroleum. But many of these facts are learned by accretion and from reading. Much of the stuff learned—memorized—in school is quickly forgotten. Worse, it leads kids to become anti-intellectual, hating school, teachers, reading, and writing. Our fast-food nation has epidemic ill health. It also has an endemic anti-intellectualism rooted in a culture that worships celebrity and replaces reason and judgment with brand identification. Kids should not pledge allegiance like sheep or wear labeled clothes in sheer imitation but, rather, develop stable values that have been arrived at generatively, through trial, error, thesis, antithesis, and on-course correction. Kids need to view themselves, and their parents too, as projects, taking joy in discovery that helps them understand their places in the universe and the local community and, as well, their potential to change these worlds.

Democracy is perhaps the most neglected outcome of our rote curricula and prisonlike schools. Parents, teachers, administrators, and politicians do not educate for democracy—we call it "parenting democracy"—because our nation has become xenophobic, torn by economic and social conflicts and dominated by corporate agendas. Schools and parents reproduce the status quo when they should be teaching kids how to question it. What we learn from the 1960s (see Gitlin 2003) is that radicalism is a habit of mind, an openness to experience, an empathy with others less fortunate and sometimes simply different, and the willingness to take risks. This is a "messy" agenda that would require a great deal of parental participation in schools as well as public flexibility about the assessment of outcomes. Turning schools into training grounds for democracy and tolerance of difference would also require that families change, and workplaces too, embracing a new set of values that one might call generative and inclusive. This is certainly not a chamber of commerce view of the world, although if the Right really reflected on America's eroding place in the world, it, too, would recognize that a nation of strong democrats (small "d") would serve its own interests better in the long run.

America lags behind other Western countries in clean air, public transportation, renewable energy, public works, family/work flexibility, health benefits, and parental leave. We have abundant violent crime and a dysfunctional prison system. Too many children are "left behind" because they are nonwhite and poor. This is largely because capitalism and corporate profit have vitiated democracy, understood as personal and public involvement in the life of communities, schools, families, and workplaces. At a basic level (see Miliband 1969; O'Connor 1973) democracy and capitalism contradict each other and collide. Marx already understood the democratic state as merely "the executive committee of the bourgeoisie," and as part of the concept of state he would include what we now consider popular culture, schools, and families. There are real questions about whether our federalist conception of democracy was flawed from the beginning (see Hamilton, Madison, and Jay 1982; Kann 1982, 2005b) and needs to be corrected by a dose of Tocqueville (1966), early Marx (1964), and perhaps even Plato (1993). The transition from direct to representative democracy thwarted the sort of community control and public participation that we have in mind—the "participatory democracy" of the early Students for a Democratic Society (SDS) (Bloom and Breines 1995). It did not take long for corporations to realize that they could buy legislative and even executive patronage with bribes, gifts, and campaign contributions.

Our conception of America is taken more from Port Huron, Martin Luther King, and 1960s feminism than from neoliberalism and now the New Right. We disagree with the Right about what America should be. We want economic leveling, ample social services, health care, a livable minimum wage. We want vibrant communities stitched together by schools that are gathering points for parents, children, and citizens. Democracy trumps capitalism at a time when capitalism is primarily designed to benefit the rich and fails miserably at solving social problems using market mechanisms. Like Garrison Keillor (2004), we are "homegrown democrats."

In this sense, we oppose the "privatization" of public education, whether this involves fast-food franchises operating in our schools or the military-industrial complex setting the research agenda in public universities by requiring faculty to become entrepreneurs who pay their own way through grants. Privatization only removes the autonomy of schools, faculty, teachers, parents, and students. The corporate agenda is opposed to human values and democratic self-determination. "Public administration," the field inspired by Max Weber (1958), realigns public welfare with corporate interests (for a critical perspective see Box 2005). The problem is that seemingly neutral values of efficiency, utility, and technique are already embedded with substantive commitments to preserving the status quo and deepening inequality.

K-12 educators and administrators know this already because their curricula and textbooks are dictated by committees, agencies, and legislators. Sentences are debated, parsed, and sanitized so that students are not exposed to New Left, pro–affirmative action constructions of American history and culture. The Right's backlash against the separation of church and state, multiculturalism,* liberal professors, and overall permissiveness seeps deep into the books and curricula to which our children are exposed. These debates are thoroughly political, even if Bush and his ilk trumpet "fact-based" education as an antidote to fuzzy-headed theorizing. There are no such things as "facts" that simply present themselves to the naked eye. The social constructionists are correct: everything is a construction capable of being viewed from multiple perspectives[†] (Berger and Luckmann 1966).

Democracy, then, is a radical position in these dismal times. Educating kids for democracy is controversial because democracy, the real kind, is not equivalent to slavish patriotism, from repeating the Pledge of Allegiance every morning to wearing American-flag signed "spirit" shirts. Democracy is debate, dialogue, dissent; civil disobedience is at its core. Parenting democracy does not mean affixing yellow ribbons supporting our troops in Iraq to the bumpers of family cars. It means having serious discussions in the home and then the schools—and then the polity—about what we were told in order to justify the military incursion into Iraq. Kids should be told about weapons of mass destruction, the origins and membership of al-Qaeda, and why many abroad hate the United States. Kids need to know that Bush is dangerous, even as the Democrats stand by timidly and pretend to out-patriot the Republicans. Repeating the Pledge by rote has exactly the same political status today as it did during the war in Vietnam; it signals mindless support of a military-corporate agenda that has resulted in millions of innocent deaths. Parenting democracy means to expose kids to the truth about dead and maimed Iraqi children, children who, like their parents, bear absolutely no responsibility for the bombings of the World Trade Center.

Democracy is at stake, much as it was during the last years of the 1960s and early 1970s, when the FBI and Nixon combined in a ruthless campaign to suspend civil liberties (COINTELPRO, Watergate, and so on). Love of country quickly degenerates into the fear and hatred of foreigners, now including many Americans with Arab names and others

---

*An academic and political movement beginning in the 1980s that attempts to broaden the definition of culture to include the voices and works of minorities, women, and people from the third world.

[†]A key sociological concept indicating the importance of viewing the social world from different standpoints, especially class, race, and gender, none of which grasps the whole truth.

such as gays and lesbians who simply do not fit into a narrow version of our country.

PUBLIC-SCHOOL-PRIVATE

If the public sphere is occupied by work, politics, and media and the private sphere by the time away from work, then schools are somewhere in between. They occupy a middle or meso level that overlaps the public and private, and they are the special place in which children enter into the adult world, only to retreat to "privacy" after school. School is the place where teachers become parents, in real parents' absence, and students begin to lose their innocence and become workers and performers. School is not a happy time for many children because it borrows the worst from both public and private worlds—work discipline and overloading, on the one hand, and surrogate parental authority, on the other. At present, our schools are too much like factories and prisons, enforcing work discipline and personal performance. School needs to be more like a family, perhaps even more a family than the actual family, which has begun to implode under external pressures.

There are two ways in which schools can become families, nurturing and protecting the child against the outside world while also preparing the child for citizenship. First, schools will be like families if they include families, joining parents, teachers, and children in the codetermination of educational practices and outcomes and forming a real community that bridges public and private spheres. Although parents are asked as "volunteers" to run class parties and raise money for the school, they are often resented if they become more deeply involved with their children's education. Second, schools need to de-emphasize homework production and curricular and extracurricular performance, all the way from standardized and weekly tests to athletic performance and deference to authority. Schools should be sites of democracy, imagination, and exploration, joining people's private lives with the public life of the local community.

Schools should be regarded as sites of democracy and community, especially in the absence of an adequate public sphere. Voter turnout is low. People are apathetic and cynical. Schools can become an interstitial level below political institutions and above the level of privatized personal life, giving people somewhere to go, something to care about, and a rich interpersonal life. Schools can become public gathering points for theater, recreation, and festivals.

Schools inhabit both public and private spheres; they are funded publicly and their curricula are matters of legislative and administrative oversight. They are sites of voting and other public activities and events. They have taken over some of the functions of parents and families, especially where parents are absent because of work and/or neglect. They address children's development and they are sites of what sociologists call primary socialization—learning social norms from peers and intimate adults such as teachers. Our argument is that schools can provide shared intimacy based on mutuality and prepare children for democratic citizenship, indeed becoming a democratic community that overlaps both public and private spheres. Schools can become democratic families and nurture democratic personality types. They will "teach" not only children but also parents, teachers, and administrators about generativity, mutuality, and interdependence. This reconfiguring of schools has radical implications not only for children but also for families, public institutions, and society generally. The notion that educational practices can play a vital role in the democratic public sphere is shared by "unschoolers," discussed earlier, who criticize the compartmentalization and confinement of education to what takes place within the walls of traditional schools.

Our perspective on schooling as vital to the public sphere and unschooling's perspective on the stultifying effects of traditional schools converge with the early 1970s radical critiques of education offered by Ivan Illich (1971) and Paulo Freire (1970). Illich's call for "deschooling" and Freire's urging for a "pedagogy of the oppressed" are explicit contributions to a critical social theory of education that inspire our own. We share their view that teachers can be in the forefront of social change, just as we also believe that everyone can teach and everyone is always already a student.

Schools can thus be in the vanguard of social change, filling gaps in people's harried, hurried lives created by the decline of the public sphere and both modeling and becoming democratic institutions. Although it is difficult to imagine the PTA as a latter-day version of the SDS, parent-teacher alliances can address children's needs, as well as adults' needs, in the context of what the SDS's Port Huron Statement termed participatory democracy. Instead of debating only where to put the new playground equipment and how to staff the school carnival used as a fund-raiser, the PTA, which would become a committee of the whole, would discuss the implications of a school dress code for class and gender identity; it would address tracking in terms of class and childhood development; and it would spark dialogue about standardized and other tests, homework, and how we can move from a rote curriculum—and culture—to a more imaginative, open-ended one.

Such "public" public schools would do more than talk. They would host events, celebrations, and recreation; they would help the poor; they would reach out into the community and deal with neglected populations and kids (much as the Black Panthers provided a meal program to poor kids in the Bay Area during the late 1960s and early 1970s). Schools would become political and public venues in which debates would be held not just about curriculum and educational practices but also about public policy. In these ways, schools would take over some of the roles of churches, which have largely abdicated the responsibilities for social change since the hard-right evangelical turn of recent times.

Both children and adults would "teach" each other and themselves. These 1960s images of free schools grounded in the community need to be resurrected at a time when the public sphere has collapsed, the family is imploding, and school is becoming another bureaucratic nightmare. The New Right's solution to all this—the free market, an evangelical version of "family values," and teacher accountability, standardized testing, and a lockdownlike culture of fear in the schools—is, of course, all wrong. Authoritarianism will not solve the collapse of authority in fast capitalism. It is a premodern perspective flowing from the assumption, discussed earlier, that people, especially children, are bad and need to be regulated.

We cannot "fix" education without interrogating the role of schools in society, particularly as middle institutions between public and private. Schools have taken on functions of the family, such as authority and discipline, and they have had utilitarian and anti-intellectual agendas imposed on them by the state. Teachers cannot be parents, and the corporate privatization of education will not engender students who think creatively and become citizens of a democracy. This is the worst of all worlds: schools are expected to do things they cannot, and they are constrained by the custodians of fact-based education, who want to produce clones and ciphers.

CHILDREN'S RIGHTS, PARENTAL RESPONSIBILITIES

We believe that children have six basic rights and that parents have six corresponding responsibilities. Our children's bill of rights accords them citizenship and inserts them into the polity. Here are the six basic rights.

- The right to be naïve.
- The right to be idealistic.
- The right to be imaginative and creative.
- The right to empathize.
- The right to health.
- The right to participate democratically.

The following are corresponding parental responsibilities.

- The responsibility to protect.
- The responsibility to avoid cynicism.
- The responsibility to avoid rote learning and rote culture.
- The responsibility to teach social and political awareness.
- The responsibility to provide health and good self-care.
- The responsibility to provide kids occasions for democracy.

The Right to Be Naïve

Children need to be protected from a hurried adult world. They should not have to view advertisements for sexually oriented products during prime-time family television viewing hours. There is nothing wrong with being naïve; seasoning, based on experience and careful nurturance, will come in time. When we say that kids should be allowed to be naïve, we do not mimic the Right's desire to plug children's ears and prevent them from hearing "street" and sexual lyrics. We are not in favor of censorship, but we think that parents and schools should take seriously children's right to be children, which only happens once. Kids should not learn too early about sex, violence, drugs, and cynicism. They should be allowed to view the world positively and with great hope. Children are infinitely optimistic and they should remain so for as long as possible.

The Right to Be Idealistic

Children are happy and positive by nature. They should not become cynical too early. Their parents' cynicism must not become corrosive. Wounded adults reinforce this in their children, who become codependent. As adults undergo emotional vicissitudes, they carry their children along with them. Idealism means that you see the best in people and you hope for the best for yourself and those around you. Idealism is contrasted with "realism" only because reality so often disappoints, especially for the poor. One can be idealistic, about oneself and others, and still be realistic and pragmatic. Idealism is the energy you spend to imagine and then work toward a better world. Children have this in abundance. They live on a high plateau of kindness and positive expectations. It is not natural to lose this; cynicism is a response to a disappointing world.

The Right to Be Imaginative and Creative

Fill-in-the-blank questions provoke a fill-in-the-blank world. Drag-and-drop term papers, purloined and pasted together from the Internet, provoke a drag-and-drop world. Kids are naturally creative, and their education and life with peers and adults should nurture this. The strongest enemy of a mimetic culture that prizes the regurgitation of knowledge is thinking and acting outside the lines. Give kids a blank piece of paper and tell them to write their reactions to a story they just read or one they just wrote. Do not grade their answers harshly or from a predetermined and inflexible list of grading criteria. Better yet, do not grade them at all. Make schooling, and life, a pass/fail enterprise, where you pass if you show up and give it your all. Grades promote an obsession with them. Abolish grades and children's faces will light up. Ask them to draw, paint, and color their stories and they go for it. Ask them to read Dickens and then see a movie about his story. Do not test students on what some minor character in a book said or did, which will make them hate literature and culture; instead, have a conversation about Dickens. Write about him and his story. Write like him. Pretend that you are writing the next chapter of his story for him. Act out a play, don't read it. Shakespeare came alive for one of us in junior high when we enacted *A Midsummer Night's Dream* in the classroom. You kill Shakespeare when you reduce him to factual answers.

The Right to Empathize

Kids are taught to be self-oriented and self-absorbed by pushy parents without a social conscience, but kids are naturally empathetic and caring. Explain to them that others are different and are often suffering. Help them want to help. Do not teach them only to look out for number one. Personal ambition is fine in measured doses, but teaching young kids that they must outperform other kids is both destructive of community and collegiality and a recipe for disaster: there will always be someone "better." Self-esteem must not be allowed to hinge on performances and grades, which are chimerical and illusory. We live in a society based on winning. This is a problem because the glory of the win fades immediately, and the scars of losing—viewing oneself as a loser—are often permanent. Kids must put themselves in the shoes of all the players, including adults such as parents and teachers. We are not saying that they must learn to cooperate as good "team players"; that is business-world fascism.* But cooperation and mutuality stem from the ability to empathize with people who do not walk in your shoes.

The Right to Health

Kids do not get enough sleep. They eat fast and fatty foods. They do not exercise enough. Not only do they not exercise enough to maintain good health, such as cardiovascular fitness and low blood pressure, they also do not exercise enough in playful ways. Kids do get some exercise through organized sports leagues, but these are adult games with adult rules, organized and pressured by adults. Kids do not enjoy health because we overschedule them with our expectations of productivity and performance and because kids are an important market for fast food and entertainment technologies. Again, markets do not solve all problems; here, they create them. Remove all advertising directed at children from television and tax fast foods heavily, much as we tax cigarettes. Expand recess and physical education in the schools, especially recess because it allows for undirected play. Limit our kids' exposure to vegetative electronic entertainments. Encourage them to read, write, and daydream. Once kids lose their health and the verve to play, it is often too late for them in their teenage and adult years to rediscover the rambunctious, tireless child within them.

The Right to Participate Democratically

Kids must be viewed, and view themselves, as effective political agents capable of having input into the decisions that affect them. They need a voice and sometimes a vote in family and school matters. Ask kids what they think of a school dress code or a family vacation destination. Although kids still need guidance—they need it now more than ever

---

*A political theory, for example Hitler's, that recommends a powerful state with authoritarian leadership that unilaterally organizes the people and tends to make scapegoats of visible minorities and external enemies.

in our "media-ted" world that distorts everything—they must feel like valued partners in a dialogue. Sure, they will make mistakes, but so do their parents. Kids must also learn how to deal with their friends and larger groups of children, being neither bullied nor rendered passive. This does not necessarily mean that they play leadership roles, for that smacks of college-entrance résumé building. But they must learn to think for themselves, make persuasive arguments, and participate in consensus building. These are Jürgen Habermas's (1990) goals for democracy. They apply particularly to children, who are likelier by nature to be democratic, share, and take turns than adults.

Parents have responsibilities, too, which correspond to these rights of children.

The Responsibility to Protect

Kids cannot be naïve and unworldly in the best sense without parents who protect them from growing up too quickly. By the same token, kids must be taught the realities of our society in order to empathize, which we also value highly. Protecting kids does not mean insulating them. Banning *Catcher in the Rye* only makes kids want to read it. (And, by comparison with today's unvarnished popular culture, that book is a walk in the park.) Parents need to protect their kids against the acceleration of childhood, which is an important developmental stage to which children have a right. Hearing the phrase "erectile dysfunction" during an ad for Viagra on network television in the evening robs kids of innocence and puts their parents in the position of having to explain this term—and the purpose of the drug—before they should have to do so. Exposure to spam and Internet pop-ups selling sex drugs and sex itself seriously compromises children's ability to grow into these things gradually, in good time. Although we strongly believe that our society should be more sensual ("erotization") and open-minded, the premature sexualization of children makes it difficult for them to come to grips with their sexual natures in the slow unfolding of adolescence and young adulthood. Of course, those who market sex (and address sexual dysfunction with their products) do not care about children's well-being. They are simply trying to turn a profit.

Our culture is sexualized for two interrelated reasons: people are unsatisfied in their work and family lives and they turn to cheap thrills as an inauthentic substitute, and they are encouraged to seek these cheap thrills by companies looking to make a profit. Sex sells, and it sells to people frustrated with their lives. What Herbert Marcuse

(1955) called "erotization" is similar to our concept of "familization." Marcuse wants all of our interactions with others and with nature to take on sensuous, "touchy" components instead of focusing all of our attention on genital sex (and its avoidance). Implicit in this is a critique of Puritanism, which views the body, and other bodies, with shame. Similarly, familization takes intimacy and mutuality out of the family per se and informs all of our relationships, in public and in private, with this ethos. We would not necessarily join other people's families but we would experience our friendships and work relationships as familylike—caring and nurturing.

The Responsibility to Avoid Cynicism

Cynics view the world as irremediably gloomy, and they regard people as bad or at least venal. One becomes cynical through one's own misfortunes, which are often totally unjustified. Cynicism is a psychic scar, which can become an unfortunate worldview through which one processes everything in only the most negative terms (see Sloterdijk 1987). Kids are not cynical, at least not at the beginning. They are idealistic and view dogs, cats, and people with adoring and open eyes. Kids become cynical by watching corrosive television and movies and by hearing their parents talk about their own misfortunes in fatalistic terms—"It always has to be this way." Sometimes cynicism flows from religions that portray people as fallen and immoral. Adults need to model hopeful, trusting behavior for their children, who are inveterate idealists.

The Responsibility to Avoid Rote Learning and Rote Culture

Parents must encourage kids to think unconventionally, even reward them for it. Parents and teachers must not promote a fill-in-the-blank or drag-and-drop world, as if the "correct" answer always already exists and only waits to be discovered. We are a nation of sheep, beginning in early childhood. We slavishly follow political leaders who are stupid and dangerous; we swallow advertising claims hook, line, and sinker; we view education as the accumulation and ingestion of "facts" that exist in discrete bits and bytes and have only to be assembled, like a jigsaw puzzle. Kids should be encouraged to question authorities and not believe everything they read or are told. They should be encouraged to think in sweeping terms and see the big picture. They must theorize, which means seeing the world as if one is at thirty thousand feet, even if that means sacrificing some ground-level details. Kids must be taught to think historically, tracing today to yesterday and to the many yesterdays before that. The world needs vertical depth, and kids should be encouraged to dig beneath present appearances to real causes, structures, and historical sedimentation. We need to understand the twenty-first century in broad terms, as well as the industrial revolution, the Middle Ages, and antiquity. It is next to useless to memorize the location of the Euphrates River; much more pertinent would be to trace Western-Arab conflicts to ancient religious and cultural differences.

The Responsibility to Teach Social and Political Awareness

Empathy is putting yourself in the other person's shoes. Particularly important is putting yourself in the shoes of less fortunate people, whether classmates, neighbors, or people around the world. Kids must be taught social and political awareness, appreciating diversity, acknowledging differences, and empathizing with the poor and powerless. It is impossible to keep politics out of the classroom and textbooks; it is always already there, encoded in the sanitized language and representations of value freedom. But, as postmodernism instructs us, truth is always born of perspective and must be conditional. Kids need to understand these contexts and controversies so that they can make up their own minds. Teaching social and political awareness does not mean preaching a party line but simply alerting students to the impossibility of being totally objective. Skepticism will make them better citizens and it will instill in them a passion for being clear in their arguments and iconoclastic when necessary. Teaching empathy helps mitigate the effects of self-absorption, which is characteristic of a culture of narcissism. Kids need to look outside of themselves and to recognize their common humanity with people who appear to be very different but who are really in search of the same goals, truths, and freedoms.

The Responsibility to Provide Health and Good Self-Care

Who has not had the experience of driving along and noticing a toddler or preschooler in an adjacent car sucking down a bottle of Coke or some other soft drink? Most kids do not drive themselves to fast-food restaurants, at least not until they turn sixteen. But parents buy for their children processed, refined foods that are high in fat and sodium and low in fiber and complex carbohydrates from supermarkets and fast-food restaurants. Adults are cutting back recess and physical education in the schools, and they are buying kids video games and televisions and installing phone lines in their kids' bedrooms. These electronic prostheses are babysitters.

Parents must provide kids with good health and with information for effective self-care to promote long life. This includes exercise and a diet low in fat and high in complex carbohydrates that includes plenty of fresh fruits and vegetables. Parents are just as susceptible to the rhetoric of advertising as their kids, and frequently their diets and lack of exercise are not much better than their children's. And parents are likelier to be unfit, having spent a lifetime making the wrong lifestyle choices. It takes a lot of effort to start and maintain an exercise regimen and eat healthfully, and it may take even more effort to teach your children to do so, especially if you are an imperfect role model.

Good health is a human right, although we in the United States largely restrict quality health care to the middle class and the wealthy. One can live well on a modest diet, as people in poor cultures have demonstrated for years. Poor countries often have very low rates of heart disease because their people derive little of their protein from marbled meat and eat fibrous beans, unprocessed rice, and unleavened bread with low fat content, such as tortillas. These can be supplemented with leafy green vegetables and fruit. Top this kind of diet off with exercise and one can achieve health and vitality inexpensively. However, in America the poor are likelier to be obese and unhealthy than the rich. This is because they lack information about self-care, diet, and exercise. It is also because fast-food chains, with their convenient and inexpensive but unhealthful offerings, have targeted poor neighborhoods.

The Responsibility to Provide Kids Occasions for Democracy

Adults, perhaps naturally, want to make all the decisions. Compulsive yuppie parents begin assembling their children's résumés as soon as they are out of diapers and perhaps even sooner. Where alienated people lack control over their own lives, it may be natural to control one's kids in the hope of providing them with "more." However, parents need to involve kids in these decisions not only in order to prepare them for democracy but also to turn families and schools into democracies. For example, instead of telling your daughter that she has been signed up for figure skating or gymnastics lessons, inquire of her what type of exercise or sport she prefers. Explain the health and psychic benefits of regular workouts and then give her some freedom of choice. Of course, she needs to try out various options in order to make an informed decision. Once a decision has been made, though, encourage her to stick with it so that she develops perseverance and also to give the activity enough time to win her over.

Too many parents do not examine their own motives, which largely involve projection and resolving their own inadequacies, as they plan their children's lives and futures and refrain from giving them input. Being compulsive may be a normal response to feeling out of control, as many adults are. However, compulsive parenting takes a large toll in the loss of autonomy, ego strength, and creativity among children whose lives are scripted for them by doting parents. We suppose that compulsive parents are better than neglectful ones, although leaving kids to their own devices can sometimes encourage them to be inventive and playful outside the purview of media and incessant parental involvement. These are tough choices for parents to make because well-informed parents recognize that media, peers, and schools weigh heavily on children and rob them of autonomy in the name of "consumer choice." But no ten-year-old or even sixteen-year-old is mature enough—theoretical enough—to resist advertising and peer pressure. Parents have to help them, but not so much that the children become mindless conduits of their parents' own insecurities.

CONCLUSIONS: HARRIED PARENTS, HURRIED CHILDREN— THE FAMILY/SCHOOL/SOCIETY NEXUS

In this book, we have examined families that have lost their functions and their boundaries, work that is invasive, schools that are points of production and performance, and an electronic culture that steals childhood from children. We have also suggested a children's bill of rights. Sometimes, adults do this "to" children, perhaps unwittingly. Any critical social theory worth its salt must consider childhood and children as important topics, although these topics have nearly always been neglected by theorists, even feminists, who profess to be writing and organizing on behalf of a universal humanity. No truly universal humanity is possible if we leave out children, much as feminists have argued persuasively that a social theory that ignores women ignores more than half the human race.

Civil rights for children are part of a larger perspective that we term a critical sociology of the family. Indeed, as we have been arguing, we cannot isolate the family or childhood from the larger social context. Hence, we use the term "the family/school/society nexus" to refer to the ensemble of interweavings of public and private, political and personal.

These interactions are increasingly complex, as a postmodern capitalism uses rapid information and communication technologies to tether people to the workplace and, after hours, their home media centers. In a fast society, there are no "after hours." People are always plugged in, thus diminishing their abilities as selves to resist and reconstruct their lives screened for them by those who promote a certain version of "reality." If adults cannot usually resist, how can children?

One of the key issues in understanding and then transforming the family/school/society nexus is the use of time and its compression. Adults are harried, having too much to do and too little time in which to do it. They then hurry their children, not only out the door in the morning but out of childhood and out of the family. Both adults and their children are alienated in that their time is not their own. Our 24/7 wired world leaves little downtime and, thus, little opportunity to recover from the rigors of work and home/work, commuting, and activities. Families rush by each other and, like atoms in Brownian motion, occasionally bounce off each other. This is not an issue restricted to, or originating in, the family; it is a dynamic engulfing families but emanating from outside the household. It is a dynamic set in motion by a frenzied fast capitalism that is now global and nearly instantaneous. This laptop capitalism allows people to work and consume anytime, anywhere. Private life is swallowed up in the tidal wave of frenzied production and performance.

But our agenda is not simply to restore "the family," as if we could. The family has never been a haven in a heartless world but a transmission belt for capitalism that relies on women's and children's bodies for its reproduction. We do not want to turn back the clock but, rather, move it forward using the imagery of family and school as intimacy, community, and mutuality, a model of a good and decent society. Family is a radical idea because there is so little of it today. Family stands for nonalienated relationships. We have refused to restrict these activities and sensibilities of intimacy, community, and mutuality to the home but infuse them into all human relationships, especially those found in schools and workplaces.

Part of this familylike agenda is children's civil rights—their right to be children and not hurried or harried. This is good not only for children but also for democracy because it creates intermediate or interstitial institutions, such as schools, that are in between home and work. This is a new public sphere, or, to be exact, a sphere that is both public and private. Schools can be the sites of Tocqueville's New England town meetings, especially if they are reconfigured to serve children's needs and to operate on democratic principles of imagination, expression, and codetermination. Schools can be in the vanguard of social change, restoring community to public life and serving the developmental needs of young minds and bodies. For these schools to function well, we need to have families involved and not shunned as troublemakers. We need the doors kept open on the weekends and during the summers for extension, adult education, and children's preparatory work. We need schools to be operated on the model of Chautauquas, an intriguing institution of an earlier American democracy (see Schultz 2002). They would be sites of freedom, self-expression, and self-development. Schools would no longer be modeled on the prison, with codes of silence and ceaseless surveillance.

The school lies at the intersection of family and society. Changing the schools will have impact in both directions, transforming the family into a learning community and involving parents in schools and in their children's lives. Rethinking schooling would also have impact on larger public institutions such as work because kids will be democratic and expressive personalities no longer fixated on résumé building and the bottom line. And we will begin to open up school curricula to open-ended answers, questions, essays, paintings, poems, and dreams.

Changing schools is a way of transforming the family/school/society nexus, promoting the overall agenda of family/families. One way to change schools is by revamping curricula to emphasize expressiveness and creativity. We need to deal with "a mind at a time" (Levine 2002) and avoid standardization where possible. We need to abandon compulsive testing and grading, perhaps even moving to a high pass/pass/fail model as some schools, such as Roosevelt Middle School in Eugene, Oregon (see Roosevelt Middle School Home Page 2006), have done. We also need to transform and upgrade the occupation of teacher, raising salaries in order to attract highly motivated college graduates, including more with master's degrees, into the profession. K–12 teaching is currently a "pink-collar" career—it is filled primarily by women who tend to have low pay and poor benefits. Teaching should be professionalized, but perhaps not via the route of schools and colleges of education, which are bureaucratically entrenched and for the most part not sites of progressive thinking about the relationship between curriculum and social change (for prominent exceptions see Goodson 1997; Allan Luke 1988). The best teachers are radicals who get to the root of things; they empower, enhance democracy, and assist children in developing horizontal, not vertical, relationships. The worst teachers are martial, punitive, devoted to a negative and cynical view of human nature, overly utilitarian.

Changing schools will have ripple effects in the direction of private life (families, personality) and in the direction of public life (work, culture, politics). These ripples cannot be contained in institutional compartments. Education is as much about families, children, politics, power, class, gender, and race as it is about curriculum and administration. It is the everyday ground on which the politics of personal life plays out. Where kids and adults during the 1960s were galvanized by the Vietnam War, civil rights, and rock music, today they can be energized by the politics of schooling, which is at once a public and private site. The issues are not only whether kids should be allowed (or forced) to pray, play sports even if their grades are low, wear uniforms, or enjoy more or less recess and physical education but also whether we should train kids to practice democracy, challenge authority, exercise independent judgment, and involve their parents in this interstitial institution.

Should schools remain drab institutional sites of rote learning, testing, grading, and discipline or should they become gathering points—town meetings—for children and adults who care about the everyday life of democracy? We believe that schools should be, in effect, "alternative" institutions that coax us to question the other more established institutions. In short, schools should become radical forces that have impact on both family and society. This will have huge impact on the life and times of children and on their parents, who will no longer send their kids off to dreary days of ever-the-same fact-based learning with strict codes of discipline and punishment. Kids will become free (again—they are born free). And their parents will willingly participate in a codetermining public and private institution that not only sets the curricular agenda but also becomes a site of democratic learning and living involving imagination, skepticism, and critique. Parents, and of course children too, will become healthier if we abolish grades and rigid discipline and thus deny adults the vicarious gratification of comparing their own kids—and themselves—with others. Democracy can only be inculcated in free schools that free children to grow up slowly and to participate in the body politic. Schools will slow down what capitalism has sped up.

At present, schools are surrogate families; parents have abdicated responsibility for raising kids and setting limits. After all, they have their own problems of overload. We must change families, but only in the context of what we are calling the family/school/society nexus, which is manifest on the boundary of private and public life—school. Changing schools will change families and work, and change in families and work will occasion changes in schools. These are overdetermined relationships that cannot be simplified into single causes and singular solutions. Children need a bill of rights, schools need to be freeing, and capitalism must be slowed and rendered less invasive. Turning off the cell phone and computer is certainly a beginning, but it is not the only place to begin.

We must broaden the definition of family to reflect current realities—single-parent, gay and lesbian, extended. Family/families is a useful metaphor for rebuilding all social relationships along lines of intimacy and community. "School," as we have demonstrated, is also a utopian ideal, referring to a living and learning community that goes beyond the school building's walls. We must upgrade teaching as a profession, throw out most of the existing curriculum, eliminate rote learning and testing, and transform schools into Chautauquas and New England town meetings, or perhaps even the Port Huron convention that in 1962 brought the SDS into public life. Our leaders should be teachers, and teachers should lead. Parents should head families in which open discussion is encouraged. These families will be rebounced so that the external world does not invade the psyches and bodies of our children, who should be kept naïve and unworldly at least until they are ready for the world. And work must be buffered by "familizing" relationships not only among peers but also between labor and management so that democracy takes hold and with it new agendas of the public interest.

Fast capitalism, like the slower version that preceded it, flows along, globalizing itself and instantaneizing everyday life. This impoverishes whole sections of the human race, perhaps permanently. And it vaporizes the virtual self, who becomes merely a receptacle of superficial knowledge and culture. But, like nineteenth-century capitalism, this "postmodern" version also creates contradictions and conflicts not easily defused—between premodern and modern, women and men, people of color and whites, children and parents. These conflicts can combine and evolve in volatile ways that issue in social change, if appropriately understood. Seizing on families, childhood, and schooling as twenty-first-century sites of struggle is only the most recent version of Marx's earlier model of class struggle, which would spring from the factory floor. Now as before, we must remain utopian and visionary and not allow the pressing weight of events and constraints to turn us into either conservatives or cynics. Conservatives confuse the present state of affairs with social fate, ever the agenda of ideologists. For them, nothing can or should be different. Cynics believe that change will only make things worse. We remain idealists: change is necessary and even likely, given the contradictions of fast life, fast families, and virtual childhood. When schools fail to educate and kids and their parents are stressed and sinking under the weight of their production and performance, something has to give. That historical moment is the opening to real democracy, which is both a lifestyle and a learning style.

As we near the end of Bush's second term, "family values" and a back-to-basics approach to education represent an attack not only on women, gays, and lesbians but also on children—the forgotten minority group. In this book, we have tried to "liberate" the concepts of family/families and schooling in order to provide progressive people with an imagery and agenda of attainable social change. This effort extends the project of the 1960s New Left, especially of the SDS, which made "participatory democracy" its rallying cry. The Right in America today has no monopoly on family and school; these become progressive concepts once we take them out of their functionalist compartments and allow them to extend into a host of public and private spheres. And the student movement that the early civil rights movement and SDS started during the 1960s can be reborn as a movement of women, progressive men, gays, and even children who refuse to be marginalized in the name of so-called traditional values. We who believe in children's rights, good schools, and familylike social relationships need to take back these values and claim them as our own, as we have tried to do in this book.

References

Abowitz, Deborah A. 2002. "On the Road to 'Happily Ever After': A Survey of Attitudes toward Romance and Marriage among College Students." Paper presented at annual meeting of the Southern Sociological Society, Baltimore, April.

Adorno, Theodor W. 1973. *Negative Dialectics*. Trans. E. B. Ashton. New York: Seabury.

———. 1978. *Minima Moralia: Reflections from Damaged Life*. London: Verso.

Adorno, Theodor W., Else Frenkel-Brunswik, Daniel Levinson, and R. N. Sanford. 1950. *The Authoritarian Personality*. New York: Harper.

Agger, Ben. 1989. *Fast Capitalism: A Critical Theory of Significance*. Urbana: University of Illinois Press.

———. 1990. *The Decline of Discourse: Reading, Writing, and Resistance in Postmodern Capitalism*. New York: Falmer.

———. 1992. *The Discourse of Domination: From the Frankfurt School to Postmodernism*. Evanston, Ill.: Northwestern University Press.

———. 1993. *Gender, Culture, and Power: Toward a Feminist Postmodern Critical Theory*. Westport, Conn.: Praeger.

———. 2002. *Postponing the Postmodern: Sociological Practices, Selves, and Theories*. Lanham, Md.: Rowman & Littlefield.

———. 2004a. *Speeding Up Fast Capitalism: Cultures, Jobs, Families, Schools, Bodies*. Boulder, Colo.: Paradigm.

———. 2004b. *The Virtual Self: A Contemporary Sociology*. Malden, Mass.: Blackwell.

———. 2005. "Beyond Beltway and Bible-Belt: Re-imagining the Democratic Party and the American Left." *Fast Capitalism* 1.1. www.fastcapitalism.com.

———. Forthcoming. *The Sixties at 40: Radicals Remember and Look Forward*. Boulder, Colo.: Paradigm.

Apple, Michael W. 2000. 2nd ed. *Official Knowledge: Democratic Education in a Conservative Age*. New York: Routledge.

———. 2006. *Educating the "Right" Way: Markets, Standards, God, and Inequality*. New York: Routledge.

Arendt, Hannah. 1959. *The Human Condition*. Garden City, N.Y.: Doubleday.

———. 1964. *Eichmann in Jerusalem: A Report on the Banality of Evil*. New York: Viking.

Atkinson, Ti-Grace. 1974. *Amazon Odyssey*. New York: Links Books.

Ball, Howard. 2000. *The Bakke Case: Race, Education, and Affirmative Action*. Lawrence: University Press of Kansas.

Baron, Jonathan, and M. Frank Norman. 1992. "SATs, Achievement Tests, and High-School Class Rank as Predictors of College Performance." *Educational and Psychological Measurement*. 52:1047–55.

Baudrillard, Jean. 1981. *For a Critique of the Political Economy of the Sign.* St. Louis: Telos Press.

————. 1983. *Simulations.* New York: Semiotext(e).

Baumgardner, Jennifer, and Amy Richards. 2000. *Manifesta: Young Women, Feminism, and the Future.* New York: Farrar, Straus and Giroux.

Becker, Gary S. 1981. *A Treatise on the Family.* Cambridge, Mass.: Harvard University Press.

Bell, Daniel. 1973. *The Coming of Post-Industrial Society: A Venture in Social Forecasting.* New York: Basic.

Bendix, Reinhard. 1956. *Work and Authority in Industry: Ideologies of Management in the Course of Industrialization.* New York: Wiley.

Berger, Peter L., and Thomas Luckmann. 1966. *The Social Construction of Reality: A Treatise in the Sociology of Knowledge.* Garden City, N.Y.: Doubleday.

Berk, Sarah Fenstermaker. 1985. *The Gender Factory: The Apportionment of Work in American Households.* New York: Plenum.

Berle, Adolf A., and Gardiner C. Means. 1932. *The Modern Corporation and Private Property.* New York: Macmillan.

Bernstein, Basil B. 1975. *Class, Codes, and Control: Theoretical Studies towards a Sociology of Language.* New York: Schocken.

Best, Steven, and Douglas Kellner. 1991. *Postmodern Theory: Critical Interrogations.* New York: Guilford.

Blair-Loy, Mary. 2003. *Competing Devotions: Career and Family among Women Executives.* Cambridge, Mass.: Harvard University Press.

Blau, Francine D., Marianne A. Ferber, and Anne E. Winkler. 2006. *The Economics of Women, Men, and Work.* 5th ed. Upper Saddle River, N.J.: Pearson/Prentice-Hall.

Bloom, Alexander, and Wini Breines, eds. 1995. *"Takin' It to the Streets": A Sixties Reader.* New York: Oxford University Press.

Bloom, Allan. 1987. *The Closing of the American Mind: How Higher Education Has Failed Democracy and Impoverished the Souls of Today's Students.* New York: Simon and Schuster.

Blumstein, Philip, and Pepper Schwartz. 1983. *American Couples: Money, Work, Sex.* New York: William Morrow.

Bourdieu, Pierre. 1977. *Outline of a Theory of Practice.* Trans. Richard Nice. Cambridge: Cambridge University Press.

Bourdieu, Pierre, and Jean-Claude Passeron. 1990. *Reproduction in Education, Society, and Culture.* Trans. Richard Nice. London: Sage.

Bowles, Samuel, and Herbert Gintis. 1976. *Schooling in Capitalist America: Educational Reform and the Contradictions of Economic Life.* New York: Basic.

Box, Richard C. 2005. *Critical Social Theory in Public Administration.* Armonk, N.Y.: M. E. Sharpe.

Bradbury, Ray. 1967. *Fahrenheit 451.* New York: Simon & Schuster.

Braverman, Harry. 1974. *Labor and Monopoly Capital: The Degradation of Work in the Twentieth Century.* New York: Monthly Review Press.

Brody, Jane E. 2006. "Children, Media, and Sex: A Big Book of Blank Pages." *New York Times,* January 31. www.nytimes.com.

Brooks, Andree. 1996. "For Teen-Agers, Too Much to Do, Too Little Time for Sleep." *New York Times,* October 31. www.nytimes.com.

Buchmann, Claudia, Vincent J. Roscigno, and Dennis Condron. 2006. "The Myth of Meritocracy? SAT Preparation and College Enrollment in the U.S." Paper presented at the annual meeting of the American Sociological Association, Montreal, Canada, August.

Cheney, Lynne V. 1995. *Telling the Truth: Why Our Culture and Our Country Have Stopped Making Sense, and What We Can Do about It.* New York: Simon & Schuster.

Child Welfare Information Gateway. 2004. "How Many Children Were Adopted in 2000 and 2001." www.childwelfare.gov/pubs/s_adoptedhighlights.cfm.

Chodorow, Nancy. 1978. *The Reproduction of Mothering: Psychoanalysis and the Sociology of Gender.* Berkeley: University of California Press.

Coleman, James S. 1990. *Foundations of Social Theory.* Cambridge, Mass.: Harvard University Press.

Collins, Randall. 1979. *The Credential Society: A Historical Sociology of Education and Stratification.* New York: Academic Press.

Coltrane, Scott. 2004. "Elite Careers and Family Commitment: It's (Still) about Gender." *Annals of the American Academy of Political and Social Science* 695:214-20.

Coupland, Douglas. 1991. *Generation X: Tales for an Accelerated Culture.* New York: St. Martin's Press.

Cowan, Ruth Schwartz. 1983. *More Work for Mother: The Ironies of Household Technology from the Open Hearth to the Microwave.* New York: Basic.

Cutler, David M., Edward Glaeser, and Karen Norberg. 2000. "Explaining the Rise in Youth Suicide." National Bureau of Economic Research Working Paper 7713. http://ideas.repec.org/p/nbr/nberwo/7713html. Copyrights held by Cutler, Glaeser, and Norberg.

Dalla Costa, Mariarosa, and Selma James. 1975. *The Power of Women and the Subversion of the Community.* Bristol, U.K.: Falling Wall Press.

Davis, Kingsley. 1937. "The Sociology of Prostitution." *American Sociological Review.* 11:744-55.

Day, Jennifer Cheeseman, and Eric C. Newburger. 2002. "The Big Payoff: Educational Attainment and Synthetic Estimates of Work-Life Earnings." U.S. Census Bureau. www.census.gov/prod/2002pubs/p23-210.pdf.

Debord, Guy. 1973. *Society of the Spectacle.* Detroit: Black and Red.

Deiner, Paige Lauren. 2006. "Local Views on School Uniforms Far from Uniform." *(Yuma) Sun,* June 22.

Della Cava, Frances A., Norma Kolko Phillips, and Madeline H. Engel. 2004. "Adoption in the U.S.: The Emergence of a Social Movement." *Journal of Sociology and Social Welfare* 31(4): 141-60.

Derrida, Jacques. 1978. *Writing and Difference.* Trans. Alan Bass. Chicago: University of Chicago Press.

———. 1994. *Specters of Marx: The State of the Debt, the Work of Mourning, and the New International.* New York: Routledge.

Descartes, Rene. 1976. *A Discourse on Method.* Indianapolis: Bobbs-Merrill.

Dewey, John. 1917. *Creative Intelligence: Essays in the Pragmatic Attitude.* New York: Holt.

Dill, Bonnie Thornton. 1988. "Our Mothers' Grief: Racial-Ethnic Women and the Maintenance of Families." *Journal of Family History* 13(4): 415-31.

Donlan, Anne E. 2005. "In Switch, Mitt Goes Anti-Gay Union." *Boston Herald,* June 17, News, p. 6.

Doucet, Andrea. 2000. "'There's a Huge Gulf between Me as a Male Carer and Women': Gender, Domestic Responsibility, and the Community as an Institutional Arena." *Community, Work and Family* 3(2): 163–84.

Douglas, Susan J., and Meredith W. Michaels. 2004. *The Mommy Myth: The Idealization of Motherhood and How It Has Undermined Women.* New York: Free Press.

D'Souza, Dinesh. 1991. *Illiberal Education: The Politics of Race and Sex on Campus.* New York: Free Press.

Durkheim, Émile. 1947. *The Division of Labor in Society.* Glencoe, Ill.: Free Press.

Dworkin, Andrea. 2002. *Heartbreak: The Political Memoir of a Feminist Militant.* New York: Basic.

Dyer-Witheford, Nick. 1999. *Cyber-Marx: Cycles and Circuits of Struggle in High-Technology Capitalism.* Urbana: University of Illinois Press.

Ehrenreich, Barbara. 1983. *The Hearts of Men: American Dreams and the Flight from Commitment.* Garden City, N.Y.: Anchor/Doubleday.

Ellul, Jacques. 1964. *The Technological Society.* New York: Knopf.

Engels, Friedrich. 1972. *The Origin of the Family, Private Property, and the State.* New York: Pathfinder Press.

Faludi, Susan. 1992. *Backlash: The Undeclared War against American Women.* New York: Anchor Books.

Fields, Jason. 2004. *America's Family and Living Arrangements: 2003.* U.S. Census Bureau, Current Population Reports. www.census.gov/prod/2004pubs/p20-553.pdf.

Foucault, Michel. 1977. *Discipline and Punish: The Birth of the Prison.* New York: Pantheon.

Frankfurt, Harry G. 2005. *On Bullshit.* Princeton, N.J.: Princeton University Press.

Fraser, Nancy. 1989. *Unruly Practices: Power, Discourse, and Gender in Contemporary Social Theory.* Minneapolis: University of Minnesota Press.

Freire, Paulo. 1970. *Pedagogy of the Oppressed.* New York: Herder and Herder.

Freud, Sigmund. 1958. *Civilization and Its Discontents.* Garden City, N.Y.: Doubleday.

Friedan, Betty. 1974. *The Feminine Mystique.* New York: Dell.

Galbraith, John Kenneth. 1984. *The Affluent Society.* 4th ed. Boston: Houghton Mifflin.

Gardner, Marilyn. 2003. "Where Gay Unions Are Legal, What Lessons?" *Christian Science Monitor,* November 20.

Garfinkel, Harold. 1967. *Studies in Ethnomethodology.* Englewood Cliffs, N.J.: Prentice-Hall.

Gatins, Deborah E. 2005. "Adolescent Substance Use: Current Rates and Personal Impact." *North American Journal of Psychology* 7(3): 449–56.

General Accounting Office. 2003. "Title I: Characteristics of Tests with Influence Expenses; Information Sharing May Help States Realize Efficiencies." www.gao.gor/cgi-bh/getrpt?GAO-03-389.

Gerstel, Naomi. 2000. "The Third Shift: Gender and Care Work Outside the Home." *Qualitative Sociology* 23(4): 467–83.

Giroux, Henry A. 1988. *Schooling and the Struggle for Public Life: Critical Pedagogy in the Modern Age.* Minneapolis: University of Minnesota Press.

Giroux, Henry A., Colin Lankshear, Peter McLaren, and Michael Peters. 1996. *Counternarratives: Cultural Studies and Critical Pedagogies in Postmodern Spaces.* New York: Routledge.

Gitlin, Todd. 1987. *The Sixties: Years of Hope, Days of Rage.* New York: Bantam.

————. 2003. *Letters to a Young Activist.* New York: Basic.

Goffman, Erving. 1959. *The Presentation of Self in Everyday Life.* Garden City, N.Y.: Doubleday.

Golding, William. 1954. *Lord of the Flies: A Novel.* London: Faber and Faber.

Goldman, Robert, and Stephen Papson. 1995. *Sign Wars: The Cluttered Landscape of Advertising.* New York: Guilford.

Goldman, Robert, Stephen Papson, and Noah Kersey. 2005. "Speed: Through, Across, and In—The Landscapes of Capital." *Fast Capitalism* 1.1. www.fastcapitalism.com.

————. 2006. "Landscapes of the Social Relations of Production in a Networked Society." *Fast Capitalism* 2.1. www.fastcapitalism.com.

Goodson, Ivor. 1997. *The Changing Curriculum: Studies in Social Construction.* New York: P. Lang.

Gramsci, Antonio. 1971. *Selections from the Prison Notebooks of Antonio Gramsci.* Trans. Quintin Hoare and Geoffrey Nowell Smith. New York: International Publishers.

Grantham, Andrew, and George Tsekouras. 2004. "Information Society: Wireless ICTs' Transformative Potential." *Futures* 36:359–77.

Greenaway, Norma. 2006. "Provinces, Feds Squabble over Child-Care Funding." *Ottawa Citizen,* May 30.

Griffith, Mary. 1998. *The Unschooling Handbook: How to Use the Whole World as Your Child's Classroom.* New York: Three Rivers Press.

Grossman, Lev. 2005. "They Just Won't Grow Up." *Time,* January 24.

Gurstein, Penny. 2001. *Wired to the World, Chained to the Home: Telework in Daily Life.* Vancouver: University of British Columbia Press.

Habermas, Jürgen. 1970. *Toward a Rational Society: Student Protest, Science, and Politics.* Trans. Jeremy J. Shapiro. Boston: Beacon.

————. 1971. *Knowledge and Human Interests.* Trans. Jeremy J. Shapiro. Boston: Beacon.

————. 1984. *The Theory of Communicative Action.* Volume I. Trans. Thomas McCarthy. Boston: Beacon.

————. 1987a. *The Philosophical Discourse of Modernity: Twelve Lectures.* Cambridge, Mass.: MIT Press.

————. 1987b. *The Theory of Communicative Action.* Volume II. Trans. Thomas McCarthy. Boston: Beacon.

————. 1990. *Moral Consciousness and Communicative Action.* Trans. Christian Lenhardt and Shierry Weber Nicholsen. Cambridge, Mass.: MIT Press.

Hamilton, Alexander, James Madison, and John Jay. 1982. *The Federalist Papers.* New York: Bantam.

Harvard Health Letter. 2006. "Video Games Are Not So Bad." Harvard Health Publications. August, p. 7.

Harvey, David. 1989. *The Condition of Postmodernity: An Enquiry into the Origins of Cultural Change.* New York: Blackwell.

Hayden, Tom. 1988. *Reunion: A Memoir.* New York: Random House.

Hegel, George Wilhelm Friedrich. 1967. *The Phenomenology of Mind.* Trans. J. B. Baillie. New York: Harper & Row.

Hobbes, Thomas. 1950. *Leviathan.* New York: Dutton.

Hochschild, Arlie Russell. 1997. *The Time Bind: When Work Becomes Home and Home Becomes Work.* New York: Metropolitan Books.

182   REFERENCES

Hofstadter, Richard. 1963. *Anti-Intellectualism in American Life*. New York: Knopf.

Horkheimer, Max. 1974. *Eclipse of Reason*. New York: Seabury.

Horkheimer, Max, and Theodor W. Adorno. 1972. *Dialectic of Enlightenment*. New York: Herder and Herder.

Horowitz, David. 2006. *The Professors: The 101 Most Dangerous Academics in America*. Washington, D.C.: Regnery.

Huizinga, Johan. 1966. *Homo Ludens: A Study of the Play-Element in Culture*. Boston: Beacon.

Huyssen, Andreas. 1986. *After the Great Divide: Modernism, Mass Culture, Postmodernism*. Bloomington: Indiana University Press.

Hwang, Suein. 2005. "White Flight in Silicon Valley as Asian Students Move In." *Wall Street Journal*, November 19-20.

Illich, Ivan. 1971. *Deschooling Society*. New York: Harper & Row.

Jacobs, Jerry A., and Kathleen Gerson. 1998. "Who Are the Overworked Americans?" *Review of Social Economy* 66(4): 442-59.

Jacobson, Joyce P. 1998. *The Economics of Gender*. 2nd ed. Malden, Mass.: Blackwell.

Jacoby, Russell. 1975. *Social Amnesia: A Critique of Conformist Psychology from Adler to Laing*. Boston: Beacon.

——. 1976. "A Falling Rate of Intelligence?" *Telos* 27:141-46.

——. 1987. *The Last Intellectuals: American Culture in the Age of Academe*. New York: Basic.

——. 1999. *The End of Utopia: Politics and Culture in an Age of Apathy*. New York: Basic.

——. 2005. *Picture Imperfect: Utopian Thought for an Anti-Utopian Age*. New York: Columbia University Press.

Jaggar, Alison M. 1983. *Feminist Politics and Human Nature*. Totowa, N.J.: Rowman & Allanheld.

Jameson, Fredric. 1991. *Postmodernism, or, The Cultural Logic of Late Capitalism*. Durham, N.C.: Duke University Press.

Jefferson, Thomas. 1944. *Basic Writings of Thomas Jefferson*. Ed. Philip S. Foner. New York: Willey.

Kamerman, Sheila B., and Alfred J. Kahn, eds. 1991. *Child Care, Parental Leave, and the Under 3s: Policy Innovation in Europe*. New York: Auburn House.

——. 1995. *Starting Right: How America Neglects Its Youngest Children and What We Can Do about It*. New York: Oxford University Press.

Kann, Mark E. 1982. *The American Left: Failures and Fortunes*. New York: Praeger.

——. 2005a. "From Participatory Democracy to Digital Democracy." *Fast Capitalism* 1.2. www.fastcapitalism.com.

——. 2005b. *Punishment, Prisons, and Patriarchy: Liberty and Power in the Early American Republic*. New York: New York University Press.

Kant, Immanuel. 1987. *Critique of Judgment*. Trans. Werner S. Pluhar. Indianapolis: Hackett.

——. 2003. *Critique of Pure Reason*. Trans. Norman Kemp Smith. New York: Palgrave Macmillan.

Kay, Jane Holtz. 1997. *Asphalt Nation: How the Automobile Took over America and How We Can Take It Back*. Berkeley: University of California Press.

Keillor, Garrison. 2004. *Homegrown Democrat: A Few Plain Thoughts from the Heart of America*. New York: Viking.

Keller, Bess. 2001. "Schools Seen as Out of Sync with Teens." *Education Week* 20(33): 17.

Kellner, Douglas. 1995. *Media Culture: Cultural Studies, Identity, and Politics between the Modern and the Postmodern.* New York: Routledge.

Keystone Center. 2006. "The Keystone Forum on Away-from-Home Foods: Opportunities for Preventing Weight Gain and Obesity." Final Report, May. www.keystone.org/spp/documents/Forum_Report_FINAL_5-30-06.pdf.

Kimmel, Michael S. 2000. *The Gendered Society.* New York: Oxford University Press.

Klein, Julie Thompson. 1990. *Interdisciplinarity: History, Theory, and Practice.* Detroit: Wayne State University Press.

Kralovec, Etta, and John Buell. 2000. *The End of Homework: How Homework Disrupts Families, Overburdens Children, and Limits Learning.* Boston: Beacon.

Kroker, Arthur, and Marilouise Kroker, eds. 1997. *Digital Delirium.* New York: St. Martin's.

Kroker, Arthur, and Michael A. Weinstein. 1994. *Data Trash: The Theory of the Virtual Class.* New York: St. Martin's.

Kuhn, Thomas S. 1970. *The Structure of Scientific Revolutions.* 2nd ed. Chicago: University of Chicago Press.

Lakoff, George. 2002. *Moral Politics: How Liberals and Conservatives Think.* 2nd ed. Chicago: University of Chicago Press.

Lareau, Annette. 2003. *Unequal Childhoods: Class, Race, and Family Life.* Berkeley: University of California Press.

Lasch, Christopher. 1977. *Haven in a Heartless World: The Family Besieged.* New York: Basic.

——. 1979. *The Culture of Narcissism: American Life in an Age of Diminishing Expectations.* New York: Norton.

——. 1984. *The Minimal Self: Psychic Survival in Troubled Times.* New York: Norton.

——. 1991. *The True and Only Heaven: Progress and Its Critics.* New York: Norton.

Lavigne, Paula. 2005. "The Price of Prosperity." *Dallas Morning News,* August 14.

Leavis, Frank Raymond. 1933. *Culture and Environment.* London: Chatto & Windus.

Lehmann, Jennifer M. 1994. *Durkheim and Women.* Lincoln: University of Nebraska Press.

Lehrer, Evelyn L. 1999. "Married Women's Labor Supply Behavior in the 1990s: Differences by Life Cycle Stage." *Social Science Quarterly* 80(3): 574-90.

Leiss, William. 1976. *The Limits to Satisfaction: An Essay on the Problem of Needs and Commodities.* Toronto: University of Toronto Press.

Levine, Mel. 2002. *A Mind at a Time.* New York: Simon & Schuster.

Lin, Biing-Hwan, Joanne Guthrie, and Elizabeth Frazio. 1998. "Popularity of Dining Out Presents Barrier to Dietary Improvements." *Food Review,* May–August 1998.

Linn, Susan. 2005. *Consuming Kids: Protecting Our Children from the Onslaught of Marketing and Advertising.* New York: Anchor Books.

Lively, Tarron. 2006. "Uniform Policies Fit Well for High Schools." *Washington Times,* April 22, A1.

Locke, John. 2003. *Two Treatises of Government; and, A Letter Concerning Toleration.* Ed. Ian Shapiro. New Haven, Conn.: Yale University Press.

Lombroso, Cesare. 2006. *The Criminal Man.* Trans. Mary Gibson and Nicole Hahn Rafter. Durham, N.C.: Duke University Press.

Luke, Allan. 1988. *Literacy, Textbooks, and Ideology: Postwar Literacy Instruction and the Mythology of Dick and Jane.* London: Falmer Press.

Luke, Timothy W. 1989. *Screens of Power: Ideology, Domination, and Resistance in Informational Society.* Urbana: University of Illinois Press.

Lyotard, Jean-François. 1984. *The Postmodern Condition: A Report on Knowledge.* Minneapolis: University of Minnesota Press.

Macpherson, C. B. 1962. *The Political Theory of Possessive Individualism: Hobbes to Locke.* Oxford: Clarendon Press.

Marcuse, Herbert. 1955. *Eros and Civilization: A Philosophical Inquiry into Freud.* Boston: Beacon.

———. 1964. *One-Dimensional Man: Studies in the Ideology of Advanced Industrial Society.* Boston: Beacon.

———. 1969a. *An Essay on Liberation.* Boston: Beacon.

———. 1969b. "Industrialization and Capitalism in the Work of Max Weber." In *Negations: Essays in Critical Theory.* Boston: Beacon.

———. 1972. *Counterrevolution and Revolt.* Boston: Beacon.

Marx, Karl. 1964. *Early Writings.* Trans. and ed. T. B. Bottomore. New York: McGraw-Hill.

———. 1967. *Capital: A Critique of Political Economy.* Ed. Frederick Engels. New York: International Publishers.

Marx, Karl, and Friedrich Engels. 1967. *The Communist Manifesto.* Trans. Samuel Moore. Harmondsworth, U.K.: Penguin.

May, Martha. 1982. "The Historical Problem of the Family Wage: The Ford Motor Company and the Five Dollar Day." *Feminist Studies* 8(2): 399–424.

Meskell, Matthew W. 1999. "An American Resolution: The History of Prisons in the United States from 1777 to 1877." *Stanford Law Review* 51(4): 839–65.

Miliband, Ralph. 1969. *The State in Capitalist Society.* New York: Basic.

Mill, John Stuart. 2003. *On Liberty.* Ed. David Bromwich and George Kateb. New Haven, Conn.: Yale University Press.

Miller, James. 1987. *"Democracy Is in the Streets": From Port Huron to the Siege of Chicago.* New York: Simon and Schuster.

Mills, Andrew. 2005. "Gay Marriage Now Legal, but Fight's Not Over." *Toronto Star,* July 21, A6.

Mills, C. Wright. 1959. *The Sociological Imagination.* New York: Oxford University Press.

Moen, Phyllis, and Patricia Roehling. 2005. *The Career Mystique: Cracks in the American Dream.* Lanham, Md.: Rowman & Littlefield.

National Sleep Foundation. 2006a. "Adolescent Sleep Needs and Patterns: Research Report and Resource Guide." www.sleepfoundation.org/hottopics/index.php?secid=18&id=185.

———. 2006b. "Sleep in America Poll." National Sleep Foundation. Washington, D.C. www.sleepfoundation.org/hottopics/index.php?secid=16&id=392.

Negroponte, Nicholas. 1995. *Being Digital.* New York: Knopf.

Neilan, Terence. 2003. "Massachusetts Court Rules for Gay Unions; Legislature Given 6 Months to Act." *New York Times,* November 19, p. 6.

NewsHour. 2001. "Bad Examples." January 5. http://www.pbs.org/newshour/bb/sports/jan-june01/badexamples_01-05.html.

Newton, Sir Isaac. 1931. *Opticks: or, a Treatise of the Reflections, Refractions, Inflections and Colours of Light.* London: G. Bell and Sons.

Nietzsche, Friedrich. 2001. *The Gay Science: With a Prelude in German Rhymes and an Appendix of Songs.* Trans. Josefine Nauckhoff. New York: Cambridge University Press.

O'Connor, James. 1973. *The Fiscal Crisis of the State.* New York: St. Martin's.

O'Neill, John. 1985. *Five Bodies: The Human Shape of Modern Society.* Ithaca, N.Y.: Cornell University Press.

————. 1994. *The Missing Child in Liberal Theory: Towards a Covenant Theory of Family, Community, Welfare, and the Civic State.* Toronto: University of Toronto Press.

Orwell, George. 2003. *Nineteen Eighty-Four: A Novel.* New York: Plume.

Ostry, Aleck. 2006. *Change and Continuity in Canada's Health Care System.* Ottawa: Canadian Healthcare Association Press.

Packard, Vance. 1957. *The Hidden Persuaders.* New York: David McKay.

Padavic, Irene, and Barbara Reskin. 2002. *Women and Men at Work.* 2nd ed. Thousand Oaks, Calif.: Pine Forge.

Pardon, Carol J., and Kathy Roberts Forde. 2005. "Sexual Content of Television Commercials Watched by Early Adolescents." www.unc.edu/depts/jomc/teenmedia.

Pareto, Vilfredo. 1991. *The Rise and Fall of Elites: An Application of Theoretical Sociology.* New Brunswick, N.J.: Transaction.

Parsons, Talcott. 1937. *The Structure of Social Action: A Study in Social Theory with Special Reference to a Group of Recent European Writers.* New York: McGraw-Hill.

————. 1951. *The Social System.* Glencoe, Ill.: Free Press.

Parsons, Talcott, and Robert F. Bales. 1955. *Family, Socialization, and Interaction Process.* Glencoe, Ill.: Free Press.

Penny, Laura. 2005. *Your Call Is Important to Us: The Truth about Bullshit.* New York: Crown.

Petrini, Carlo. 2003. *Slow Food: The Case for Taste.* Trans. William McCuaig. New York: Columbia University Press.

Plato. 1993. *Republic.* Trans. Robin Waterfield. Oxford: Oxford University Press.

Poster, Mark. 2001. *What's the Matter with the Internet?* Minneapolis: University of Minnesota Press.

Postman, Neil. 1985. *Amusing Ourselves to Death: Public Discourse in the Age of Show Business.* New York: Viking.

Princiotta, Dan, and Stacey Bielick. 2003. "Homeschooling in the United States: 2003." National Center for Educational Statistics. http://nces.ed.gov/Pubsearch/pubsinfo. asp?pubid-2006042.

Remez, Lisa. 2000. "Oral Sex among Adolescents: Is It Sex or Is It Abstinence?" *Family Planning Perspective* 32(6): 298–304.

Rippin, Hannah. 2005. "The Mobile in Everyday Life." *Fast Capitalism* 1.1. www. fastcapitalism.com.

Roosevelt Middle School Home Page. 2006. http://schools.4j.lane.edu/roosevelt/ aboutourschool/aboutourschool.html.

Rorty, Richard. 1982. *Consequences of Pragmatism: Essays, 1972–1980.* Minneapolis: University of Minnesota Press.

Rosenfeld, Alvin, and Nicole Wise. 2001. *The Over-Scheduled Child: Avoiding the Hyper-Parenting Trap.* New York: St. Martin's Griffin.

Rothstein, Jesse. 2001. "Assessing the Informational Content of the SAT Scores." Paper presented at the "Rethinking the SAT" conference, University of California, Santa Barbara, November 16-17.

Rousseau, Jean-Jacques. 1987. *The Social Contract.* New York: Penguin.

Sappenfield, Mark. 2001. "Kickball Game? I Can Pencil One in Next Month." *Christian Science Monitor* 93(149): 1.

Sayer, Liana C. 2005. "Gender, Time, and Inequality: Trends in Women's and Men's Paid Work, Unpaid Work, and Free Time." *Social Forces* 84(1): 285-303.

Scheler, Max. 1961. *Ressentiment.* Ed. Lewis A. Coser. Trans. William W. Holdheim. New York: Free Press of Glencoe.

Schlosser, Eric. 2002. *Fast Food Nation: The Dark Side of the All-American Meal.* New York: HarperPerennial.

Schultz, James R. 2002. *The Romance of Small-Town Chautauquas.* Columbia: University of Missouri Press.

Schumpeter, Joseph A. 1976. *Capitalism, Socialism, and Democracy.* New York: Harper and Row.

Seidman, Steven. 1996. *Queer Theory/Sociology.* Cambridge, Mass.: Blackwell.

Sennett, Richard, and Jonathan Cobb. 1972. *The Hidden Injuries of Class.* New York: Knopf.

Sheehan, George A. 1978. *Running and Being: The Total Experience.* New York: Simon & Schuster.

Sheeran, Thomas. 2006. "Study Says School Uniforms May Help Attendance, Graduation Rates." Associated Press. January 12.

Shorter, Edward. 1975. *The Making of the Modern Family.* New York: Basic.

Simplico, Joseph S. C. 2005. "Homework in the 21st Century: The Antiquated and Ineffectual Implementation of a Time Honored Educational Strategy." *Education* 26(1): 138-42.

Sloterdijk, Peter. 1987. *Critique of Cynical Reason.* Trans. Michael Eldred. Minneapolis: University of Minnesota Press.

Smith, Adam. 1998. *An Inquiry into the Nature and Causes of the Wealth of Nations: A Selected Edition.* Oxford: Oxford University Press.

Smith, Dorothy E. 1987. *The Everyday World as Problematic: A Feminist Sociology.* Boston: Northeastern University Press.

Sonenstein, Freya L., Gary J. Gates, Stefanie Schmidt, and Natalya Bolshun. 2002. "Primary Child Care Arrangements of Employed Parents: Findings from the 1999 National Survey of America's Families." Occasional Paper Number 59, The Urban Institute, Washington, DC. http://www.urban.org/publications/310487.html.

Spurlock, Morgan. 2005. *Don't Eat This Book: Fast Food and the Supersizing of America.* New York: Penguin.

Stacey, Judith. 1990. *Brave New Families: Stories of Domestic Upheaval in Late Twentieth Century America.* New York: Basic.

Steinberg, Jacques. 2002. *The Gatekeepers: Inside the Admissions Process of a Premier College.* New York: Viking.

Stepp, Laura Sessions. 1999. "Parents Are Alarmed by an Unsettling New Fad in Middle Schools: Oral Sex." *Washington Post,* July 8, p. A1.

Stockwell, Michele. 2005. "Childhood for Sale: Consumer Culture's Bid for Our Kids."

Policy report, Progressive Policy Institute. www.ppionline.org/documents/MARKETING_0804.pdf.

Talbot, Margaret. 2005. "Best in Class." *The New Yorker,* June 6. Posted on May 30, 2005, at www.newyorker.com/printables/fact/060606fa_fact.

Tocqueville, Alexis de. 1966. *Democracy in America.* Trans. George Lawrence. New York: Harper & Row.

Touraine, Alain. 1971. *The Post-Industrial Society: Tomorrow's Social History: Classes, Conflicts, and Culture in the Programmed Society.* Trans. Leonard F. X. Mayhew. New York: Random House.

Turkle, Sherry. 1997. *Life on the Screen: Identity in the Age of the Internet.* New York: Touchstone.

Tyre, Peg. 2006. "The New First Grade: Too Much Too Soon?" *Newsweek.* September 11.

U.S. Census Bureau. 2003. "Who's Minding the Kids: Child Care Arrangements." Spring 1999. Table 3A. www.census.gov/population/www/socdemo/child/ppl-168/tab03A.pdf.

U.S. Department of Labor. 2005. *Women in the Labor Force: A Databook.* Table 1. Washington, D.C.: U.S. Department of Labor. www.bls.gov/cps/wlf-databook.-2005.pdf.

Veblen, Thorstein. 1979. *The Theory of the Leisure Class.* New York: Penguin.

Walby, Sylvia. 1990. *Theorizing Patriarchy.* Oxford: Blackwell.

Weber, Max. 1958. *From Max Weber: Essays in Sociology.* New York: Oxford University Press.

Wexler, Philip. 1987. *Social Analysis of Education: After the New Sociology.* London: Routledge & Kegan Paul.

Wiggershaus, Rolf. 1994. *The Frankfurt School: Its History, Theories, and Political Significance.* Trans. Michael Robertson. Oxford, U.K.: Polity Press.

Wittgenstein, Ludwig. 1953. *Philosophical Investigations.* Trans. G. E. M. Anscombe. Oxford: Blackwell.

Wright, George C. 2001. "E-Mail Communication." Memo sent April 30, 2001. University of Texas at Arlington.

Wulfhorst, Ellen. 2006. "Laptops in Tow, More Americans Work on Vacation." www.boston.com/business/technology/articles/2006/07/26/laptops_in_tow_more_americans_work_on_vacation/.

Young, Michael. 1958. *The Rise of the Meritocracy, 1870-2033: The New Elite of Our Social Revolution.* New York: Random House.

Index

About the Authors

Ben Agger is professor of sociology and humanities at the University of Texas at Arlington. He also directs the Center for Theory there. Agger works in the areas of critical theory, cultural studies, and media studies. Among his recent books are *Postponing the Postmodern* and *Speeding Up Fast Capitalism,* and he is currently working on a book about the 1960s titled *The Sixties at 40: Radicals Remember and Look Forward.* Agger edits the online journal *Fast Capitalism* (www.fastcapitalism.com).

Beth Anne Shelton is professor of sociology and director of women's studies at the University of Texas at Arlington. Her primary areas of research include gender, work, and family. Shelton's published work has focused primarily on the relationship between work and family, with emphasis on the household division of labor between women and men and the implications of this division of labor for women's employment and earnings.